Reflective Practice in the Sport and Exercise Sciences

Within the Sport and Exercise Sciences (SES) and allied disciplines, reflective practice has become firmly established as a fundamental aspect of education, professional training and development, and applied service delivery. This has resulted in an emerging, context-specific evidence base that has attempted to make sense of the application and utility of reflective practice as a mechanism to facilitate personal and professional growth through experiential learning, and subsequently develop the knowledge required to navigate the complexities of applied practice.

This new and fully revised edition of *Reflective Practice in the Sport and Exercise Sciences* explores the contemporary conceptual landscape, critical perspectives, pedagogy, and applied considerations in reflective practice in the SES and allied disciplines. Contributions from scientists, researchers, practitioners, and academics offer innovative perspectives of reflective practice, founded on a synthesis of the contemporary empirical evidence base and applied practitioner experience.

These contributions challenge academic and/or practice-based audiences regarding the utility, research, and representation of reflective practice, while offering critical insights into the application of different approaches to reflective practice. Based on exploring the crucial interface between learning and practice, this book is important reading for all who work in the SES and allied disciplines, and, more widely, any professional aiming to become a more effective practitioner.

Brendan Cropley, PhD, FBASES, is Professor of Sport Coaching in the Faculty of Life Sciences and Education at the University of South Wales. He is also Head of the Centre for Football Research in Wales, and the Coaching Science Research Steering Group Lead for the Welsh Institute of Performance Science.

Zoe Knowles, PhD, FBASES, is Professor of Engagement and Learning at Liverpool John Moores University. Zoe is Strategic Lead for External Engagement in the School of Sport and Exercise Sciences and a National Coordinating Centre for Public Engagement (NCCPE) Public Engagement Professional. Zoe is also a HCPC Registered Practitioner Psychologist.

Andy Miles, PhD, FBASES, is a part-time Principal Lecturer in the School of Sport and Health Sciences at Cardiff Metropolitan University where he previously managed the School's enterprise activities. He continues to engage with a wide range of stakeholders through his own education and training company, which provides products and services to a variety of sectors including sport, the military, the NHS, and the private sector.

Emma Huntley, PhD, is a Senior Lecturer in Sport and Exercise Psychology and Member of the Sport and Exercise Science Team in the Department of Sport and Physical Activity at Edge Hill University. She is a British Association of Sport and Exercise Sciences Accredited Practitioner.

This book is endorsed by the British Association of Sport and Exercise Sciences.

BASES

The British Association of
Sport and Exercise Sciences

Reflective Practice in the Sport and Exercise Sciences

Critical Perspectives, Pedagogy, and Applied Case Studies

Second Edition

Edited by
**Brendan Cropley, Zoe Knowles,
Andy Miles, and Emma Huntley**

Routledge
Taylor & Francis Group

LONDON AND NEW YORK

Designed cover image: petrelos

Second edition published 2023
by Routledge
4 Park Square, Milton Park, Abingdon, Oxon, OX14 4RN

and by Routledge
605 Third Avenue, New York, NY 10158

Routledge is an imprint of the Taylor & Francis Group, an informa business

First edition published by Routledge 2014

ISBN: 978-1-032-05695-1 (hbk)
ISBN: 978-1-032-05694-4 (pbk)
ISBN: 978-1-003-19875-8 (ebk)

DOI: 10.4324/9781003198758

Typeset in Galliard
by Apex CoVantage, LLC

Dedications

Brendan Cropley: First, to my fellow editors – the golden sky, the sweet silver song of the lark. Second, to my colleagues past and present – thank you for the opportunity. Third, to my friends and family – thank you for the inspiration. Most importantly, to my wife, Maria – thank you for the love . . . poetry in motion!

Zoe Knowles: To Professors Gilbourne, Stratton, Fairclough, Boddy, and Baltzopoulos for their academic support and wisdom. I am paying this support forward to others daily with real privilege having learned from you all. To my co-editors (#Team RP), we did it!! To my family and friends who make me reflect, strive, and challenge for the better.

Andy Miles: A big thanks to Ads for her ongoing love and support – she can now believe that those "just popping upstairs to do book stuff" evenings were genuine – here is that book! To my five children, all "growed up" now but loved more than ever, and to my fellow editors – "They said, 'I bet they'll never make it', but just look at us . . ."

Emma Huntley: To my biggest professional champions, my co-editors (aka "Team RP") – thank you for telling me "You can!" when I believed I couldn't. To my biggest champions at home . . . Tabo – thank you for your endless love, support and words of wisdom. My parents and sister – thank you for everything! And my amazing children – may my ceiling be your floor.

As an editorial team we would like to thank all the contributing chapter authors, who have also helped to drive the development of our community of reflective practitioners. We would also like to sincerely thank Professor Dave Gilbourne, not only for the Foreword, but for supporting us all along our journeys at one time or another.

We dedicate this book in the loving memory of Professor Lindsey Dugdill. Lindsey sadly passed away between the previous text and this current one, yet her inspiration is felt through the book from that of the Editors' ideas to all contributors in shaping the words they wrote. Thank you.

Contents

Figures

Tables

About the Contributors

Dr Tegan Adams has a Master's degree in sport psychology and a Doctorate in clinical psychology with over ten years of experience supervising advanced degree trainees. She is a Certified Mental Performance Consultant via the Association of Applied Sport Psychology (AASP). At Holy Names University (HNU) she has supported the supervisors as a meta-supervisor.

Dr Andy Borrie works as a Senior Lecturer in Coaching and Professional Practice at the University of Derby alongside running his own consultancy business. Andy has worked as an applied sport scientist on world class programmes, performance managed a suite of talent programmes and been a Board director for three NGBs. Currently his research is focused on understanding talent development philosophies.

Dr Emma S. Cowley was the PhD candidate leading on the HERizon project. She is a mixed-methods researcher, whose primary area of interest is understanding adolescent girls' relationship with physical activity. Through her PhD, with collaboration from a multidisciplinary supervisory team, The HERizon Project was developed and evaluated. She has experience with reflective practice through her background in secondary school teaching.

Dr Brian Gearity is an Associate Professor, Founder, Director of online graduate degrees in sport, and an undergraduate minor in Kinesiology and Sport Studies at the University of Denver. He has co-edited the book, "Coach Education and Development in Sport: Instructional Strategies" and co-authored, "Understanding Strength and Conditioning as Sport Coaching: Bridging the Biophysical, Pedagogical and Sociocultural Foundations of Practice."

Professor Sheldon Hanton is a Professor of Psychology at Cardiff Metropolitan University and became the Pro Vice-Chancellor for Research in 2012. As PVC (Research & Innovation) he is responsible for all research strategy at the University including the Research Excellence Framework. Sheldon remains research active and lists his main interests as competition and organisational stress, mental toughness, injury psychology, and professional practice.

Dr Clayton Kuklick is a Clinical Associate Professor in the Master of Arts in Sport Coaching and Kinesiology and Sport Studies programmes at the University of Denver. His research interests centre on the sociology of sport coaching, coach learning, and reflection. Clayton is on the editorial board of the International Sport Coaching Journal.

Amelia K. McIntosh is currently a trainee sport and exercise psychologist, having recently begun a Professional Doctorate at Liverpool John Moores University (LJMU). She has completed a B.Sc. (2020) and M.Sc. (2021) in sport psychology also at LJMU. Prior to her studies she competed in rhythmic gymnastics, having since qualified as a coach, she now teaches at her local club.

Professor Stephen D. Mellalieu is a Professor of Sport Psychology at Cardiff Metropolitan University. He is the former editor of the Journal of Applied Sport Psychology and co-founder and editor of the World Rugby Science Network. His primary research interests lie in the area of athlete welfare, including stress, coping and performance, psychological skills training and behaviour change, and the organisational environment of elite sport.

Matthew Miller is a Professional Doctorate student in sport and exercise psychology at the University of Portsmouth. His primary research focus is organisational resilience in elite sport. In addition, he works as a practitioner psychologist (in training) within the professional football talent development pathway.

Professor James Morton is a Professor of Exercise Metabolism at Liverpool John Moores University, where he has authored over 180 research publications. In addition to academia, James has also worked in several performance support related roles, including performance nutritionist to Liverpool FC (2010–2015); and nutrition and physical performance lead for Team Sky (2015–2019). James also sits on the Technical Steering Panel for the English Institute of Sport and is a high-performance mentor for the Premier League.

Laura Needham completed both her Undergraduate and Postgraduate sport and exercise science degrees at Cardiff Metropolitan University and then after a successful internship with Sport Wales joined the physiology team within the Welsh Institute of Sport in 2011. She moved to join the English Institute of Sport (EIS) in 2013 where she worked as the physiologist for GB boxing for the Rio Olympiad. Laura is now both co-head of physiology at the EIS and senior physiologist for British Triathlon. Laura is also undertaking a Professional Doctorate at the University of Portsmouth.

Dr Gareth Picknell is Head of Operations for a physical readiness department within the United Arab Emirate's Ministry of Defence. Gareth completed his PhD at Cardiff Metropolitan where he examined mechanisms and processes linked to effective practice of health practitioners. He is an Accredited Sport & Exercise Scientist (British Association of Sport & Exercise Sciences) and Chartered Scientist (Science Council, UK).

Dr Alison Pope-Rhodius is the Programme Director for the Applied Sport and Performance Psychology master's degree at Holy Names University (HNU) in Oakland, California. Her career highlights include travelling the world working with elite archers and coaches, including at the Olympics. She was made a fellow of the Association for Applied Sport Psychology (AASP) and is a Certified Mental Performance Consultant (CMPC).

Professor Alessandro Quartiroli is a Professor of Psychology at the University of Wisconsin – La Crosse (USA) and a Visiting Reader in Applied Psychology at the University of Portsmouth (UK). Ale completed his academic and professional training in Italy, Spain, and the United States. Ale's research is primarily focused on practitioners' development, well-being, and ethical and effective practice. Ale also engages in applied practice and in the applied supervision of early-career practitioners and trainees.

Dr Emily Ryall is a Reader in Applied Philosophy, at the University of Gloucestershire. Emily is currently the associate editor for the Journal of the Philosophy of Sport and is former chair of the British Philosophy of Sport Association. Emily has authored many book chapters and peer reviewed journal articles as well as appearing on, and writing for, national, local, and international media such as The Moral Maze, BBC News 24, and BBC Radio 4's Today.

Amelia K. Simpson has completed a B.Sc. and M.Sc. in sport and exercise psychology at Liverpool John Moores University (LJMU), experiencing reflective practice throughout. She is now a trainee sport and exercise psychologist having taken a Professional Doctorate route at LJMU. Amelia has interests in behaviour change, self-determination theory, and physical activity promotion.

Dr Hamish Telfer is a coach who has operated at grass roots and international levels. Training initially as a Physical Education teacher, he survived schools, training venues and high-level competition to amass 50+ years' experience. He moved into work as a GB National Coach, then into higher education specialising in applied sports coaching including methodologies, practice ethics and leadership. He now is 'retired'.

Dr Jo Trelfa is a skilled facilitator with 35+ years' experience working with individuals, groups, and communities in a range of contexts, two decades of which have been in higher education, specifically professional education. Currently Principal of a specialist independent college in England, her area of expertise is reflective practice continually developed and shared through rich research, workshops, training, presentations, and publications.

Dr Christopher R. D. Wagstaff is a Reader in Applied Psychology at the University of Portsmouth (UoP). He divides his time between research, supervision, and practice. His research is primarily on organisational sport psychology and professional development, and he is the editor for the Journal of Applied Sport Psychology and Sport and Exercise Psychology Review. He supervises researcher-practitioners on his doctorate programme at UoP while also working as a HCPC Registered Practitioner Psychologist within the UK's high performance sport system.

Dr Paula Watson is a HCPC Registered Practitioner Psychologist with an interest in physical activity and health behaviour. Having been employed in higher education for 17+ years, Paula recently left academia to run her own exercise psychology practice – Made Up To Move Ltd. Since her M.Sc. in 2004, reflection has played an integral role in Paula's research, teaching, and applied practice. Paula also enjoys facilitating critical reflection in others.

Dr Amy Whitehead is a Reader in Sport Psychology and Coaching and is the lead of the Coaching and Pedagogy Research Group at Liverpool John Moores University. Her research focuses on athlete and coach cognition, reflection, and education, and more specifically the application of the Think Aloud method within these contexts. She is also a BPS Chartered (HCPC Registered) Sport and Exercise Psychologist working in a range of sports.

Dr Amanda J. Wilding is a BASES Accredited and HCPC Registered Practitioner Psychologist. Amanda has worked with a plethora of elite athletes including Premier League football players and masters' world champions in weightlifting and athletics. Amanda is also a Senior Lecturer in Sport and Exercise Psychology at Bournemouth University and has taught on various undergraduate and postgraduate programmes as well as supervising postgraduate research degree students.

Dr Kate Williams is a Senior Lecturer in Sports and Exercise Therapy in the Faculty of Life Sciences and Education, University of South Wales. Kate has over 20 years of experience working as a Graduate Sports Therapist and musculoskeletal clinician across a range of sporting contexts and has been the Head of Rehabilitation for a professional rugby union team for the last ten years.

Hannah C. Wood undertook her M.Sc. sport psychology degree at Liverpool John Moores University, during which she worked on the HERizon Project; her first experience of engaging with reflective practice. Having discovered a passion for research during her studies, she is now pursuing an exercise psychology PhD at Kings College London.

Foreword

First, I would like to thank Professor Zoe Knowles for inviting me to compose this foreword. In my past career I have been very fortunate to meet and work alongside all the present editorial team and many of the contributors. In those times I always regarded myself as privileged to be in their company.

The scope of topics explored in this book serves as a testament to the way philosophic, practical, and pedagogic exploration has progressed. There is little doubt that reflective practice has gained traction across a range of disciplines and institutions. On a more cautious note, the underlying pitch of many chapters contained here serve as a reminder that reflective practice is not necessarily an easy thing to do. At a more strategic level, different authors also stress, directly or indirectly, the important role of institutional structure (as enabler) to promote participation in reflective exercises or workshops.

Despite these advances, at some level, at some time those who facilitate or support reflection may have to confront and overcome an undercurrent of sorts. In my early research days, I would often find myself explaining (sometimes defending) reflective issues. Some colleagues even asked why reflecting on practice was deserving of any form of inquiry. Often my explanation would be met with a shrug of the shoulders. At this time, workplace practitioners often seemed underwhelmed. I constantly sensed resistance. In such moments I wondered if the widespread use of the terms 'reflective' and 'practice' made the concept of reflective practice seem little more than common sense, something everyone already knew about and had been doing anyway.

Maybe times have changed. This book makes it clear that reflective practice is a well-researched discipline, one that is increasingly understood and appreciated. The opening chapters detail how reflective practice is underpinned by an extensive philosophical base and can now boast an impressive peer review history. Many of the authors demonstrate a generous approach to their writing. They openly discuss challenges they have experienced, as such, many applied stories are included in this book. These sometimes make reference to difficulties both personal and professional. Reflective stories always draw me in and remind me of the close proximity between reflective writing and auto-ethnography. In other sections of the book, topics such as: core reflective skills; attitudes toward reflection; organisational culture as a conduit to reflection; and meaningful personal development through reflection; offer critical messages and illustrate how difficult it might be for people to engage in reflective practice. All of the above suggests reflective practice has developed in a mature and critically progressive manner. Clearly there are many barriers to overcome at academic, pedagogic, personal, and/or organisational levels. But that just seems normal to me.

A final few words if I may. I offer my congratulations and best wishes to all of those involved in bringing this important project to a successful conclusion and hope readers find the book informative and helpful in a personal and professional sense.

Professor David Gilbourne

Professor David Gilbourne specialises in critical qualitative inquiry. He was a Reader in Qualitative Research at Liverpool John Moores University before moving on to professorship roles in qualitative inquiry at Cardiff Metropolitan University and the University of Hull. David acted as a Visiting Professor at Copenhagen University in 2010, and cofounded *Qualitative Research in Sport and Exercise*, the first peer-reviewed journal dedicated to disseminating qualitative research from all sport-based disciplines. David took early retirement in 2016 and lives with his wife Janette on their plant-based small holding in the rolling hills of North Wales.

Section 1

Exploring the Conceptual Landscape of Reflective Practice in SES and Allied Disciplines

1 Introduction
Reflecting on Opportunities and Journeys

Brendan Cropley, Zoe Knowles, Andy Miles, and Emma Huntley

"It's on the strength of observation and reflection that one finds a way. So we must dig and delve unceasingly."

– Claude Monet (n.d.)

Introducing the Text

Within the sport and exercise sciences (SES) and allied disciplines, reflective practice is becoming increasingly established as a fundamental aspect of education, training, and professional service delivery. Despite this progress, several issues concerning the nature, integration, and pedagogy of reflective practice remain. For example, reflective practice is often found aligned to the discipline of sport and exercise psychology more so than those disciplines favouring more positivistic frameworks for practice (e.g., physiology, biomechanics). Reflective practice is, however, a pedagogical and developmental approach that lies at the heart of applied practice in all SES disciplines. Further, professional applied practice is often dictated by a "hurry-up mentality" whereby practitioners are expected to be engaged in practical action rather than in critically reflective thought. The very nature of working in sport and exercise settings can, therefore, lead to a view that reflective practice is more important and accessible during training and formal professional development rather than as an integral aspect of daily practice. Finally, through our (editorial team) experiences of delivering reflective practice education events for neophyte and professional practitioners in SES and allied disciplines globally (e.g., sports therapy, strength and conditioning), we have been party to ongoing concerns relating to how reflective practitioners can be developed and how individuals and organisations might engage in the reflective process in ways that are meaningful enough to elicit effective learning and improvements to practice. It is arguably a critical time for the genre, therefore, because such considerations emphasise the ongoing necessity to establish a context specific evidence-base that embraces different epistemological positions, as well as the enduring need to better understand both the application of reflective practices and what it means to be a reflective practitioner.

DOI: 10.4324/9781003198758-2

With these considerations in mind, we would like to welcome you to *Reflective Practice in the Sport & Exercise Sciences: Critical Perspectives, Pedagogy, and Applied Case Studies*, which has been purposefully constructed as an evolution from our original Routledge text: *Reflective Practice in the Sport & Exercise Sciences: Contemporary Issues* published in 2014 (Knowles et al., 2014a). We (editorial team) understand that this "Second Edition" has been long in the making – this is despite the gargantuan efforts made by Professor Knowles to (re) build *Team RP* and mobilise us all to begin the preparation of the current text some time ago. However, as the saying goes, "All good things come to those who wait" – certainly nearly a decade has passed, which, given the developments in the SES and allied disciplines, has furnished us with ample opportunities to advance and shape this text.

Perhaps one contributing factor regarding the time between editions was the onset of the global COVID-19 pandemic, which challenged everyone physically, mentally, emotionally, and socially. We (editorial team) recognise, therefore, that we bring this text into a very different world, one in which people have had to adapt to new ways of living, new ways of working, and new ways of being. We understand that many of our perspectives will have changed (or evolved), and the way in which we all experience our personal and professional lives is now different. We believe that these developments (in some way) can be recognised throughout our current text, with contributing authors sharing, at times, very different views about reflective practice, professional service delivery, and meaning within the SES and allied disciplines. For us, it is these different perspectives and understandings that add to the rich tapestry of this text. Indeed, it was never our intention to offer "answers" in this edition (e.g., to how we "do" reflective practice; or the most beneficial frameworks for reflective practice). Instead, our aim has been to embrace and explore the contemporary conceptual landscape, pedagogy, and applied considerations in reflective practice in the SES and allied disciplines. In attending to this aim, our intention has been to facilitate discussion concerning the concept of meaningful reflective practice and the dilemmas and challenges faced by reflective practitioners in a way that allows the genre to move forwards.

To ensure that diverse, innovative, and critical perspectives of reflective practice could be garnered in this edited text, we invited a mix of global scientists, researchers, practitioners, and academics from across a range of SES and allied disciplines. Adding to this diversity, we invited contributions from those beginning their professional journeys through to esteemed professionals, and actively encouraged our contributors to collaborate with others on their chapters. In doing so, to potentially counter the impact that the pandemic had on *togetherness* and to facilitate a *sense of collective endeavour* amongst the authors, we sought to develop a *community of reflective practitioners*. Here, we asked all authors to move beyond the traditional approach of simply preparing a chapter, and instead engage more widely with each other, the construction of this text, and the concept of reflective practice. As an editorial team, forming a community of passionate and engaged individuals was important to us as we attempted to create meaningful and lasting collaborations both for the betterment of the discussions presented in each chapter and more widely the field. To operationalise this community, we arranged to meet all authors collectively during the preparation of their chapters. This meeting allowed us to bring everyone together to share ideas and understandings, positively challenge perceptions regarding reflective practice and associated professional training and service delivery, and develop new collaborations and lines of enquiry aimed at furthering research and insight in the area of reflective practice in the SES and allied disciplines. Beyond the publication of this text, it is our intention to continually engage in, and with, this community, building its membership and level of output. Through this we will provide opportunities to engage with you the readership also.

A Guide to the Chapters Ahead

We have heeded to calls presented in the recent literature and those proposed in the first edition of this text in preparation of this current edition. Specifically, we considered it important to: (a) review the current reflective practice literature in the SES and allied disciplines as a way of presenting an understanding of "where we currently are" and where the area might "need to go"; (b) provide greater evidence of the impact of reflective practice on service delivery effectiveness; (c) offer novel insights into pedagogy and applied issues relating to reflective practice; and (d) present bespoke case examples of the utility of reflective practice in a variety of different applied contexts in SES and allied disciplines. Working with the contributing authors, we wanted them to feel free to take our initial ideas in the direction that best fit with their perspectives and experiences. During the process of agreeing the content and delivery of their chapters, however, we advocated that contributions should be designed to challenge, contest, and offer innovative perspectives of reflective practice founded on a synthesis of the contemporary empirical evidence base and applied practitioner experience. Thus, this book aims to challenge both academic and practice-based audiences regarding the utility, research, and representation of reflective practice, while offering critical insights into the mechanisms and efficacy of different approaches to reflective practice. Each chapter is free flowing in design, and the book structured in a way that allowed contributors to present their work through a varied range of writing approaches. Some tell stories from their own experiences through reflective excerpts, others supplement their arguments with conversations, and others compile their discussions through reference to more traditional research-based information.

This book consists of five sections and 17 chapters, with all chapters contributing to the achievement of the aims of the book whilst also being prepared in a way that allows them to standalone as critical discussions on distinct topics related to reflective practice in the SES and allied disciplines. Section 1 – "Exploring the Conceptual Landscape of Reflective Practice in SES and Allied Disciplines" – aims to frame this text by offering conceptual insights into reflective practice and, more specifically, the reflective practitioner, as well as provide an analysis of the current reflective practice literature that has been published since the first edition of this text. In this section, we offer insights into "what it means to be a reflective practitioner" through a novel approach to chapter construction whereby all authors contributing to this text provided their own perspectives through a vignette, on which the editorial team subsequently offered a summative analysis to facilitate ongoing critical discussion in this area. Section 2 – "Critical Perspectives" – this collection aims to provide contemporary debate regarding reflective practice, focusing specifically on the evidence underpinning the advocated efficacy of reflective practice, and critically explore the meaning of reflective practice and its evolution within SES and allied disciplines. Section 3 – "Pedagogical and Applied Issues" – given that reflective practice has become more widely embedded within education, professional training, and professional proficiency standards, chapters in this section explore the importance of reflective practice in preparing practitioners for the nature of applied SES service delivery, as well as issues relating to organisational reflection, facilitating reflective practice in others, and novel approaches to reflective practice. Section 4 – "Applied Case Studies" – this collection offers a variety of personal insights into reflective practice, including examples of: how reflective practice facilitates effective service delivery; how reflective practice underpins organisational practices; the impact of reflective practice on personal and professional sense making and growth; and context specific approaches to reflective practice. Finally, Section 5 – "Reflecting Forwards" – concludes the text by offering reflective analysis on the preceding sections in light of the aims of the book, and outlines future directions appropriate to researchers, practitioners, educators, and consumers of reflective practice.

Reflecting on Reflective Practice

It is not our (editorial team) intention in this introduction to engage in a full conceptual debate regarding the origins, application, and importance of reflective practice in the SES and allied disciplines – such discussion can be located in the previous edition (see Knowles et al., 2014b), the growing research base in the area (see Huntley et al., 2014, 2019), and in the chapters presented in the current text. However, we do feel it important to (re)consider our position regarding the nature of reflective practice. We do this not only to frame the forthcoming contributions, but also provide you (the reader) with an opportunity to reflect at this early stage of the book on your own understanding of reflective practice.

It may seem somewhat confusing, given the burgeoning size of the reflective practice literature across fields (including SES), that debates regarding how we should define the concept persist. Indeed, in response to the growing need for practitioners across fields to submit documentary evidence of reflective practice as part of the requirements of professional accreditation/certification, Marshall (2019) recently posited that, "It is important to . . . consensually validate the concept and definition of reflection" (p. 399). We do understand the importance of conceptual clarity, having previously presented that of the 179 research manuscripts published between 2001–2012 on reflective practice in sport and exercise settings only 68 demonstrated what might be classified as an appropriate conceptual and applied understanding of reflection (see Huntley et al., 2014). We also accept, however, that given the varied modalities of reflective practice (e.g., on- and in-action) and the multiple purposes that it may serve (e.g., personal growth, sense making, practice improvements) that an encompassing definition is difficult to locate.

In an attempt to address this issue, in the first edition of this text, following analysis of the process and outcome elements presented in many definitions of reflective practice constructed by authors in different fields, we proposed that reflective practice is:

> A purposeful and complex process that facilitates the examination of experience by questioning the whole self and our agency within the context of practice. This examination transforms experience into learning, which helps us to access, make sense of and develop our knowledge-in-action in order to better understand and/or improve practice and the situation in which it occurs. (Knowles et al., 2014b, p. 10)

While we stand by this definition as it moved our understanding beyond the often-accepted literal view (at the time) that reflective practice is simply a matter of pausing for thought, or the mere evaluation of self and/or practice, we appreciate that on its own it may add further confusion into the "conceptual mix." Thus, to add clarity to our conceptual view, we do not offer a new definition but instead have broken this definition down into its constituent process and outcome elements and provided additional layers of insight to confirm our position regarding reflective practice (see Table 1.1).

Introducing the Team

You will read elsewhere about the origins of reflective practice (RP) and how and when it made the leap into the SES literature. However, the origins of *Team RP*, the group that has come together to edit this book, is a little less clear and shrouded in mystery. Where and how we came together is not certain, but Liverpool is almost certainly involved as are Leeds and Cardiff, and there can be no doubt that there was input from Hamish Telfer, Dave Gilbourne, and Andy Borrie with a significant cameo from Ailsa Niven (nee Anderson). Somewhere and somehow though the team came together. A glance through the history books shows that I (Andy), had some role to play in the PhD's of each of my co-editors as either Director of Studies (Brendan), Examiner (Zoe), or Supervisor (Emma) – not bad for a lapsed physiologist! Thus, it falls to me as the more 'senior' member of *Team RP* to offer some comment on the band's history and on the various team members and their involvement in this book.

If we draw the lines that link the people and events, then we can probably start in the mid to late 1990s when sport coaching started to adopt RP as a means of

Table 1.1 Constituents of Reflective Practice and Their Application

Constituent	Meaning	Application
Purposeful	Reflective practice is something that we* *consciously* decide to engage in, which distinguishes reflection from the subconscious processes of daydreaming. Additionally, there should be a *purpose* to the reflection (an aim) to give the reflection focus and make the process purposeful and meaningful.	Many believe that they reflect "all of the time" usually through subconscious, implicit processes that they cannot explain. To really make sense of and examine practice in a meaningful way, however, reflective practice must be purposeful. It must be about something (e.g., an experience) and for something (e.g., exploring personal meaning). Identifying a purpose (e.g., to examine congruence between values and actions), instead of aimlessly gazing back can result in a more meaningful approach.
Complex process	Reflective practice is complex due to the need for individuals to consider personal cognitions, emotions and behaviours, their interaction and impact on the situation, as well as the impact of the context on these – rather than simply focusing on what they did and what happened as a result.	We must excavate beneath the surface of our observable behaviours (e.g., the use of certain modes of intervention) and examine why these behaviours occur, how they have come to be that way, and what impact they have. For example, exploring how personal values and beliefs may influence the way that we practice, the decisions we make, and the way that we react in situations, while not easy, allows us to develop a level of awareness that can facilitate sense making.
The importance of questions	Thinking in an un-structured way about experience is complicated. The lack of a guide through the "swampy lowlands" often results in individuals unable to process and make sense of a series of connected but random thoughts. Good questions can offer this *guide.*	(Good) questions, those that encourage deeper, critical thought and examination, initiated through a reflective conversation (with the self or in a process of shared reflection) helps to guide the reflective process. Such questions can help to facilitate the *checking of blind spots* and encourage individuals to engage meaningfully in the reflective process.

Focusing on the self and agency	Through reflective practice individuals need to consider the *self* as an agent of change. Reflective practice is about who you are, what you do, why you do it, and how it has come to be that way. Indeed, *reflexivity* – the exploration of self and development of self-awareness – is fundamental within the process.	Many individuals focus too much on the external (e.g., the client, the setting) without considering themselves and the way in which they have impacted on these external factors. To engage in deeper, more critical reflective practice, individuals have to question their own practice and the values that underpin it. By placing the self at the centre of the reflective process individuals can elicit a level of developmental control that facilitates improved practice.
Change as an outcome	Change represents: (a) a change in behaviour, values, or beliefs; (b) confirmation or rejection of a particular theory or practice; and/or (c) a change in knowledge of the self, the context of practice or the environment in which the practitioner is working.	The outcome of reflective practice should result in a form of learning or understanding depending on the nature and purpose for reflection. This learning should be expressed, and sense should be made about how this will impact on future practice and/or thinking. Individuals should commit to ensuring that the outcomes of their reflective practices become the content of their future actions, which can be supported by a process of goal setting, action planning, and goal-striving.

*Note: By "we" in this table, the editorial team refer to all individuals and/or organisations irrespective of discipline, purpose, or role.

developing coaches. What was the National Coaching Foundation (NCF, now UK Coaching), drawing on the athletics coaching expertise of the likes of Hamish Telfer, established a distance learning degree programme (see Miles, 2001) with key modules on RP written and managed by myself and Andy Borrie. The seedlings of *Team RP* were starting to sprout in the suburbs of Leeds. With both Andy Borrie and I seconded to the NCF from our respective higher education institutions in Worcester and Liverpool, "pockets of RP" began to emerge across the country, and we vied for "RP supremacy." Andy Borrie worked with Dave Gilbourne and a budding sport psychologist by the name of Zoe Knowles and developed work on RP in coaching and published their first work in 2001 (see Knowles et al., 2001) whilst around the same time Ailsa Niven had "transferred" from Liverpool to Worcester to conduct a PhD with me as supervisor, which explored RP as a means of measuring sport psychology consultant effectiveness and in 2002 the first publication regarding RP in sport science was published (see Anderson et al., 2002). My move to Cardiff paved the way for Brendan to start his PhD further exploring the role of RP in sport psychology consultancy and at the same time Zoe started her PhD work continuing the exploration of RP in coaching contexts with the two of them racing each other to completion in 2009. There may be certainty about when Paul McCartney first played alongside John Lennon in the Quarrymen, but there is no such certainty around when Zoe, Brendan and I first "jammed" together, and the mists of time seem to swallow up the early exchanges. What we do know is that along the way we took the opportunity to develop a RP workshop for the British Association of Sport and Exercise Sciences (BASES) as an outlet for research dissemination and the founding line-up of *Team RP* was up and running.

For a lengthy period through the mid 2000's to the mid 2010's, just like *Take That*, we each pursued solo projects whilst still managing to come together regularly to continue to record some of our greatest hits. The prolific Zoe and Brendan (Gary and Robbie!!) churned out the "hits" and together in 2014 "released" the memorable First Edition of this text, on which this new release is built. Brendan and I enjoyed a working partnership at Cardiff with Brendan penning a few classics along the way and Zoe recruited a new member in the form of a PhD student of her own – Emma – and the trio became a quartet. Numerous outputs, including a BASES Expert Statement (see Huntley et al., 2019), professional development workshops, and book chapters (e.g., Cropley et al., 2018) have followed and then came the idea of the Second Edition. Just like the Oasis reunion, it was on the table for a long time as an idea and many said it could never happen but with no feuding brothers in *Team RP* not even a global pandemic could stop us. Once the notion was verbalised to the publishers there was no going back and suddenly here we are. This book sees the culmination of a lot of hard work (mainly Brendan's – he is more studious!), many sleepless nights (mainly Emma's – doing a PhD and editing a book with a new young daughter has an effect), lots of feedback (mainly Zoe's – she reads quicker!) and many bad jokes (mainly mine – I am not funny!) and comes to you the reader with a request that you enjoy reading it as much as we enjoyed editing it.

As the "instrumental break" kicks in I will take the opportunity to offer some comments on each individual member of *Team RP* and then I am sure one of them will step in to chide the old man with some comment on my contribution (or lack of) and humour (or lack of). In so doing, it also seems appropriate to offer a word of thanks to former band member David Gilbourne for his insightful comments in the Foreword of this edition and it would be hugely remiss of me not to acknowledge the wonderful Lindsey Dugdill whose sad passing served as an inspiration and motivation to us all to get this book across the line and to whose memory we dedicate wholeheartedly this Second Edition.

Professor Brendan Cropley has established himself as arguably one of the leading names in the RP literature and has the unique ability to not only publish highly reputable academic discourse on the subject but also to provide insightful applied advice and instruction on the most effective ways for practitioners to engage in critical RP. The impact of his work has been widely felt across several disciplines including SES, coaching, and academia, as well as across public, private, and third sector organisations. As a former footballer himself, Brendan heads the Centre for Football Research in Wales and I am sure that he developed his interest in reflection from his time as a goalkeeper – he spent so much time looking back to see the ball in the net that he must have felt he could make a living out of looking behind him! Brendan is my professional "pay it forward" and all that was good that was done for me I would do for him although he will always remain my second favourite PhD student!

On a personal note, Brendan will always have a special place in my heart – present at both the best day of my recent life and the worst, he always offers that moment of support and humour, and our mutual love of the same football team means that neither of us will ever walk alone. I frequently smile to myself when I recall a day at the Vale of Glamorgan hotel when he and I went to watch the British Lions train. Armed with his replica shirt Brendan ran from player to player getting their autographs and with just coach Rob Howley to go for the full set Brendan eagerly joined the queue and, in his impatience, the way he elbowed the line of eight-year-olds out of the way to secure his quest was worthy of a place on the Lions tour.

Professor Zoe Knowles is, in scholarly terms, prolific, and both well regarded and highly credible. It seems like she has spent pretty much all her academic lifetime researching in, commenting on, and providing training for, RP. Her championing of RP has spanned the academic fields of coaching science, sports psychology and children's play with numerous publications and successful PhD students moving her thinking and appreciation of the importance of RP in professional development forward in each field. As an academic, she has strongly advocated public engagement with sport science through not only her formal role as a Professor of Engagement and Learning but also through her applied practitioner role and as an active member of BASES. Her continued contribution to BASES has seen her gain the ultimate recognition from her peers in the industry by being elected as the Association's first female Chair, a role in which she continues to support and promote all aspects of both SES to academic and practitioner communities as well as ensuring that the profession has high standing in the eyes of the public.

A lasting memory of Zoe will always be the level of respect she garnered from her family, friends, peers, and colleagues at her inaugural professorial lecture. The manner in which her personal family and professional family acknowledged her contribution to their lives was truly awe-inspiring and made those of us who know her and who have the privilege of working with her feel extremely humble – any person who can get Hamish Telfer on a train from the wilds of Scotland to hear them speak must have something special to say! Zoe is a woman who truly lives and breathes the sporting campaign strapline, "This girl can" – and has expanded it with her own statement – "This woman has."

Dr Emma Huntley is the future of *Team RP* and as such the direction and quality of the work in this field is in safe hands. As a Senior Lecturer in sport and exercise psychology, Emma retains a keen interest in all aspects of the sport and exercise profession being a highly respected teacher, researcher, and applied practitioner. Being the "junior" member of *Team RP*, Emma gets all the jobs nobody else wants but that's OK because she does them so well – the evidence for that is clear in her solo chapter in this book updating and building on her previous extensive back catalogue of reviews of the RP literature. There is no doubt that the delegates passing through the current iteration of the BASES workshop on RP owe the quality of their experience to Emma as a result of her rigorous and insightful evaluation of its effectiveness, its impact on professional development, and the professional manner in which she championed the inclusion of her findings.

I am sure Tabo, her ever supportive husband and their children don't need any mirrors in the Huntley house because there is already so much RP going on! If Emma has a weakness (and that is a big if!) it is that she does not realise how good she is. Maybe the rest of us have not told her this enough but Emma, hopefully you will now realise we are not bluffing, and you are that good – the baton is yours for the Third Edition.

And so, it has fallen to me (Zoe) to offer some words about Andy the "senior" member of the team, the Admiral, and in fact one of my PhD examiners "back in the day". **Dr Andy Miles** has worked for over 30 years in Higher Education with a focus initially on physiology and latterly reflective practice. I see Andy as someone determined to promote the values of interdisciplinary focus to SES and he lives that through his own practice, curriculum management work, and leadership. He has developed a passion for people/practitioner professional development and worked in applied settings to train tutors and early career practitioners to be the best that they can be and for the benefit of the people they deliver to and work with. Andy has created two business ventures: Sport Education Solutions Ltd to facilitate this training and development ethos in the SES domain, and Made to Measure Mentoring Ltd to apply the professional development and training concepts to a wider audience, which now includes the British Army, NATO, and the NHS, as well as sport. As an editorial team we have benefitted from his experience of these settings, consultancy, and working with people beyond those in SES. Indeed, the text here is richer in focus and writing because of that. Finally, Andy's contribution on the #TeamRP social media group is legendary. Amongst the periodic challenges of compiling this book, a gif, joke or "one liner" was just what was needed . . . here's hoping you stick around for book three, it's fair to say we couldn't have done any of this without you.

Summary

In summary, it has been a pleasure to work collectively as an editorial team to bring you this text. We have thoroughly enjoyed working with all the contributing authors on this endeavour and our collaborative interactions have certainly helped us to appraise and question our understanding of reflective practice. We believe that the diversity of perspectives, the level of critical insight, and the varied directions taken in the ensuing chapters will provoke interest, further understanding, and raise debate about education, training, and professional practice in the SES and allied disciplines and the position of reflective practice within these areas. If this is the case, and in recognition of our intention to grow the community of reflective practitioners in the SES, we invite you to work with us, not only through the preceding chapters by engaging in your own reflection and sense making on what the discussions mean for you, but also by contributing to future research and debate – please feel free to get in touch!

2 Where Are We Now and Where to Next?

A Strategic Pause Amongst the Reflective Practice Literature in Sport and Exercise

Emma Huntley

Introduction

Over the last two decades, and more specifically, since the first edition of this book (Knowles et al., 2014a), a significant increase in the volume of reflective practice (RP) research within a sport and exercise context has been published (see Huntley et al., 2019; Huntley, 2021). Whilst there is continued acceptance that RP is a valuable and important mechanism for all disciplines and for practitioners of varying levels of experience, the extant literature has been dominated by self-reflective and opinion/experiential pieces, methods associated traditionally with the social sciences. This is perhaps because such research has been typically dominated by the disciplines of sport coaching and sport psychology (Huntley et al., 2014). As a result, there have been understandable calls for more empirical research in the area, with the aim of exploring in detail, and perhaps verifying, the value that RP has for facilitating the personal and professional growth of practitioners working in the sport and exercise sciences (SES; Huntley et al., 2019). It has previously been proposed that by addressing this need researchers should consider how their work might assist novice practitioners' initial engagement in the process and extend into other disciplines outside of coaching and psychology to ensure that research findings can be better disseminated across the SES as a whole.

Twenty years have passed since the inaugural RP papers were published within sport and exercise (e.g., Holt & Strean, 2001; Knowles et al., 2001). Huntley et al. (2014) systematically explored the literature published during this early period (2001–2012), and it now seems appropriate to stop and reflect on the RP literature to date, and in doing so answer the questions, "Where are we now?" and, "Where to next?" This chapter, therefore, aims to review the most recent RP literature, written within or from a sport and exercise context, published from 2013 to 2022, as well as consider areas for future examination regarding RP.

Locating RP Research in the SES

Let's start with the question – *where is RP found in the SES?* Huntley et al. (2014) reported that whilst initial studies in the early 2000s were mainly focused on

DOI: 10.4324/9781003198758-3

sport coaching, from 2004, the most frequent research concerning RP emanated from the discipline of sport psychology. This may have been because of the heightened emphasis placed on practitioners working (or training) in a sport psychology setting (arguably more so than those working in other disciplines) to engage in, and provide evidence of, RP as part of their respective professional regulations (e.g., British Association of Sport and Exercise Sciences [BASES]; British Psychological Society [BPS]). Further, given the opportunities for publishing *professional practice* research (and insights) in sport psychology, many individuals saw an opportunity to publish the output of their RP as a way of furnishing the field with accounts of lived experience. Consequently, many publications prior to 2012 were focused on the self-reflections of practitioner experience, mainly from trainee or neophyte populations, with a noticeable absence of reports from those more experienced (Knowles et al., 2012). Conversely, whilst sport coaches engaging in coaching courses would be required and/or encouraged to engage in RP as part of their respective awards, requirements were less formal and remained 'hidden' amongst academic outputs. Indeed, during this period (2001–2012), those writing about RP from a coaching perspective were mainly researchers from coach education/coaching science (e.g., based in Higher Education Institutions, HEIs), or in some cases, were individual coaches sharing their experiences via personalised accounts.

More recently, however (e.g., since 2013), the sport and exercise literature relating to RP has been heavily dominated by work from the field of sport coaching. There are perhaps several possible explanations for this surge in RP research in this area. First, sport coaching, and those researching in this field, have undergone somewhat of an epistemological shift to a position that understands coaching as a complex, contested, and subjective process requiring individuals to develop locally owned knowledge to be able to navigate the challenges they experience in their roles. Thus, RP has become more formally embedded in coach education programmes and reflective accounts have gained increased recognition as valuable practical research insights into coaches' lived experiences. Second, the ongoing professionalisation of sport coaching has seen a global increase in the number of undergraduate and postgraduate degree programmes, which has augmented the need to develop a specific knowledge base regarding the theory and practice of coaching. Finally, there has been an increase in the number of research outlets accepting of personalised accounts of practice, which are thought to add interpretative insights into the enactment and management of the coaching process.

The narrative presented in this chapter thus far demonstrates the ebb and flow of the focus placed on RP by researchers and practitioners across a relatively short period of time (2001–present). Notably, prior to 2014, RP research in the SES domain was not representative of the disciplines that make up this domain, even though RP has become more widely embedded into education and professional training pathways for practitioners working across the SES (e.g., BASES). However, there have been recent developments in the RP literature in the SES, perhaps due to the recognition that all practitioners training and working in the SES operate in contexts and environments characterised by complexity that those in sport psychology and sport coaching have embraced for some time. It is important (and timely), therefore, to explore the RP literature from a wider SES perspective, particularly as there is a historical practice of borrowing from other fields to understand one's own context. To readers, this may help you understand 'what we do now' as a SES community more widely.

The 'New Players' in RP

The following section aims to explore some of the 'younger' disciplinary areas of sport and exercise, and related allied health whereby RP is starting to become prevalent and is being actively explored. Specifically, these 'new players' include physiology, nutrition, biomechanics, strength and conditioning (S&C), and allied health disciplines, with specific reference to clinical exercise physiology, physical activity promotion, and sports therapy.

Sport & Exercise Science Disciplines

The SES traditionally encompass the three branches of psychology, physiology, and biomechanics, either in isolation or through interdisciplinary approaches (BASES, 2022). However, when considering RP, psychology has led the way in the literature for some time (Huntley et al., 2014; Huntley, 2021), with very few (if any) published contributions from the more positivistic branches of physiology (e.g., Doncaster, 2018; Morton, 2009, 2014) and biomechanics (Lees, 2019). In addition, some researchers have used an overarching SES title (e.g., Doncaster, 2018; Huntley & Kentzer, 2013; Lees, 2019), which upon further inspection, reveals authors or participants are most typically aligned with a specific discipline. For example, in Huntley and Kentzer (2013), the authors are BASES Accredited Sport and Exercise Scientists, hence the paper title is reflective of this. However, their disciplinary specialism is that of psychology. Therefore, here, I consider the literature in its truest sense, considering the skills, competencies, and alignment of the practitioners' discipline to provide maximum clarity for the RP community in a SES context.

Perhaps one of the earliest RP contributions from a sport physiologist was by Morton (2009) and more recently in the first edition of this textbook (Morton, 2014). In both outputs, Morton provided self-reflective accounts of experiences of academia, transitioning from a research student to a lecturer (Morton, 2009), and as a practitioner working in the field with elite athletes (Morton, 2014). More recently, Doncaster (2018), working in a SES role by title, highlighted a distinct lack of RP literature in his respective discipline of physiology to draw upon. Consequently, he decided to share his own reflections, utilising a variety of methods (e.g., written, audio, video, individual, shared), adapting a bespoke framework (based on Gibbs, 1988), which helped him to navigate differing roles (e.g., intern, researcher, academic), stages of development, and associated challenges faced in each. In doing so, Doncaster provided an account of self-exploration in which he sought a better understanding of the working context and of the concept of impactful service delivery. Further, drawing on the *Conscious Competence Learning Matrix* (Howell & Fleishman, 1982), Doncaster was able to describe his transition from stages of *incompetence* towards *competence* across the different roles he fulfilled.

Practitioners in fields related to physiology, such as sports nutrition, have also begun to explore the potential of RP. Specifically, Martin (2017) shared reflections on the challenges of working simultaneously as a performance nutritionist in professional horseracing and as a HEI lecturer. Through his research, Martin aimed to showcase the development of a bespoke process of RP, which helped him navigate through and deal with the demands associated with both aspects of his dual career. Indeed, Martin highlighted the importance of practitioners drawing on several RP models and frameworks as a toolbox where the most relevant approach can be adopted depending on the nature of the situation to be reflected upon. Martin's work suggests that RP is (and should be) a dynamic and individualised process rather than a 'one size fits all' approach.

Doncaster's (2018) and Martin's (2017) articles share some common messages. First, they both describe the challenges of navigating multiple roles, which is common in the SES (e.g., practitioner, intern, researcher, lecturer), and highlight that RP is a fundamental process to managing oneself (and others, where applicable) when working in such diverse settings and contexts. Second, both authors advocated the use of an individualised, bespoke RP process; whether that be in using a variety of RP methods to align with the purpose of/for the reflection, or in creating/adapting an RP model/framework for supporting one's own RP. The importance of an individualised approach to RP has been explored elsewhere (e.g., Cropley et al., 2012; Huntley, 2021), and it has been proposed that the method of RP (e.g., written, verbal, shared) should be aligned with the purpose and focus of the reflection to support more effective and meaningful engagement (Huntley et al., 2019).

Perhaps the first RP focused manuscript published in the area of biomechanics offers a personal reflection, through a narrative style, on the evolution of racket sport science (cf. Lees, 2019). However, upon critical review, the article appears to provide a somewhat 'person-absent' view, more akin to an opinion piece of the external context, rather than an introspective, self-reflective view on oneself (and others) in a given context. This contrasts with the other literature reviewed in this section, in which authors do provide such introspective and critical insights into their lived experiences. Similar issues (e.g., proposing the use or exploration of RP and not offering accounts akin to widely accepted conceptualisations of RP) can be seen in other articles in the wider SES. For example, Pettersson and Ekström (2014) published an article in the context of sports nutrition that attested to discuss the potential importance of RP in the context of offering support to athletes. Nevertheless, little reflective insight or discussion was presented or framed in the manuscript.

Despite the papers presented in this section, there are still very few examples of RP research manuscripts from across the (non-psychology) SES practitioner community. This paucity of insight perhaps continues to support the erroneous perspective held by some that RP is only for psychologists (Huntley et al., 2019). Given that all literature reviewed in this section are single-author outputs, an opportunity for augmenting RP research across SES lies in the potential of collaborative outputs. In collaborating, individuals may feel more confident in opening themselves, their RP, and their professional practice up for analysis and discussion. Thus, valuable insights into the professional practice of SES across disciplines can be garnered to support better education, training, and service delivery in these areas. To note, more RP examples from the perspectives of physiology and nutrition can be found in the present text (see Chapters 13 and 14).

Strength & Conditioning

Another area that has seen some considerable interest and focus on RP in recent years is strength and conditioning (S&C; e.g., Handcock & Cassidy, 2014; Kuklick et al., 2015a; Kuklick et al., 2015b). S&C practitioners arguably crossover between traditional sport coaching, in that they require an understanding of coach philosophy and psychosocial behaviours, but also must have underpinning knowledge and experience of SES principles (e.g., anatomy, physiology, biomechanics/movement analysis) in order to successfully improve athletic performance (see Carson et al., 2021). In addition to discussion-based papers advocating for RP use in S&C settings (e.g., Handcock & Cassidy, 2014), empirical studies have begun to emerge, considering both the *process* and *outcome* of RP for S&C service delivery. For example, Szedlak, Smith et al. (2019) examined the benefits of a research-based vignette of an elite S&C coach attempting to explore effective practice, presented in different formats (written, audio, video), to disseminate information to S&C coaches. The researchers asked participants to reflect on the utility of the approach and on the preferred format, with findings suggesting that: (a) vignettes are useful in translating knowledge and encouraging action; and (b) video vignettes are most powerful. In a follow-up, Szedlak and colleagues (2020) examined how experienced S&C practitioners develop coach behaviours and characteristics through the *process* of reflection. Each participant was interviewed regarding their process of learning from a video vignette and from their subsequent reflections. The researchers reported that the RP process enhanced the participants' level of self- awareness. In another study, Szedlak, Smith et al. (2021) requested several experienced S&C practitioners to write a letter to their younger self, asking each to reflect on their careers and write about what and how they had learned during this time. Participant letters were thematically analysed and blended into one composite letter, which was next distributed to a group of S&C students who engaged in a focus group to further explore their perceptions and learning experiences upon reading the letter. This process resulted in learners feeling more encouraged to reflect, showing that the *process* of RP can indeed lead to a new *outcome* relating to RP. It was proposed, therefore, that such a tool could be used in pedagogical settings to stimulate trainee/novice practitioners to reflect, as well as provide motivation to continue to work on their development moving forwards.

Building on this work, Szedlak, Batey et al. (2021), through interviews with experienced S&C practitioners, highlighted the importance of RP (as an outcome) for the development of practitioner psychosocial behaviours, which included understanding athlete's needs, communicating effectively, caring and connecting with the athlete, and practicing what you preach. Szedlak, Batey et al.'s (2021) findings also suggested that current development programmes for S&C practitioners are limited in facilitating the development of such behaviours and made a call for educators to further facilitate RP processes in order to develop more critically *reflective practitioners* (see Chapter 3). Such facilitation in this context could include, as suggested by Roy et al. (2021), reflective diaries (e.g., Cronin et al., 2020), reflective cards (e.g., Koh et al., 2017), video analysis (e.g., Partington et al., 2015), shared and conversational reflection (e.g., Huntley & Kentzer, 2013), or *think aloud* as an approach to explore 'in-action' reflections (e.g., Whitehead et al., 2016; see Chapter 10). Roy et al. (2021) also called for several factors (e.g., motivation to engage with RP, level of experience or stage of learning of the coach, time and availability of resources, access to peers to support the RP process, and the context in which one operates) to be considered when facilitating RP in S&C settings.

Whilst RP in the context of S&C is relatively new, the literature in this area highlights positive developments. Varied and novel RP processes and research methods are being used, including some perhaps not previously seen in the more mature RP settings of sport coaching and psychology (e.g., a letter to myself; Szedlak, Smith et al., 2021). Further, key principles about appreciating contextual factors and individual preferences to enhance RP engagement, that have taken almost 20 years to generate (Huntley et al., 2019) are, relatively speaking, being discussed much earlier in its evolution within S&C and this is certainly encouraging (for further S&C RP see Chapter 15).

Allied Health Disciplines

In addition to the traditional disciplines of SES, there are areas in allied health settings within which RP research could be enhanced. One such setting is clinical exercise physiology (CEP) where practitioners are defined as "university qualified health professionals who specialise in the prescription and delivery of evidence-based exercise interventions to optimise the prevention, treatment and long-term management of acute, sub-acute, chronic and complex conditions" (CEP-UK, 2022). Recently, within Australia, where exercise physiology has been recognised as an accredited health profession for over twenty years (Jones et al., 2021), RP was deemed important enough by experts in the field to be listed as a sub-competency of professionalism, one of six broader competencies in a study aiming to establish core clinical learning competencies for exercise physiology students (Raymond et al., 2020). Contrastingly, at present, CEP in the UK is not regulated in the same way, thus RP is not a mandatory aspect of training, which is perhaps a factor in the limited RP research in this field. However, a recent call to action has been made to try and rectify this, building upon the successes of the

Australian system (Jones et al., 2021). Therefore, it is hoped (and called for) that through the development of internationally collaborative relationships, more RP research within CEP can be conducted and disseminated to support the growth of professional service delivery and practitioners' personal development.

Another area for future RP research is that relating to exercise intervention and physical activity promotion. In one of the only examples of such research in this area, Rogers et al. (2021) used a confessional tale approach to reflect on the time spent over a one-year period in a secure mental health hospital to inform the future design of a physical activity intervention. Rogers et al. (2021) shared some of the challenges of engaging in the RP process, which involved a reflexive journal to hold fieldnotes, such as feeling "awkward":

> Initially, I found my inexperience and lack of knowledge on reflective prac-
> tice to be both daunting and frustrating. I felt awkward documenting my
> thoughts and emotions on paper, struggled to accurately articulate how I felt,
> and experienced continual self-doubt around whether I was conducting the
> process correctly. The notes I wrote in initial stages of the process merely
> offered a descriptive narrative of daily events and did little to acknowledge
> my position within the research or extend my understanding of data collec-
> tion within the setting. (p. 239)

However, the authors reported more positive moments of deeper reflection facilitated through the supervisory process:

> There were times in which opportunities for reflection would have been
> missed without prompts from my supervisor . . . Supervisory discussions
> allowed me to recognise the importance of analysing seemingly insignificant
> experience whilst acknowledging the contribution or influence these experi-
> ences made to knowledge production. (p. 239)

The benefit of supervisors to the RP process is a notion described elsewhere (e.g., Woodcock et al., 2008). Reflecting with a *more capable other* is thought to provide alternative perspectives or more critically reflective depth and thereby increase ensuing knowledge and understanding gains compared to reflecting in solitude (Knowles et al., 2012; Rogers et al., 2021). Such lessons that are supported across disciplines (e.g., sport psychology) and fields (e.g., allied health) have the potential to have a positive influence on those working across the SES and thus transfer and corroboration of such benefits appears important.

One allied health area yet to receive any specific attention with regards to RP in the literature is the discipline of *sports therapy*, which is in contrast to the related fields of physiotherapy, physical therapy, and athletic trainers. The UK's Society for Sports Therapy (SST) stipulates that their members engage in RP to ensure that standards of proficiency are maintained, and members' annual CPD submissions could be audited at any point to check such engagement. Indeed, as indicated by Dr Kate Williams (see Chapter 7), RP is being utilised 'on the ground' by sports therapy students and practicing therapists. Therefore, individual sports therapists, and the wider discipline of sports therapy, are challenged to step forward, take the learnings from other allied disciplines and that of the RP community, and explore (and share) how RP may work for you!

Contemporary RP Themes: New Lines of Enquiry

Whilst the previous section highlighted both the dominant and more sparsely populated areas of RP literature in SES settings, it is apparent that over the last decade, some new lines of enquiry have begun to be explored. These include the consideration of RP for personal well-being and self-care, RP for athletes, and RP methods.

RP for Personal Well-Being & Self-Care

Full time sport practitioner roles are highly demanding, fast-paced, often take place in ever-changing dynamic settings (e.g., Cropley et al., 2016; Williams & Andersen, 2012), and in some cases, are tenured or short-term positions where job security can be lacking. The susceptibility for work-related stress or burnout is, therefore, high (Hägglund et al., 2021). Equally, trainee practitioners often find themselves working in multiple roles simultaneously in part-time jobs to fund professional or formal education fees whilst also often engaged in formal education and trying to have a social life to encompass a form of work life balance. In such instances of busyness and holding multiple responsibilities, self-care can be overlooked in favour of meeting the demands of formal roles, which can result in an impact to one's mental or physical health. Managing oneself both personally and professionally in such settings should, therefore, be of high importance (McDougall et al., 2015; Morton, 2014 – see Chapter 14 too). In doing so, self-awareness is key to understanding one's thoughts, feelings, behaviours, actions, and consequently managing stressors that may occur when learning and practicing (or competing) in such settings.

Self-awareness, gained through RP, was highlighted by McDougall et al. (2015) as crucial for sport psychology practitioners to be able to make sense of their experiences, manage themselves, and to maintain personal and professional effectiveness, especially in the face of adversity, much of which is unknown prior to entering the profession. However, practitioners working in challenging/ adverse environments need the skills or strategies to be able to navigate the possible (or actual) challenges faced. Cropley et al. (2016) identified RP as key in the development of coping strategies, specifically in providing the link between professional knowledge (theory) and knowledge-in-action (practice). This is particularly imperative for less experienced practitioners who may not yet have coping strategies to draw upon, as alluded to by Martin et al. (2022). However, problem solving, identified as a preferred coping style by participants in Cropley et al. (2016), through a shared reflective process offers an opportunity to work through the challenges faced when working in SES contexts. Such shared RP approaches reduce feelings of isolation, and perhaps lead to increased understanding, the development of new perspectives and the normalisation/validation of emotions and experiences. Shared reflection is thus thought to support the development of coping through problem solving and managing anxiety (e.g., Knowles et al., 2007; Huntley et al., 2019).

Given that the reality of applied service delivery can be (and often is) very different to that which is expected and understood by trainee practitioners, it seems ever more important that SES disciplines support the production of reflective accounts. It is these accounts that can furnish trainees and neophytes with valuable insights into the context of professional practice in sport and exercise, and thus support individuals to develop the necessary knowledge and skills to navigate these dynamic contexts. Following calls for such insights by Cropley et al. (2016), Uphill and Hemmings (2017) shared their critical reflections of being a sport psychologist, with a specific focus on vulnerability. Historically, there appears to be a perception that being vulnerable is a sign of weakness, and could have negative repercussions, personally or professionally. In contrast, however, the sharing of vulnerabilities has the potential to be transformative, either for oneself, or for others in the author's influence. Certainly, I have tried to advocate this in my earlier work (see Huntley & Kentzer, 2013), offering reflective insights into a situation in which I felt panic, fear, and worry, brought on by a momentary sense of not knowing how to best act in a potentially unethical interaction. In this article, I noted that rather than simply adopting an "I'm fine" approach in a bid to maintain face (a notion explained by Uphill & Hemming, 2017), and keep any vulnerabilities silenced, I opted to publicly share (locally and later, publicly) and reflect on my vulnerabilities by sharing my reflections in a bid to hopefully help others in some way. There are other examples of SES practitioners openly reflecting on their vulnerabilities in a positive and adaptive way (e.g., Morton, 2014; also see Chapter 14). Such reflections are powerful and provide real synthesis (or indeed highlight the dichotomy) between the professional and the personal, displaying vulnerability to the reader, which in turn can bring about new outlooks and perspective transformation (Mezirow, 1991).

These personal reflective accounts of vulnerability, well-being, and self-care have recently been substantiated with empirical research using wider (and larger) populations. For example, the development and support of vulnerability using reflection was described by Hägglund et al. (2021), who designed and investigated the use of a novel, short messaging service (SMS) or text-message based RP intervention with high performance sport coaches. Specifically, participants completed a daily or weekly SMS-based diary over a period of eight weeks, each in response to questions about mood, energy levels, and a short reflection, including a highlight of the day. Findings demonstrated high fidelity, reach and perceived value of the intervention for the participants. Additionally, participants self-reported greater engagement with their own well-being, with specific references made about self-awareness, self-compassion, and a positive view on vulnerability. Facilitation and support for those working as practitioners, or indeed as athletes, in high performance or pressure settings in sport and exercise contexts is imperative to ensure that well-being and mental health is supported for both personal and professional reasons. Based on the literature presented in this section, it appears that RP is a vital mechanism in supporting this process. A drive for self-care, referred to in a psychology context as an ethical imperative for practitioners (Martin et al., 2022), has been observed in the sport-based literature of late, perhaps contributed to by a global pandemic (e.g., Covid-19), whereby exercise, sleep, mindfulness, social interaction, as well as RP have all been identified as methods of achieving care of the self (Martin et al., 2022). What RP, as a method of self-care, offers above the others listed here, however, is a flexibility to not have to rely on other people (e.g., social support), or specialist resources/money (e.g., gym membership fees/spaces), or a large amount of time (e.g., sleep), therefore providing a readily accessible approach to prioritising one's mental health, well-being, and personal welfare, for practitioners and athletes alike.

RP for Athletes

While the main beneficiaries of RP research have typically been applied practitioners (e.g., psychologists, coaches; see Huntley et al., 2014), one area that has observed some growth in recent years, particularly since 2013, is that of the use of RP within athletic populations. For example, Neil and colleagues (2013) provided a double case study approach to sharing their first-hand experiences of the implementation of RP interventions with athletes. The first case focused on an individual cricketer whose self-efficacy, focus of attention during performances, and self-awareness were all improved after a process of guided and unguided written reflection. Similarly, in Fletcher and Wilson's (2013) work, reflective diaries were found to be beneficial for a group of professional cricketers who explored the impact of this approach over a one-month period during a competitive season. Specifically, participants reported that the reflective diaries provided an opportunity to enhance oneself, as well as a form of cathartic release, which facilitated progression and a quest to find one's personal patterns of success. Further, Threlfall (2014) offered a different approach to written reflection, by engaging in an email-based reflective conversation with two elite athletes from track and field athletics, utilising a similar methodology to that observed in Knowles et al.'s (2012) work. Outcomes of this approach revealed that the two athletes had different preferences for RP, which is an important consideration for those in faciliatory roles regarding RP. However, regardless of different preferences, both athletes agreed that reflecting-on-action was most helpful (whereas in-action reflection could be detrimental to performance in their respective events of pole vault and 800m), but also that reflecting in *collaboration* with their coach was important and beneficial.

In contrast, the second case study presented by Neil et al. (2013) utilised a variety of RP methods within a female rugby team, with a particular focus on goal setting. During two focus groups to explore perceptions of the RP intervention, which involved a combination of written, verbal, individual, and shared RP, athletes reported increased ownership and control over goal achievement, a shift in goal focus from outcome to performance orientation, increased awareness of strengths and weaknesses, and increased confidence. Similarly, a series of research studies across a variety of sports (e.g., archery, basketball, badminton) using mixed methods approaches and several modes of RP were conducted by Tan et al. (2016), Koh et al. (2017), and Koh and Tan (2018). Only one study out of the three reported improvements to sport-specific (badminton) performance, which examined the impact of a six-week group-based RP intervention, based on verbal use of the Gibbs' (1988) framework of questions (Koh & Tan, 2018). In this study, all measures of skill-based performance significantly improved, and in follow-up interviews about perceptions of RP utility participants also reported improved skill consistency, increased self-confidence, self-awareness, and motivation in learning. In the earlier studies, declines in performance (Tan et al., 2016) or no change (Koh et al., 2017) were attributed to either athletes working on technical aspects of performance around the same time as the RP intervention, therefore performance was already being impacted, or the notion that not all individuals liked to reflect in the same way, so some participants may not have found the stipulated RP process to be helpful. In addition, no in-person facilitation was provided to support individual RP processes in these earlier studies. This contrasted with Koh and Tan's (2018) study where group RP was used, thus providing a more interactive and supportive process, and the opportunity for any negative issues commonly associated with individual RP to be eradicated (e.g., feelings of isolation, focusing on negative issues).

Whilst the research reviewed thus far in this chapter provides insight into that of individual athlete or team experiences of RP, it is also important that research helps to build a wide-reaching knowledge and evidence base, and as such, studies emanating from a variety of epistemological and ontological positions are required. In considering the philosophical positions that perhaps traditionally less frequently underpin RP research (cf. Huntley et al., 2014), to the author's knowledge, only two quantitative studies exist within the current timeframe under review (2013–2022) which consider RP and athletes as participants (Cowden & Meyer-Weitz, 2016; Wang, 2021). Both studies used the Self-Reflection and Insight Scale (SRIS) with large populations of athletes, and both studies found positive correlations between SRIS subscales (e.g., insight) with resilience as a comparable variable. Wang (2021), however, additionally reported a positive relationship between reflection and self-efficacy, suggesting that developing athletes' reflective ability could help them to manage competition anxiety. Wang (2021) was not able to suggest how such improvements in reflective ability could be achieved (as this was beyond the scope of the study) yet such work demonstrates the importance of varied research questions, approaches, and methods in order to develop a more holistic evidence base for the use of RP with athletes.

RP Methods

What perhaps is evident in the literature reviewed thus far and considering that which has been discussed in the literature previously (e.g., Huntley et al., 2014), is that over time, more novel methods and approaches to RP have emerged in the SES and related allied disciplines. For example, now more than ever we are seeing, reading, or hearing about practitioners' experience of or support for *shared/facilitated/guided* approaches to RP (e.g., Hägglund et al., 2021; Koh & Tan, 2018; Neil et al., 2013).

When reading about experiences of shared forms of RP, in most cases, this is through verbal or conversational methods (e.g., Doncaster, 2018; Koh & Tan, 2018). In some instances, this shared approach can include written RP, as seen in Neil et al.'s (2013) case study where an athlete's reflective diary was guided/facilitated, and subsequently verbally discussed, resulting in positive outcomes. Hägglund et al. (2021) also illustrated a written form of shared RP by using an SMS-based approach to a reflective diary, which based on the modality, kept the reflections short and time efficient. Another approach to guided RP that could be used with athletes on a larger scale was outlined by Chow and Luzzeri (2019), who developed a post-event reflection tool, aimed to facilitate self-awareness, self-monitoring, and self-regulation. This one-page tool offers an approach to RP that is objective, considers strengths and weaknesses in performance, and claims to increase self-regulation skills after successful completions. However, no evidence of the tool's success has yet been provided.

Generally, *written* reflection (e.g., diaries, case reports, self-reflections) is still the most reported RP format. Within education settings, RP is typically introduced as a written process, and it is often only once individuals are 'out in the field', if fortunate enough to have a placement opportunity, or be in supervised practice, or working as a SES or allied discipline practitioner, that other methods of RP become available, recognised, or introduced. Perhaps this is based on pragmatic issues. For example, teaching hundreds of undergraduates how to engage in shared RP is potentially more difficult and time consuming than using the more traditional written format, which from an assessment perspective is logistically easier to navigate (or is it!?). However, at postgraduate level where student numbers are lower, or as part of a smaller professional practice or supervision group, or working individually with a supervisor/mentor, interactive meetings and discussions become more 'normal', and offer a natural space for reflective conversations to take place.

In a digital and technology orientated world, it is not surprising that such approaches to RP are becoming more popular. Barriers to RP have been frequently discussed (e.g., Cropley et al., 2012), with time being one of the most reported. Therefore, approaches to make RP more time-efficient have been considered, such as using audio recording devices (e.g., Dictaphone, voice recorder) instead of handwritten/typed diary formats as such recordings can be captured whilst simultaneously engaging in other activities (e.g., recording one's reflections whilst driving or walking to make the better use of that time). However, an alternative viewpoint, perhaps fitting with the well-being and self-care section above is, should we be striving to fit more in? Would a drive or a walk without simultaneous recording of reflections be better use of time? A balance must, therefore, be struck so that the meaning of RP is not lost or the descriptive accepted at the expense of the meaningful simply to 'fit RP in'. Another approach designed to facilitate better RP, is that of video reflection, which has been reported to capture more emotion/sensory information which is an aspect of RP that some struggle to articulate when using written approaches (e.g., Doncaster, 2018). Finally, another technology-based approach to RP that is becoming more prominent in research and practice is *think aloud* (e.g., Whitehead et al., 2016), a process where in-moment reflections are captured using a microphone and recording device, allowing individuals (e.g., practitioners, athletes), alone, or with facilitation (e.g., from a mentor, supervisor or peer), an opportunity to explore reflection in action, allowing sense making to take place.

Summary

When compared to that of sport psychology and sport coaching for some SES and related allied disciplines there remains less discipline specific literature to draw upon with regards to RP. This may lead to the discipline, or individuals within, having a sense of feeling alone, lost, or confused when it comes to trying to understand RP in one's relevant context. Therefore, an invitation for additional RP literature in less mature disciplinary areas, such as CEP, physical activity, nutrition, physiology, biomechanics, and sports therapy is made. This invitation is presented with the aims of extending the RP community, developing our knowledge and understanding of RP, and exploring how we, collectively as reflective practitioners, can continue to be more effective in our respective roles. In addition, the current chapter also presents new developments and areas of exploration within the SES literature, including RP use for personal well-being and self-care, a focus on the athlete as a reflective 'practitioner', and a summary of the most recently utilised RP methods.

3 The Reflective Sport and Exercise Science Practitioner

*Zoe Knowles, Andy Miles, Emma Huntley,
Gareth Picknell, Stephen D. Mellalieu, Sheldon
Hanton, Emily Ryall, Andy Borrie, Jo Trelfa,
Hamish Telfer, Kate Williams, Tegan Adams,
Alison Pope-Rhodius, Christopher R. D. Wagstaff,
Matthew Miller, Alessandro Quartiroli, Amy
Whitehead, Amanda J. Wilding, Paula Watson,
Laura Needham, James Morton, Brian Gearity,
Clayton Kuklick, Hannah C. Wood, Amelia K.
Simpson, Amelia K. McIntosh, Emma S. Cowley,
and Brendan Cropley*

Introduction: The Reflective Practitioner

The increasing recognition of reflective practice as a fundamental aspect of the education, training, and practice of applied practitioners in the sport and exercise sciences and allied disciplines, has been coupled with continued growth in reflective practice research and discussion in both the empirical and grey literature as well as in popular media (e.g., podcasts) in these fields (e.g., Doncaster, 2018; Wadsworth et al., 2021). Much of this work has explored the various typologies of reflective practice (e.g., reflection-in- and -on-action; Stephenson et al., 2020), the value of different approaches to reflection (e.g., journaling; visual sociology; Lee et al., 2020), the potential impact of reflective practice on service delivery (e.g., Cropley, Hanton et al., 2020), and the value of reflective practice for facilitating practitioner development and growth (e.g., Martin, 2017). Collectively, this body of research, and ensuing discussion, has helped those working in the sport and exercise sciences and allied disciplines to further establish the importance of reflective practice, better understand the efficacy of different modalities of reflection, and comprehend issues that may facilitate or hinder engagement.

Given that some conceptual disparity is still evident (e.g., concerning the philosophy, meaning, and purpose of reflective practice), the *value* of such developments in understanding come with a caveat. Specifically, as reflective practice becomes more formally integrated into education and training pathways in the sport and exercise sciences and allied disciplines, as well as into associated professional standards (see Health and Care Professions Council, 2019), there is a

DOI: 10.4324/9781003198758-4

realistic prospect that focus will (or maybe already has) shift(ed) to a fixation on the *mechanics* of reflective practice at the expense of furthering understanding of what it means to be a *reflective practitioner*. This position is potentially problematic as viewing reflective practice as a technical requirement for trainees and professionals alike is not likely to result in the commitment required to extrapolate the benefits of reflective practice for personal and professional growth. Instead, it is more likely to result in individuals seeking to understand 'what they need to do' to be compliant with professional standards, resulting in insipid, descriptions of practice, rather than exploring the whole person and that of 'who they are' and 'what they do' as professional practitioners, and why these things have come to be this way. This is some distance away from that of description or competency demonstration.

It is argued that becoming a reflective practitioner is of "primary importance" for those engaged in professional service delivery (Rowe et al., 2020, p. 784). This is because reflective practitioners possess the attitudes, and are able to develop the self-awareness, knowledge, and skills, required to cope with the challenges associated with applied practice, adapt to the contextual demands of their roles, and build the necessary expertise to engage in effective practice (Rowe et al., 2020). It is important to recognise, however, that becoming a reflective practitioner requires more than mere engagement in a collection of techniques (Lee et al., 2009). Rather, being a reflective practitioner involves an all-encompassing attitude to practice that requires individuals to commit to professional and personal development (Anderson et al., 2004). Indeed, a reflective practitioner is "someone who lives reflective practice as a way of being" (Johns, 2017, p. 3). It seems timely, therefore, to (re)focus attention on what it means to be a reflective practitioner in the sport and exercise sciences and allied disciplines. In doing so, a lens can be placed upon the significance of individuals adopting a disposition for reflective practice that facilitates constructive and meaningful transformation rather than simply seeing reflective practice as something to be done.

Purpose and Approach

With a pre-defined word limit to focus the narrative, all authors contributing to chapters in this text were invited, as individuals and/or teams, to present their understanding of *what it means to be a reflective practitioner* within their particular disciplines (e.g., physiology, psychology, coaching) and areas of work (e.g., professional practice, education, supervision). To note for context and perspective, encouraged by the editorial team, some contributors have subsequently extended their views beyond the points they raise in their vignettes within their own chapters. We (editorial team) have presented each of these vignettes as they were submitted by the chapter authors, in the order the authors appear in this text, to provide you (the reader) with an opportunity to understand their nuanced perspectives regarding the concept of the reflective practitioner. We hope that this approach allows you to immerse yourselves within the authors' own experiences, perspectives, and developmental journeys, while allowing your own understanding of the reflective practitioner to be constructed. In doing so, we invite you to 'reflect on' and note what resonates, surprises, challenges, and provokes you as you read the vignettes. As members of the reflective practice community ourselves, the editorial team have also engaged in such reflective consideration and consequently, following the presentation of the vignettes, we have offered our own analytical summary to draw together some of the common ideas and themes. Our (editorial team) intention in offering this summary, was to add to current conceptualisations regarding the nature of *being a reflective practitioner* and provide insights that may support an individual's ongoing personal and professional development. Finally, we encourage you to challenge these summative insights in accord with your own understandings as a way of continuing discussion in this area.

What It Means To Be a Reflective Practitioner in Sport & Exercise Science and Allied Disciplines: Author Vignettes

Dr Gareth Picknell, Professor Stephen D. Mellalieu & Professor Sheldon Hanton

The journey from neophyte to seasoned applied practitioner is paved with experiences that afford opportunities to learn about oneself, those we work with, and the environments we operate in. How we interact with those experiences directly influence our trajectories across necessary career transitions. Sure, 'tipping one's hat', thinking about, or paying attention to certain experiences can be useful and meaningful. However, learning how to examine experiences with purpose and commitment elevates our expectations as professionals and is considered seminal in developing effective applied practice. Becoming a reflective practitioner requires a mind-set that is open to creative processes for acquiring new understanding, knowledge, behaviours, skills, attitudes, and/or preferences. Whilst the mechanisms for how reflective practice impacts applied practice warrants further examination, it appears that reflective practice aligns professional philosophies with individual's theoretical orientations that guide practice. In doing so, decisions and behaviours adopted in practice are more likely to be in harmony with individual's personal values and beliefs. To become a reflective practitioner requires actively developing skills (e.g., problem solving, critical thinking) associated with reflective practice, which, over time facilitate the ability to reflect at more advanced levels. Therefore, a reflective practitioner is someone who has developed proficiency in using reflective practice and commits to integrating its principles into their ongoing professional endeavours.

Dr Emily Ryall

Being a reflective practitioner is ultimately about thinking critically, asking questions, and questioning assumptions in an attempt to make sense of the world and one's place within it. As a philosopher by training, some of my scepticism about reflective practice and the way is it often conceptualised and taught has come about because it often does not get to these core aspects of critical thought. As a result, reflective practice is unable to generate the change in perspective that underpins a radical or meaningful change in practice. Reflective practitioners go beyond superficial layers of thought, which requires a genuine desire to dig down to difficult and philosophical issues about what is valuable and important in life, and to accept that this process is exhausting and interminable; but not to give up in a sense of frustration or despondency. Instead, it is to recognise that understanding the world and one's place within it, as well as how one's agency can create change. This requires ongoing commitment to a deeper philosophic thought and method. This conception [the reflective practitioner] can be both therapeutic for the self, and can influence change in others, which is what most proponents challenge it to do.

Dr Andy Borrie

I have two main interests now relating to how we develop practitioners and how we develop talented young athletes. [As a reflective practitioner] reflective practice is absolutely at the heart of my work within both these areas and without a long-term commitment to reflective practice I wouldn't be the practitioner I am today. However, that answer is superficial and doesn't reflect all my current thinking about reflective practice. Whilst I believe wholeheartedly in the importance of reflective practice it is easy for it to lack depth. Too often we let our reflective practice work stop at evaluating an immediate technical challenge rather than looking more closely at issues of underpinning philosophy, social justice, or how people draw meaning from a situation. I know that as I have reflected on deeper questions about purpose, philosophy, and meaning creation I have radically altered my approach to practice. I now automatically start to look at underpinning cultures and power dynamics in any new practice environment and seek an understanding of core philosophies of key stakeholders. Reflective practice still helps me with technical challenges but more importantly it helps me position my practice within a deeper, comprehensive, and possibly ethical, world view.

Dr Jo Trelfa and Dr Hamish Telfer

Whilst we (Jo and Hamish) come from different professional disciplines (social care and sport coaching), where we join, the root to our 20+ years collaboration, is: *professional* practice; practitioner experience; and reflective practices as a developmental tool. We have always questioned the role and function of reflective practices in 'authenticating' practice, indeed, questioning the use of reflective practice as a 'tool' at all. We continue to explore the validity (ethically and technically) of using reflection *of* and *about* practice as a means to ensure boundary compliance (leading to, for example, accounts worked to fit professional expectations and education standards). Instead, practice is messy, unpredictable, fast moving – and whilst fixing this into deliberated (and controlled, censored) stories through critical thinking after the event has utility, we also recognise its limitations. For us, [being a] reflective practitioner requires a rigorous approach of inquiry about practice, but also a lived, rich experience of noticing and attending to it too as practitioners in all fields seek to practice, innovate, and challenge while still wrestling with the need for compliance to accepted norms. This nuanced balance between 'what is the norm' and 'what could possibly be' is the basis of our motivation for exploring reflection within practice.

Dr Kate Williams

The Graduate Sport Therapist (GST) is a clinically autonomous practitioner. Reflective practice is central to GST's development as 'expert practitioners' however, the concept of the reflective practitioner in Sports Therapy is relatively new – trainees and graduates are expected to reflect, but being a reflective practitioner is more than simply completing a reflective framework. To be a reflective practitioner, individuals must consistently reflect, both in- and on-action and adopt the disposition (cognitive, affective, social, and physical) required for self-examination and the examination of the contexts in which they work. Reflective practitioners are those willing and able to challenge the assumptions held about applied practice and connect different types of knowledge and skills to add to and redefine what applied practice looks like in the moment for them. Knowledge and skills include those associated with the discipline (e.g., manual therapy techniques, knowledge of anatomy) as well as interpersonal (e.g., building a therapeutic alliance; communication), personal (e.g., coping, emotion regulation), and contextual (e.g., understanding organisational culture) factors. The reflective practitioner is able to combine these in different ways to meet the needs associated with current practice and, therefore, have a level of control over the effectiveness of their work.

Dr Tegan Adams and Dr Alison Pope-Rhodius

Reflective practitioners take the time to slow down, to review, analyse, and make sense of their own performance. To 'reflect' is a critical component of being an ethical supervisor, because it helps supervisors stay committed to doing their best work with trainees. I (Tegan) encourage my trainees to engage in this practice by committing to it myself, modelling it, and connecting with them on how to incorporate it in the ways that fit their style. If I don't engage in reflection regularly, I am more likely to misstep, either ethically or with unchecked micro-aggressions. I notice and share how my own biases get in the way and make it more likely for me to make assumptions about the trainee's process or about what would work best for them. Practitioners need to take their own cultural context into perspective when they think about and work with their trainees. It is paramount that they consider ways that power and privilege influence the reflective process, within their work, and the work that their trainees are doing with clients. Modelling these dialogues and recognising the value of connecting in this way will lead to healthier working relationships, and a greater degree of trust with trainees.

Dr Christopher D. Wagstaff, Matthew Miller and Professor Alessandro Quartiroli

The reflective practitioner is someone who not only embraces the *doing* of reflective practice to learn from their experiences, but someone who consistently engages in such critical exploration of the self and the context that they find themselves in. This engagement requires those who work in interdisciplinary teams to challenge what is taken for granted and make sense with others to develop knowledge that helps inform effective and ethical action across one's context. Thus, the reflective practitioner strives to uncover personal meaning in situations and deliberately seeks to construct better ways of being among and for those they work with.

Dr Amy Whitehead

As someone who works across education, sport coaching, and sport psychology the term reflection is a key part of my daily role and language. Reflection to me means questioning myself, my context, and my place within each social context I enter. In terms of self, I am questioning my own thoughts and behaviours and how they engage with the social context or environment. In addition, I am questioning where these thoughts and behaviours have come from and what has shaped them. From a social context perspective, I am questioning where and how I fit within a given environment, where the power dynamics are, and how I might best navigate each environment. In each situation it is important that we (reflective practitioners) reflect on how we are being perceived and how we are making others around us feel. Regardless of the discipline, be it coaching, sport psychology, or education, reflection is about connecting the cognitive with the social and having an understanding how both influence one another.

Dr Amanda J. Wilding

In the beginning, reflection was a tick box exercise; what went well, what could have gone better and therefore what needs changing for next time. Eighteen years on, being a reflective practitioner is an integral part of my service provision, with reflective practice embedded into every aspect of my job. At present, my reflective process evolves around four A's, (Assess, Accept, Adapt, and Apply). I constantly *assess* the situation in front of me, the task being undertaken and how the people around me are interacting within the given context. From this, I can undertake in-action reflection, but this entails *acceptance* of those factors which cannot be changed along with *adaptation* to those which can. This enables the *application* of new perspectives, tasks, or manipulation of in-the-moment factors, which bring about alternative outcomes if required. Thus, in-action reflection is a constant cycle that allows my sessions to be fluid, dynamic, and thus responsive to the current context. For me, reflection evidences my ability to cope with the situational sensitivities that each session brings enabling greater impact and effectiveness within every session. To me, the ability to adapt during sessions brings evidence-based practice to life.

Dr Paula Watson

As an M.Sc. student in 2004, I was introduced to the work of the eminent psychologist Carl Rogers. His 'personal learnings' about self-awareness and empathy have shaped my practice ever since and articulated what – to me – underpins the foundation of reflective practice, "understanding is risky. If I let myself really understand another person, I might be changed by that understanding" (Rogers, 1961, p. 20). A reflective practitioner constantly strives for personal and professional growth. As a psychologist, reflection is about understanding myself, others, and how the two interact. I soon discovered the truth of Rogers' words, when in my M.Sc. research I explored exercise experiences of people living with obesity. I wrote deep, honest reflective accounts that exposed my subconscious biases. I asked myself what I was thinking and feeling. I asked myself "why" and challenged my ingrained assumptions. I asked myself how it felt to be those individuals, and before long, I noticed my views began to change. To reflect critically requires a willingness to dig below the surface and be honest with ourselves (which may reveal uncomfortable truths). We need to ask ourselves how our values, attitudes and biases affect our clients' feelings, thoughts, and behaviours. And crucially, we need to be open to the change that may occur as a result of what we discover.

Laura Needham

Applied physiology requires a unique blend of technical expertise and exceptional people skills. Those who I have observed to be the most successful practitioners are those that can connect, engage, and translate science into practice. At the heart of the success is an incredible openness to reflect, which takes us on a journey to increased self-awareness, and subsequently it facilitates a growing trust between athlete, coach, and the practitioner; the holy grail of sport science in my humble opinion. My developmental journey as a reflective practitioner has seen significant change in the way that I engage in, process, and benefit from reflective practice. In my neophyte years, I very much engaged in written reflection on technical issues, which would then be dissected with my supervisor. However, I now very rarely focus on my technical knowledge; I can generally learn a new technical topic as it comes with each Olympic cycle. The challenge always comes with being able to influence and connect positively with my athletes and coaches. Consequently, I now engage with several executive coaches and mentors to reflect on my practice focusing on my values and behaviours. As a result, I have a heightened understanding of who I am, why I am the way I am and why I behave in the way I do. If we all understand ourselves further, I believe we can be more effective in our practice. I want to be the best I can be for the incredible athletes I have the opportunity to work with, and reflective practice is my secret weapon.

Professor James Morton

[As a reflective practitioner] I engage with reflective practice as a cognitive process in a way that helps me to review and appraise my own (and other's) technical (i.e., knowledge) and practical (i.e., delivery) attributes that are necessary to operate as a practitioner within a given situation. At a higher level of reflection (i.e., critical), reflective practice also helps me to understand, accept, and yet challenge, my own (and other's) meaning within a specific situation. In this sense, I can then embrace *why* I (and other's) feel, behave, and act the way they do, thereby allowing me to operate with greater understanding, empathy, and effectiveness in future situations. In simple terms, reflective practice is a process that helps me to 'get better'.

Dr Brian Gearity and Dr Clayton Kuklick

As a new Strength and Conditioning (S&C) coach, like so many others, I (Brian) focused on the scientifically best programming and periodisation strategies. The reps, sets, load, rest, exercise frequency and selection, proper technique – everything had to be a certain way or at least within a narrow bandwidth. Reflective practice drawing upon biology, biomechanics, motor learning, nutrition, and technology helped me to reduce athletic injury and enhance performance, but some problems endured, others emerged, and I found myself reaching out for other, hopefully discerning, explanations. What if I studied how S&C practices came into existence, if I considered that they themselves produced problems or tensions, and what if we were marginalising potentially useful ways of knowing? Becoming a reflective practitioner is more than problem solving or treating the human body and spirit as an inanimate chunk of tissue. It involves critical reflective practice, which considers deeply how knowledge and power are intertwined and how they produce S&C understandings, practices, and effects within a particular time and context. What are the taken-for-granted assumptions and unintended consequences from thinking and doing S&C in any particular way? Empirical evidence is useful for understanding what is, but what about what could be and what should be? Always-in-the-making, a reflective practitioner engages in deep role taking and experimentation from multiple perspectives.

Hannah C. Wood; Amelia K. Simpson; Amelia K. McIntosh and Dr Emma S. Cowley

As recent M.Sc. Sport Psychology graduates, we are all fairly new to reflective practice but have come to view it as integral to our development. From our perspective, being a reflective practitioner allows you to make sense of your experiences while providing a safe space to identify and challenge your own values, biases, and assumptions. Increasing self-awareness in this way is particularly important for us as neophyte practitioners to enable us to get to know ourselves, develop our professional philosophy and strive for congruence between the way we conduct ourselves and our values. We have found reflecting with others particularly beneficial because it exposes you to different perspectives and challenges you to identify what you think, as opposed to, perhaps, what you have been told to think. Being a reflective practitioner is challenging. It is a skill that takes time and consistent practice to develop (and to see the benefits of); we were surprised to look back at our early reflections and see how far we had progressed. Ultimately, without reflection we feel we would miss opportunities for learning and improving our practice, but with reflection we can work towards being the best version of ourselves, both professionally and personally.

The Reflective Practitioner: Analytical Summary

Schön's (1983) original work introduced the concept of the reflective practitioner as a challenge to the conventional epistemology of service delivery whereby professionals are encouraged to operate by applying formally learned specialist or technical knowledge. Instead, to navigate the complexities (or *swampy lowlands* using Schön's own term) associated with applied practice, caused by human, contextual, and environmental factors, Schön argued that professionals use a form of tacit knowledge that is bound within the experiences they have of doing their jobs. Schön referred to this as *knowledge-in-action*, which is constructed through reflective practice on (or within) experience. By making sense of their knowledge-in-action, the reflective practitioner can then develop repertoires of theories-in-use (courses of action built on personal beliefs, values, knowledge, and experiences) and learn how to re-frame difficult problems into those they can deal with more readily (Cheetham & Chivers, 1998). Thus, reflective practitioners are able to intelligently respond to situations based on intuitive feelings and actions that have been cultivated through experience (Hébert, 2015).

Since Schön (1983) introduced this concept, the reflective practitioner has been discussed in a variety of fields (e.g., nursing, education), and the development of reflective practitioners has widely become the "cornerstone of professional education programmes" (Williams & Grudnoff, 2011, p. 281). However, across these fields, despite apparent agreement, there lies a diversity in meaning and vision regarding the reflective practitioner (Rowe et al., 2020). In this chapter, it has not necessarily been our (editorial team) intention to attempt to clarify such nuances or offer a discussion of these. Instead, we have drawn from the insights of an informed community of individuals as a way of raising debate concerning what it might mean to be a reflective practitioner in the sport and exercise sciences and allied disciplines. In doing so, we recognise that we have added to this diversity in conceptualisation, but we hope that this too widens both discussions concerning professional training, development, and reflective practice as well as augmenting the focus placed on the individual practitioner rather than simply on the mechanics of learning from experience. Thus, in consideration of the vignettes presented in this chapter by the contributing authors, we would like to highlight several key issues that appear considerate of the authors views.

First, within the vignettes, the authors widely (and at times implicitly, which is an interesting notion in itself) refer to the *philosophical position* required by the reflective practitioner. Specifically, the reflective practitioner needs to accept that practice is complex, shaped by context, and thus in order to operate effectively they must develop and connect of various forms of knowing. In addition, the reflective practitioner is seen as someone who is willing to *challenge the assumptions* (taken-for-granted processes) held within a discipline about practice and how it is enacted. Such perspectives would indicate that *reflective practitioners adopt a relative view* (as opposed to a dualistic) of knowledge that promotes the use of evidence to reason between alternative solutions to practice-based problems, making such individuals open to a range of perspectives (Marshall et al., 2021). Further, some authors considered the philosophical position of the reflective practitioner to include an *acceptance of personal agency*. Here, it is posited that the reflective practitioner identifies themselves as an orchestrator of change and, even in the face of challenge or obstruction, irrespective of the discomfort that this may bring, remains committed to the continuous endeavour of improvement (Yagata, 2018). This commitment requires the reflective practitioner to dedicate themselves to *developing self-awareness*, as understanding their worldview, beliefs, values, and qualities positions them to make more informed decisions about their practice and how it might be developed.

Second, in line with the views of several commentators (e.g., Johns, 2017; Marshall et al., 2021; Nguyen et al., 2014), within their vignettes many authors referred to the attitudes that reflective practitioners should possess. Linked to the view that reflective practitioners adopt a relative view of knowledge, within their vignettes, the authors acknowledge that these individuals need to be *open to change*. It appears that this attitude is fundamental for reflective practitioners, given the need to be willing to consider (and accept where necessary) new meanings, possibilities, and opportunities. Others have argued that being open to change does not mean the uncritical acceptance of the alternatives but requires the individual to explore the potential of both current and new views before deciding on where to position oneself (cf. Yagata, 2018). Further, some authors in this chapter link being open to change to a reflective practitioner's motivation for *personal and professional growth*. Indeed, this attitude can allow the reflective practitioner to be accountable to themselves, their clients, those they work for, and their fields by working to evolve their understanding of what works in the context of their practice. Associated with this, the authors widely attest in their accounts that to be a reflective practitioner requires a *commitment to/towards critical reflective practice*, a *willingness to actively engage* in the process to construct new meanings. The reflective practitioner, therefore, seeks to make sense of the world and their agency within it, develop a better 'self', and improve action through personal and professional growth. For some of the authors, this commitment is inherently linked to a reflective practitioners' *ethical responsibility* as a professional. For example, being responsible by carefully considering the consequences of potential actions and interactions allows reflective practitioners to check and challenge the decisions they make (Cropley et al., 2015).

Finally, the authors acknowledged within their vignettes a range of skills required by reflective practitioners. These skills represent those required to *engage in critical reflective typologies* (e.g., in- and on-action) on a consistent basis as a way of pursuing meaningful insight and change. For example, the authors indicated that reflective practitioners need to exhibit the problem-solving, critical thinking, questioning, and modelling skills that consistently move their reflective practices from the technical to deeper philosophical thought. In accord, it is suggested here that reflective practitioners need to become comfortable with engaging in a range of reflective modalities to ensure purposeful engagement and to facilitate a process of transformation (e.g., that reflective learning is subsequently used to inform future action; Johns, 2017).

We (editorial team) appreciate that drawing on the themes discussed here has the potential of detracting from the rich insights presented by the contributing authors, and that the themes we have selected may not be representative of all perspectives. However, in drawing together some of the common ideas and themes concerning the philosophy, attitudes, and skills required by the reflective practitioner we challenge individuals, supporters, and organisations in the sport and exercise sciences and allied disciplines to engage in their own critical reflection. This should focus on: (a) how the vignettes and subsequent summative analysis supports, contrasts, and/or adds to personal constructions of the reflective practitioner; and (b) how current education, training, and development programmes are supporting or thwarting the development of reflective practitioners. In concluding this chapter, if you have, at this point (or if you will do in the future), actively engaged in such critical reflection as you read through, then thank you for 'working' with us. From here we invite you to read each chapter in this text and then to perhaps revisit the vignettes offered in this chapter to add additional layers to your own constructions regarding the reflective practitioner in the sport and exercise sciences and allied disciplines. We hope you enjoy reading (or should that be working) through the chapters as much as we did through our editorial duties.

Section 2
Critical Perspectives

4 Where's the Evidence? Contemporary Insights into the Impact of Reflective Practice on Professional Practice

Gareth Picknell, Stephen D. Mellalieu, Sheldon Hanton, and Brendan Cropley

Introduction

Reflective learning is established within the professional development literature as an essential characteristic for developing individuals' expertise within a variety of fields, including allied healthcare, medical sciences, and sport and exercise professions (e.g., Dube & Ducharme, 2015; Hazan et al., 2020; Huntley et al., 2019). Indeed, since Schön (1983) examined the development of *knowledge-in-action* (tacit knowledge) and its relationship with practitioners' judgements and decisions, extensive research interest across professions has been afforded to understanding how this type of knowledge can be garnered to be of benefit to professional practice. Accordingly, knowledge-in-action is acquired from the practice settings that individuals operate in, whereby simply applying theory and techniques derived from systematic, scientific knowledge alone, are unlikely to render practice as effective (Doncaster, 2018; Huntley et al., 2019). Instead, individuals are able to develop their knowledge-in-action, or professional artistry, from their diverse range of practical experiences following engagement with two distinct learning processes referred to as: *reflection-in-action* (takes place during the situation) and *reflection-on-action* (takes place following the completion of an event).

As a result of Schön's (1983) initial work, and subsequent support within the wider professional development literature, reflective practice has enjoyed sustained interest within the sport, exercise, and health domains over the past two decades (e.g., Butterworth & Turner, 2014; Cropley, Baldock et al., 2020; Dao et al., 2020; Dixon et al., 2016; Picknell, Cropley et al., 2022). A simple cross-examination of the professional requirements of various sport and exercise science and allied health professions highlights numerous commonalities in terms of the competencies necessary for the provision of effective support. This is unsurprising as competency frameworks are primarily adopted as a means to enhance the professionalism of individuals operating within specific domains by setting out standards that have to be achieved and adhered to in order to protect members of the public (Englander et al., 2013). Whilst similarities exist regarding competency categories across therapeutic professions, the relevant knowledge and application of skills required remain profession specific. However, one area

DOI: 10.4324/9781003198758-6

that is consistent, as well as transferable, across domains is the need for individuals to continually review and self-evaluate their practice. For example, the Health and Care Professions Council (HCPC) insist that Practitioner Psychologists and Dieticians should be able to *reflect on and review practice* as part of their Standards of Proficiency requirements (HCPC, 2013, 2015). In addition, the British Association for Sport and Exercise Sciences (BASES) stipulates that those wishing to become accredited practitioners need to demonstrate competencies for *Development of own Practice – understanding the value of reflection on practice* (BASES, 2019). Explicit, across all regulation requirements is the need for practitioners to develop their critical reflection capabilities in order to effectively and adequately examine their practice.

Whilst promising, the inclusion of reflective principles as a means of generating knowledge and learning from experiences has been primarily grounded on theoretical debate and anecdotal accounts (cf. Picknell et al., 2014). Indeed, in their recent expert statement on reflective practice, Huntley et al. (2019) emphasised the need for a wider and more encompassing evidence-base that requires various allied healthcare disciplines to value different forms of knowledge and evidence. To that end, this chapter will review contemporary research that has emerged more recently, in which researchers have attempted to add to the empirical evidence-base related to the effectiveness of reflective practice in sport, exercise, and health domains, and thus provide valuable insights into the impact of reflective practice on professional practice. The first section will provide an overview and critique of relevant research pertaining to reflective practice within the sport, exercise, and health domains. As such, this section will be structured similarly to Picknell et al.'s (2014) earlier review. Indeed, available research sourced from the sport, exercise, and health literature will be categorised and grouped into those which: (i) attempt to examine the development of reflection skills (process-oriented); and (ii) investigate the impact of reflective practice on measurable outcomes (outcome-oriented). The second section will consider the conceptual and practical implications afforded to researchers, profession regulators and applied practitioners as a result of the broader reflective practice evidence-base presented herein. Indeed, we introduce a model (i.e., integrated model of the relationship between reflective practice, cognitive structures, self-regulation, and behavioural outcomes) that aims to link together recent conceptual developments with rigorous scientific evidence to further explicate *why reflective practice works*. In doing so, it is our intention to provide practical, easy to follow guidance for navigating the process from engaging in reflective practice to bringing about meaningful change. Further, it is hoped that progress can be made within the sport, exercise, and health professions towards developing confidence, acceptance, and adoption of reflective practice as part of everyday professional activities.

Reflective Practice: The Intertwining of Reflective Skills, Applied Practice, and Client-Support Programmes

Aligned to Huntley et al.'s (2019) request for a more encompassing evidence-base within the reflective practice literature, we previously laid out recommendations for guiding future research directions (see Picknell et al., 2014). In our review of the available empirical evidence at the time we noticed that research from numerous domains could be organised into one of two categories. Specifically, researchers typically examined the benefits of reflective practice using either *process-oriented* or *outcome-oriented* designs (Picknell et al., 2014). Process-oriented investigations involve examining the development of reflective skills amongst participants following their involvement in a reflective practice intervention (e.g., Neil et al., 2013). The primary assumption of process-oriented research assumes that enhancing individuals' reflective skills ultimately has a positive impact on professional practice. Conversely, the purpose of outcome-oriented research is to examine whether improved outcomes in practice may be attributed to methods that promote reflecting-on-practice.

Development of Reflective Skills: Process-Oriented Research Findings

The general view within the literature is that reflective practice is a highly skilled activity and therefore needs to be carefully nurtured (Huntley et al., 2019). To support this process, models of reflection have previously been established (e.g., Goodman, 1984; Mezirow, 1981; Powell, 1989) that view reflection as hierarchical and developmental in that different levels of reflection exist, with higher levels being considered increasingly complex. Therefore, to evaluate whether a reflective practice programme is effective, one would expect reflective skills (e.g., self-awareness, problem solving, critical thinking) to improve, thus resulting in more advanced levels of reflections being achieved (cf. Cropley, Hanton et al., 2020). In essence, the level of reflection demonstrated by a practitioner provides a representation of their reflection skills. Whilst intuitively appealing, until recently, this contention lacked empirical support. Indeed, within our previous review in 2014, we noted that support for the developmental hypothesis of reflective skills, whilst limited in number, existed primarily within the medical sciences literature (e.g., Duke & Appleton, 2000; Sobral, 2000; see Picknell et al., 2014).

Where efforts have been made within the sport and exercise domain (e.g., Cropley, Hanton et al., 2020; Neil et al., 2013; Whitehead et al., 2016) to explicitly examine the impact of reflective practice for enhancing reflective skills, issues raised by Picknell et al. (2014) continue to persist. That is, these investigations have refrained from utilising reliable and valid psychometric assessment tools for measuring reflective skills and have not included comparison criteria as part of their experimental designs. As such, issues relating to the transferability and generalisability of findings from these types of investigations may continue to result in reluctance from some factions to fully embrace reflective practice as a worthwhile endeavour within applied service delivery. The first of these issues appears to be largely in part due to the belief that quantification of reflective practice and associated skills is difficult (Mann et al., 2009). The second is more likely associated with the philosophical foundations underpinning reflective practice. Specifically, when reflective practice is recognised as a meaningful learning endeavour, the dominant associated epistemological assumptions (e.g., constructivism, humanism); that is, what constitutes knowledge and how knowledge of phenomena is acquired, appear to be more closely aligned with qualitative modes of inquiry (Jones, 2014). Given that using comparison groups (i.e., experimental versus control) are more indicative of quantitative research designs, their exclusion within qualitative research is unsurprising.

To overcome the limitations noted, we proposed the need for more *evaluation research* rather than *evaluation of practice* designs, which have dominated the reflective practice literature. With the development of relevant measurement tools that allow reflection skills to be assessed (e.g., Lethbridge et al., 2013), researchers have begun to provide evidence for the effects that tailored reflective practice interventions have for facilitating reflective ability. Indeed, two recent studies by Picknell and colleagues explicitly examined the links between reflective practice programmes and their impact on reflection skills (Picknell, Cropley et al., 2022; Picknell, Mellalieu et al., 2022). In response to issues pertaining to the quantification of reflective skills, both investigations employed an adapted version of the *Reflection Questionnaire* (RQ; Kember et al., 2000), which was administered to participants pre- and post-involvement in reflective practice interventions. Picknell, Cropley et al.'s study, which examined reflective skills of applied practitioners, indicated improved perceptions of reflective ability not just at the end of the reflective practice programme, but also following participants' involvement in each of three phases of the intervention. Indeed, this was the case for both aspects of reflective actions – namely, reflection and critical reflection (Picknell, Cropley et al., 2022). In Picknell, Mellalieu et al.'s study, the authors examined the development of reflective skills among participants enrolled on a health improvement programme. Specifically, these individuals were obese (i.e., BMI >40.00) recruits completing their national military conscription. The experimental group, who were exposed to a reflective practice training programme, achieved higher scores for all reflection skills compared to a control group, and higher scores for critical reflection skills compared to a second experimental group (i.e., Mindfulness Training Group). To explore what contributed to the improvements in these reflective skills, Picknell, Cropley et al. (2022) included social validation interviews into their research design. It was concluded, that in order to improve the ability to reflect an effective reflective practice programme should aim to: (a) increase self-awareness; (b) increase autonomy for reflection; (c) engender an openness to change; and (d) facilitate a change in focus from appraising situations to considering the self and social interactions.

The Relationship Between Reflective Skills and Practice: Outcome-Oriented Research Findings

The growing empirical evidence-base that supports the developmental nature of reflective skills is a positive move in the right direction for the reflective practice literature. However, unless the purpose of achieving these higher skills (e.g., critical thinking and problem solving) is to bring about positive changes to practitioners' applied work, or support-seeking clients' circumstances, attempts to convince the sport, exercise, and health domains to 'buy in' to the benefits of reflective practice may remain futile (Huntley et al., 2019). To examine the potential of reflective practice for influencing quantitatively assessed dependent variables a steady stream of research has been conducted over the past 15 years (e.g., Cropley, Baldock et al., 2020; Cropley, Hanton et al., 2020; Hanrahan et al., 2009; Jonker et al., 2012; Picknell, Cropley et al., 2022; Picknell, Mellalieu et al., 2022). The research designs used in these studies have addressed criticisms relating to the lack of comparison criteria and thus to the generalisability of findings. On closer inspection the research in this area appears to be grouped into one of two categories. First, studies where researchers explored concepts of interest (i.e., competitive anxiety, motivation, self-regulation, hardiness) and examined whether reflective practice mediates between group differences (e.g., Cropley, Baldock et al., 2020; Hanrahan et al., 2009; Jonker et al., 2012). For example, Cropley, Baldock et al. (2020) examined factors that optimise hardiness among sport coaches and found that participants who were considered critical reflective thinkers scored significantly higher on all sub-components of hardiness. Given that hardiness is considered a key personal characteristic for moderating the ill-effects of stress on health and performance (Bartone & Homish, 2020) the potential value reflective practice has for harnessing it is a welcome additional benefit to applied practitioners and support-seeking clients alike. Further, the investigations by Hanrahan et al. (2009) and Jonker et al. (2012) both provide empirical evidence that engagement with reflective practice differentiates between groups' maintenance of effort and development of self-regulated learning among high and low achievers, respectively.

The second category of research empirically examining the value of reflective practice for bringing about meaningful change, has been interventional in nature and typically utilises a reflective practice training programme (e.g., Cropley, Hanton et al., 2020; Picknell, Cropley et al., 2022; Picknell, Mellalieu et al., 2022). When drawing conclusions regarding the association between reflective skills and changes to effectiveness of practice, it is worth noting Knowles and Saxton's (2010) conceptualisation of what represents change. Specifically, they suggested that change could be represented by three aspects of practice: (a) changes in values, beliefs, or behaviours; (b) confirmation or rejection of particular theories or practices; and/or (c) changes in knowledge of the self, the context of practice, or the environment in which individuals operate.

In the first study of its kind within the sport, exercise, and health science domains, Cropley, Hanton et al. (2020) explicitly combined process and outcome measures for examining the relationship between reflective skills and applied practice. For both self- and externally perceived (i.e., clients) assessments of effectiveness, all participants (i.e., applied sport psychology consultants) demonstrated some improvement post-intervention, with individuals rated as more critical reflective thinkers outperforming those with lower scores on this dimension. Specifically, through more critical levels of reflective practice individuals experienced enhanced self-awareness, improved approaches to meeting client needs, augmented professional judgement and decision making, and development in a range of other characteristics associated with effective consultants (e.g., developing rapport, communication skills). In accord with the previous section of this chapter, and in the context of previous suggestions for reflective practice research, the major limitation of this study related to the use of qualitatively assessed reflective skills. To overcome this limitation, Picknell, Cropley et al. (2022) delivered a reflective practice training programme that was found to develop the level of participants' (i.e., allied health practitioners) reflective practices. Further, as part of their quasi-experimental multiple-baseline crossover design, the participants' applied practice effectiveness, as determined by their use of communication skills were shown to be improved as a result of their involvement in the training programme and subsequent enhanced use of reflective skills. Notably, the improved use of communication skills was not determined by the practitioners themselves, but rather by the clients they engaged with and an independent allied health expert who observed their applied practice. An interesting insight that emerged from Picknell, Cropley, et al.'s research related to the eagerness of applied practitioners to employ aspects of reflective practice they acquired into services adopted with clients they encountered.

These findings provided the foundation for a subsequent investigation that examined whether a reflective practice intervention with obese participants may facilitate improvements to health outcomes, including the adoption of healthy behaviours, body composition, and physical fitness (Picknell, Mellalieu et al., 2022). Picknell and colleagues' findings suggested that developing health-seeking clients' abilities to reflect on their lifestyles and health improvement endeavours had distinct benefits associated with improving their overall health status. Indeed, the general trend indicated that the intervention, which focused exclusively on improving participants' reflective skills, contributed towards more favourable health behaviours and outcomes in the experimental (reflective practice intervention) group compared to two additional groups (mindfulness training group, control group) that did not comprise reflective practice elements. Specifically, the reflective practice group had significant improvements to various body composition measures compared to these other groups.

Whilst limited in number, these attempts to fuel empirical evidence that reflective practice improves practice effectiveness demonstrate positive findings that are in keeping with those noted more extensively within other domains including nursing (e.g., Pai, 2015; Pai et al., 2017) and the medical professions (e.g., Mamede et al., 2019; Xu et al., 2021). The value of this type of research is particularly noteworthy within the medical professions. Indeed, improving diagnostic accuracy is considered an essential competency of effective physicians. In their recent article, Xu et al. (2021) highlighted how reflective practice has been integrated unreservedly into education and professional development programmes for medical students. However, this decision had not been taken lightly, or through ignorance. Rather, Xu et al.'s (2021) systematic review demonstrated that a concerted effort by researchers to utilise robust experimental research designs to examine the benefits of reflective practice for improving diagnostic accuracy has cemented the profession's confidence that developing reflective capabilities is a worthwhile endeavour. It is our hope that the same enthusiasm for engaging in reflective practice will become seamed into the fabric of professional development within the sport, exercise, and health domains as a result of the evidence presented herein.

Why Reflective Practice Works: A Model for Change

The emerging empirical evidence of reflective practice research has provided insights into how reflective practice allows individuals to make sense of experiences that generate knowledge, which can be drawn upon during future situations. Implicit within this process is that in order to alter how we think and act in light of newly acquired knowledge and understanding requires potential changes to our cognitive structures and behavioural tendencies. Indeed, deliberately engaging in experiential learning through reflective practices seems to result in desirable perceptions and attitudes towards ensuing incidents (Cropley, Baldock et al., 2020; Picknell, Cropley et al., 2022). It would appear, therefore, that utilising reflective practice allows for developmental changes to occur based on the knowledge acquired as a result of the process. By acquiring new knowledge and using it to challenge pre-existing or automatic thought processes leads to a cascading effect that allows for rationalisation and alternative interpretations of experiences to occur.

The above contention has been recognised recently when examining the links between reflective practice and mindfulness (Picknell, Mellalieu et al., 2022) and components of hardiness (Cropley, Baldock et al., 2020). The evidence promoting the effects of mindfulness for improving health outcomes is well documented within the literature (e.g., Mantzios & Wilson, 2015; Olson & Emery, 2015). However, less is known about how to improve mindfulness beyond repeated exposure to certain principles (e.g., non-judgemental acceptance, separation from thought) through regular practice. Alternatively, outside the mindfulness context, reflective practice is considered a worthwhile endeavour for augmenting learning potential, in that it requires individuals to critique aspects of their experiences, which they may not have considered relevant without engaging in the process. Based on this sentiment, it is reasonable to assume that engaging in reflective practice following a mindfulness episode has the potential to expedite learning from the experience, subsequently resulting in an improved ability to be mindful. Indeed, the same could be said for other cognitive skills and thought processes as indicated by Cropley, Baldock et al. (2020), Hanrahan et al. (2009), and Jonker et al. (2012). When considered alongside other research studies that have investigated links between reflective practice and various cognitive processes, an evidence-base is emerging that potentially offers considerable practical implications for applied practitioners. Skills and thought processes (e.g., Think Aloud) that are known to be beneficial for promoting facilitative decisions and behaviours appear to be enhanced and utilised more efficiently when developed through the lens of reflective practice (e.g., Walsh & Driver, 2019; Whitehead et al., 2016). This is not to insist that all cognitive skills need to be added to professional education and training programmes or client-support programmes. Far from it. Instead, it is our belief that promoting and supporting the use of reflective practice with practitioners and end-user clients alike offers an evidenced-based framework to developing these types of skills (e.g., mindfulness, self-awareness, self-regulation) that can be utilised when needed to bring about positive changes to circumstances. In light of the findings from Picknell, Mella-lieu et al. (2022) and Cropley, Baldock et al. (2020), that link together reflective practice and cognitive processes, and their impact on self-regulation and health-related outcomes (e.g., Evans et al., 2019), we offer an integrated model of the relationship between reflective practice, mindfulness, self-regulation and health behaviours (Figure 4.1) that links all of these elements together for the first time.

The central theme of the model highlights the effect that the training of specific cognitive structures (e.g., mindfulness) has on psychological processes (e.g., self-awareness and self-regulation) that directly impact behavioural outcomes (e.g., physical activity). The presentation of these relationships is adapted from Tang and Leve's (2015) *Integrated Translational Framework*, which illustrated the neurobiological and behavioural mechanisms associated with cognitive training. Whilst Tang and Leve's representation is useful for understanding the processes involved between engaging in mindfulness and how that leads to altered behavioural outcomes, without a learning component, little can be gleaned about how improvements between the components occur. Therefore, Figure 4.1 includes reflective practice as a mechanism for augmenting learning required for achieving improved behavioural outcomes through initiating cognitive processes.

The inclusion of reflective practice into this model is based on two considerations. First, existing evidence supports the positive independent relationships between reflective practice and various cognitive structures (e.g., Mamede et al., 2007), mental processes (e.g., self-awareness; Cropley, Hanton et al., 2020), and self-awareness (e.g., Jonker et al., 2012). Second, the consideration that being mindful, self-regulatory and behaving, as outlined by Tang and Leve's (2015) framework, can be conceptualised as a concrete experience in accordance with Kolb's (1984) experiential learning cycle. From this perspective, the process of engaging in reflective practice enables concrete experience to be brought into a state of abstract conceptualisation. When framed, the abstract concepts guide active experimentation and subsequently lead to more concrete experiences. When learning takes place as a result of reflective practice, a new form of experience (i.e., more effective use of mindfulness, self-awareness and self-regulation) on which to reflect and conceptualise should be created. From a theoretical and applied perspective, the model presented in Figure 4.1 provides researchers and practitioners with key components considered integral for promoting positive behavioural outcomes and how they link together. Consequently, it provides areas for researchers to examine approaches to improving the efficacy of relationships between each component in the future. For applied practitioners, the model provides a guide for a phased approach to interventions. For example, instead of applying cognitive training with altered behaviours as an outcome, practitioners are encouraged to monitor the effects that the programme has on developing

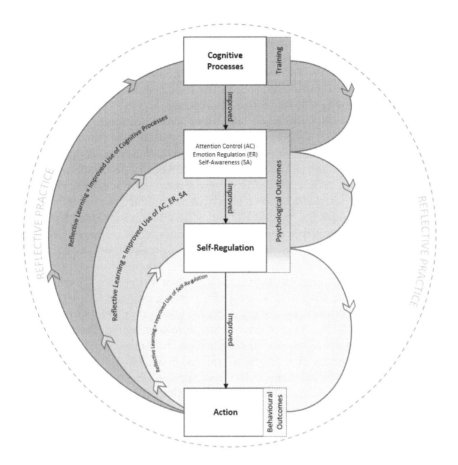

Figure 4.1 Integrated Model of the Relationship Between Reflective Practice, Mindfulness, Self-Regulation, and Health Behaviours

mental processes (e.g., attention control, emotion regulation, self-awareness), and how these lead to improved self-regulation before positive behavioural outcomes occur.

Where Do We Go From Here? Considerations for Profession Regulators

Several practical implications have emerged from this review of contemporary empirical reflective practice research and the proposal of a new model (Figure 4.1) for applied practitioners and profession regulating organisations (e.g., BASES; HCPC). These implications relate to the development of reflective skills, the refinement of practice approaches, and the potential for reflective practice for facilitating other performance and health related cognitive and behavioural skills. The evidence reviewed within this chapter should compel education and professional development providers, and profession regulating authorities to commit to ensuring that reflective practice is not only considered an essential competency associated with effective practice, and therefore a necessity for licensing and accreditation purposes, but also that adequate training opportunities and supervision are provided by experienced reflective practitioners.

Out of the profession regulating authorities across the sport, exercise, and health domains, BASES has been a leading example in the way that it has advocated and integrated reflective practice into its practitioner development programmes. Indeed, as part of the Supervised Experience route to Accreditation, *the ability to reflect, take responsibility for own actions, and to demonstrate that continuous professional development occurs* is explicitly outlined as a means towards demonstrating competence in 'Self-Evaluation and Professional Development' (BASES, 2019). Further, to support the development of this competence, BASES has added a *Reflective Practice* workshop as a core requirement of the Supervised Experience process for all candidates and provides 'would-be' supervisors with additional training for mentoring and supporting their supervisees. This approach by BASES appears to have been a result of a growing evidence base within the sport coaching and sport psychology domains, in addition to mounting pressure from within the professional practice literature warning regulatory authorities to not merely pay lip-service to reflective practice, but instead, embrace it wholeheartedly (Cropley et al., 2018; Whitehead et al., 2016). Other organisations would do well to follow in BASES' footsteps, especially when considering Mann et al.'s (2009) contention that "the most influential elements in enabling the development of reflection and reflective practice is a supportive environment, both intellectually and emotionally" (p. 608). Considering that these authorities typically set the tone for developments within a given profession, supporting the benefits of reflective practice, and providing the resources and opportunities for professionals to examine and understand their practices through reflections, should be a minimum requirement.

Future Research Directions

Although we (authors) have presented empirical data from investigations that promote the value of reflective practice in this chapter, this type of evidence is still lacking within the wider sport, exercise, and health domains. As noted previously, researchers from a variety of disciplines continue to emphasise this point even though the issue of a limited empirical evidence base has been raised on numerous occasions (e.g., Dube & Ducharme, 2015; Huntley et al., 2014; Huntley et al., 2019; Mann et al., 2009; Picknell et al., 2014). Although few in number, where quantitative data has been collected for examining either the development of reflective skills (e.g., Duke & Appleton, 2000; Sobral, 2000), or practice-based outcomes (e.g., Mamede et al., 2019; Peden-McAlpine et al., 2005), the findings have been largely positive. However, without a more diverse range of investigations across professional domains and practitioner experience levels, generalisations and transferability of findings remain limited. Potential reasons for this lack of research engagement appears to be a result of the philosophical and theoretical underpinnings of reflective practice, which traditionally are more closely aligned with interpretivism and qualitative inquiry (Sparkes, 1998). To that end, we agree with Smith and Sparkes (2009) who warned that qualitative inquiry should not be at the expense *of*, but rather in conjunction *with*, quantitative methods in order to allow for elaboration of certain issues and stimulating further thought on the topic under investigation.

Given that capabilities related to being a reflective practitioner are considered developmental in nature, it is also surprising that associated reflection skills have not been afforded more quantitative attention in the same way that other cognitive skills (e.g., imagery, mindfulness) have across psychological disciplines (cf. Tenenbaum & Filho, 2018). To our knowledge, presently, there is no specific quantitative tool within the sport, exercise, and health domains that explicitly measures skills related to reflection. Indeed, the measures (i.e., RQ & Reflection-in-learning Scale) typically used are sourced from the education domain (Kember et al., 2000; Sobral, 2000) and adapted for the specific context that the research was carried out in. It is widely recognised that quantitative inquiry, using valid and reliable assessment instruments, is considered essential for theory development. Indeed, according to Tenenbaum and Filho (2018), psychological instruments are used to develop valid theoretical frameworks, and allow scholars to propose and test different measurement models, while contrasting competing hypotheses and alternative models related to a given phenomenon. To that end, it seems timely that researchers enter a sustained period of quantitative enquiry that will contribute to the already beneficial claims of the impact of reflective practice on personal and professional development. Such research will allow scholars and practitioners to better understand the cause-and-effect relationships between reflective practice and relevant outcome measures and will also allow for the effectiveness of theoretically sound interventions to be evaluated.

With respect to the investigation of cause-and-effect relationships, it is recommended that future reflective practice research affords attention to both the process of developing reflective practice skills and how such improvements facilitate alterations to impending cognitions, decisions, and behaviours. Within the sport, health and exercise literature, this coupling of process and outcome measures has only been examined a few times (e.g., Cropley, Hanton et al., 2020; Picknell, Mellalieu et al., 2022). Indeed, most empirical studies across domains have focused primarily on evaluating the effectiveness of interventions for either developing reflection skills (e.g., Duke & Appleton, 2000; Sobral, 2000) or examining the direct link between training programmes and changes to behaviours (e.g., Mamede et al., 2019). Without linking process measures with outcome measures, conclusions regarding the effectiveness of reflective practice interventions are speculative at best, with little to no insight into questions relating to how or why a training programme worked (Picknell et al., 2014).

The issue regarding the limited research examining the benefits of reflective practice for end users within a therapeutic context has been alluded to previously. Whilst limited, previous evidence for incorporating reflective practice into support-services has suggested that recipients have demonstrated enhanced self-efficacy and management of competitive anxiety (Hanton et al., 2009), maintained effort (Hanrahan et al., 2009), and empowered self-regulated learning (Jonker et al., 2012). Although encouraging, limitations of these studies include a lack of insight into researchers' attempts to develop reflective skills, and the likelihood that participants received appropriate support from suitably trained reflective practitioners, without which conclusions regarding whether participants' thought processes were indicative of critical reflection remains limited. Such research should be commended for leading the way in considering the contributions of reflective practice for benefitting clients. Yet, in line with Hardy et al.'s (1996) previous contention, for reflective practice to be truly valued as a worthwhile contribution to the development of service provision, the advantages that it offers recipients of support-services, whether through enhanced satisfaction or facilitating positive performance and health related changes, should be of paramount concern for researchers' and practitioners' future endeavours.

5 Making Reflective Practice More Meaningful

Saying the "Unsayable"

Andy Borrie and Emily Ryall

Introduction

> "Life is a journey to be experienced, not a problem to be solved."
> – *Winnie the Pooh* (A. A. Milne)

This chapter is a collaboration between an applied philosopher with an interest in professional practice (Emily) and a practitioner with an interest in applied philosophy (Andy). Our aim is to stimulate readers to explore limitations to current approaches to reflective practice (e.g., many rarely engage in reflective practices that are meaningful) and consider alternative approaches that are better able to achieve the aims that those advocating reflective practice desire. We aim to present a different conception of reflection than those that currently dominate the sport and exercise sciences and, by changing perspectives, greater meaning is generated for the practitioner. Drawing upon the work of Martin Heidegger and Ludwig Wittgenstein we present several philosophical concepts that should influence approaches to reflective practice. What we are not doing is suggesting a new model or framework of reflective practice. Rather, we aim to reconceive of the notion of reflective practice itself. We argue that diluting the concept to models or frameworks is to misunderstand the nature of the practice itself.

The thoughts presented in this chapter have arisen from a collaboration that started with Emily's supervision of Andy's autoethnographic doctoral research looking at talent development philosophies. Within this research, Andy undertook a long and intense period of reflection on his career as a practitioner in world class sport. As a practitioner who engaged in, researched, and wrote about reflective practice in sport early in his career, part of the work became a meta-reflection on the influence of reflective practice on the evolution of his applied work. As a result of exposure to wider philosophical concepts within this meta-reflection, there was a fundamental shift in Andy's approach to reflective practice. The shift moved Andy's reflective practices from a more instrumental approach to reflection based on frameworks such as Gibbs' (1988) Reflective Cycle, to more aesthetic and creative forms of reflection.

DOI: 10.4324/9781003198758-7

The discussion that follows is presented in a dialogic form because we think it makes it more accessible and enjoyable to read. We have also used the first-person tense in the chapter as a way of supporting the critique of scientific rationalism that we present. Our exploration of the interaction between philosophy and reflective practice begins with Andy articulating his thoughts on current approaches to reflective practice in sport. We then continue by introducing the thoughts of the twentieth century philosophers' Heidegger and Wittgenstein which challenge us to think differently about reflective practice. Emily introduces each concept as a response to the question, "What can philosophy tells us that is pertinent to reflective practice?" Andy then responds by articulating how that philosophical concept has impacted on his understanding of meaningful reflective practice.

Reflective Practice – The State of Play

Andy

Reflective practice in sport has shifted from being a barely used phrase in the latter part of the 20th century to being seen as a key element in a wide range of practitioner development programmes (Marshall et al., 2021). It is now widely seen as being vital to effective practitioner development where it is commonly looked on as bridging the gap between craft knowledge drawn from experience and professional knowledge that is explicit, codified and formally taught. In sport and exercise science the importance of reflective practice has been recognised in the need for trainee practitioners to evidence their use of reflective practices to underpin learning from their practicum experiences. This evidence is required before they are accredited to work independently with athletes or members of the public (British Association of Sport & Exercise Sciences, 2021). Reflective practice is normally seen as being a proactive, deliberate act that transforms practice by supporting the practitioner in understanding their own experience, raising awareness of critical issues, and linking craft and professional knowledge (Cushion, 2018; Johns, 2017; Knowles et al., 2001). A range of reflective practice frameworks (e.g., Anderson et al., 2004; Gibbs, 1988; Johns, 2006) are commonly presented as processes for supporting systematic, rigorous reflection on experience.

However, more recently I have become aware of a number of authors who have started to question the idea that reflective practice, and dominant approaches to it, are a universal force for good. Cushion (2018) questioned the lack of clear definitions of the terms *reflection* and *reflective practice* in sport coaching and coaching's easy acceptance of reflective practice as being unproblematic. In addition, he raised concerns about the way that current approaches to reflective practice can constrain creative thinking by privileging particular perspectives on coaching. My personal experience is that this critique also holds true in the sport and exercise sciences. Outside sport, in the caring professions (social work, health care), researchers have also critiqued dominant approaches to reflective practice and have argued current interpretations may be limiting to the growth of the practitioner (e.g., Béres, 2017).

From a personal perspective, this shift in thinking mirrors my experience of reflective practice. In my early career as a practitioner, I was heavily engaged in championing a rigid and onerously systematic approach to reflective practice within the profession (cf. Knowles et al., 2001, 2005). The approach to reflective practice that is encapsulated in this early writing about reflection in sport seemed to me to just be a natural application of the critical thinking skills I had developed as a scientist. I did not see any limitations, only the power of guided introspection in creating a useful critique of practice that allowed me to enhance my professional skills. However, the engagement with key philosophical concepts, such as *monism* and *being* in the autoethnographic study of my professional career has led me to question the value of systematised and formulaic approaches to reflection. A growing awareness of the limits of my previous reflective practice allowed me to explore different ways of thinking and being, which in turn lead to richer learning. I moved beyond reflection on practice to deeper engagement *with practice* to consider much deeper issues of *value* and *meaning*.

In the rest of this chapter Emily and I want to outline some of the philosophical concepts that, when confronted, helped me generate a new perspective on my reflection.

Emily

For me, Andy's doctoral research demonstrated the power of combining deep reflection on one's own professional practice with philosophical theory. Since the most important philosophical questions are ultimately about what it is to be human and to live a worthwhile life, Andy showed why authentic reflective practice avoids attempts to distil the richness of the real-life experience down to a model or framework devoid of real meaning or sense.

In the remainder of the chapter, we would like to briefly introduce four concepts from the works of Heidegger and Wittgenstein (*technological attitude, dualism, being,* and *the unsayable*) and how they challenge current approaches to reflective practice.

Technological Attitude: Influence and Limitations

Emily

Whilst the *scientific method* – loosely defined as a systematic way of predicting and explaining phenomena in the world – is undeniably fruitful in helping us make sense of the world, both Heidegger and Wittgenstein warn us against becoming dogmatic in its use. That is not to say that they were anti-science, but rather they warn us against scientism; the belief that science can answer all questions of life. In their writings, they challenge us to think about questions of being, ethics and values differently. Heidegger (1977) used the phrase, the *technological attitude*[1] in this type of scientistic (e.g., exaggerated belief in the principles and methods of science) thinking. In this, he is critical of the way "scientific man" extracts things away from their environment, objectifying and analysing them as separate components for our service and consumption. Heidegger argues humans approach the world instrumentally, asking, "What can we use this [mineral, tree, plant, water, gene] for?" or, "What can we use as a resource to build and power our [homes, cars, entertainment facilities]?" In sport, this technological attitude can be seen in the way the body is dissected into discrete elements and seen in the context of performance. The exemplar of this is in the way the mind and the body are disconnected and seen as separate spheres. Whilst such a way of seeing the world may be fruitful for solving perceived problems (e.g., how to recover from particular injuries in some individual cases) we need to recognise that it is only one way of seeing the world, and it does not represent the way the world really is. Heidegger uses the term *standing-reserve*[2] to depict the way in which we perceive the world as a stockpile of resources waiting to be consumed. Eventually, he argues, we will take ourselves as standing-reserve and instrumentalise our own being. As such, the technological attitude can be thought of almost as a mode of existence.

Andy

Heidegger rightly questions the dominance of the *technological attitude* in societal thought processes and its influence in reflective practice is now being directly questioned (Béres, 2017). My perception is that in the sport and exercise sciences we have allowed reflective practice to become framework driven and almost exclusively sequential in nature, pursuing a positivist epistemology and the empirical realism that Heidegger and Wittgenstein warn us against (Cushion, 2018). So much of the writing about reflection in sport draws on frameworks that seek to codify and explain the process of reflection in language that is drawn from this technological attitude. We are invited to describe experience as a disembodied observer, to deconstruct experience and to separate emotion from action. Analytical processes that all stem from a natural science approach to the creation of knowledge and understanding.

In my research, recognising the technological attitude influence in my own reflective practice allowed me to see how much the use of reflective cycles (frameworks) had driven a process of always trying to break my experience into constituent parts. I realised I had stopped seeing experiences as whole entities in which my experience was embodied, with indivisible physical, emotional, cognitive, conscious, and subconscious elements. I had, therefore, imposed limits to what I could reflect upon and how I could draw meaning from that reflection through the way I had structured my reflective process.

In Table 5.1, I present a reflective vignette written during my autoethnography about the experience of doing performance analysis on a sport tour. It was an attempt to break my reflection out of a technological frame and into a more holistic frame. The vignette does not describe one specific occasion, rather it is a generalised reflection on a situation that I experienced many times in my professional work. Whilst it is in essence a fiction, it is grounded in a myriad of embodied experiences. Each time I read the vignette I see something that is far more than an abstract description of practice behaviour. My recollections in the piece were visceral, connecting touch, taste, and sound. Reading the vignette helps me

Table 5.1 Vignette Describing Undertaking Performance Analysis

The low hum from the laptop fan fills the room, it's amazing how much heat one electronic device can create. It's been crunching numbers and slicing video clips for hours now and there is a still more to get done . . . so why am I thinking about this now? My mind is starting to wander, the hum and the heat are a potent combination, I am beginning to crave sleep. I look at the clock and realise that midnight is a distant memory . . . 2.30 am . . . but it's almost done. Another 30 mins and the analysis will be complete.

I roll my neck and hear it crunch. I rub my eyes, again, and they hurt like there's a mound of grit in each one. But what should I expect? I've been in front of this screen since 10pm. I reach for my coffee . . . it's cold . . . but I drink it anyway. God knows how many cups I've had in the past four hours. If I could find a way to have it intravenously it would be so helpful.

But these are the moments when you have to concentrate harder. These are the moments when you make mistakes . . . you start to miss a couple of events and skew your stats . . . you don't "see" a critical passage of the game . . . you don't record the one example of a play that may unlock the coaches' understanding the game . . . you miss the moment that might make a difference.

It's all there in the numbers, it's all there in the sequences of events. Somewhere there's a pattern and if we can find that pattern, we can work out how to beat it.

So, you get up and move around the room, open the window and breath in some cold air. Let the draft play over your arms and face to wake you up. You move back across the room to put the kettle on again. You don't want another coffee really and your body certainly doesn't need one, but you make a cup just the same. It's the act of doing it that's important, it helps you find the energy. Your body moves and by doing so it wakes up your brain just enough to let you can concentrate for another 30 mins.

You look at the screen, but you don't see the game anymore. You muted the crowd long ago. Who wants to be distracted by the ebb and flow of the emotions of a few thousand spectators. They aren't important. Its understanding player movement that is the only thing. When did they move, where did they move, how often did they move . . . pass, feed, shoot, intercept, pass, feed, shoot . . . numbers and patterns, numbers and patterns. The players' experiences are irrelevant, the determination and effort etched on faces, the magic in a deft sleight of hand, the power in an intercept, the intensity of the contest . . . wonderful things, but not important. Numbers and patterns . . .

Another 30 mins and you can summarise ready for the morning and then you can sleep. Asleep by 3.15 sounds good. Alarm set for 7am, coaches' meeting at 7.30, players meeting at 9.00, off to training by 10 . . .

Just the three hours' sleep again but that's fine if we can crack their patterns, we can take them. It's almost within reach, the last couple of games we have been there or there about. We are starting to believe, if we can bridge the gap a little more then we are one step closer to the podium. So, you settle back into the seat, flex your fingers and start the video rolling again . . . somewhere in this data we can find another hint on how to win a medal . . . numbers and patterns . . . numbers and patterns . . .

to experience again the hum of the laptop, the sound of the kettle, the taste of cold coffee and the feeling of tired and gritty eyes. All physical sensations that spoke to an overall sense of fatigue in the moment.

If I had adopted a technological attitude using standard reflective models then I could have reflected on creating better nutritional strategies for the situation, managing sleep patterns, or maintaining work:rest ratios to alleviate fatigue. At one level those would all have been reasonable lines of reflective thought in relation to enhancing practice effectiveness. But by simply accepting and writing about my physical responses as being part of an embodied whole I allowed them to tell me a deeper story. Through the vignette I accessed my deep sense of striving to achieve a competitive outcome in that situation. I started to see how the experience was linked to a performance narrative about needing to make sacrifices to feel I was legitimately in pursuit of a performance goal. The recognition of this narrative then raised deeper questions for me about purpose and meaning. Why was I sacrificing sleep and, more importantly, why was I reducing performance to just "numbers and patterns"? By consciously stepping away from the technological attitude inherent in common reflective cycles (e.g., Borton, 1970), I accessed a more holistic form of reflection that opened a deeper appreciation of the experience.

The influence of the technological attitude on my practice also made my early reflective practice too instrumental in nature. I now appreciate that most, if not all, of my reflective practice was driven by a focus on understanding an experience for the purpose of altering it to achieve a pre-determined outcome. In essence, my reflective approach was always "if I better understand x then I can change how I do y and the end result will become the outcome I want." By thinking like this I limited the way in which I was going to see the world. I pursued a process in which I was most likely to only "see" the elements of an experience that I felt relevant to changing its outcome. Consequently, I blinded myself from seeing other aspects of an experience that may have had deeper meaning. Part of the process was also an implicit reduction of athletes or other practitioners to the status of being just a component part in a deconstructed experience. They were reduced to being objects that I could act upon, and potentially manipulate, in ways that suited my conceptualisation of the world.

The technological attitude that pervaded my reflective processes is something I now see as being problematic. By unquestioningly adopting a technological attitude I constrained myself to an instrumental view of the world and often positioned people as objects *standing-reserve*. I believe this limited my reflective process and hindered my understanding of meaning in my reflections. Now, when I step away from standard reflective cycles it becomes easier to access and feel an experience as a whole. For example, I will now more readily use metaphor as a way of expressing my understanding of an experience. A particularly contentious meeting might be described as a "storm" which gathers, then breaks, is all encompassing for a while and then passes on. The metaphor captures the flow of the experience, its intensity, its impact and its aftermath but without attempting to break it down in to specific components.

Dualism

Emily

The starting point for the technological attitude is Cartesian *dualism* where the human is both at the centre of the world and apart from it. Current approaches to reflective practice seem to assume that dualism holds true to allow us to stand back from our experience and analyse it as an external observer. However, for Heidegger the idea of the human existing apart from, or outside, the world makes no sense (Mulhall, 2000). Such a conception of the world will undoubtedly produce difficulties when we consider who or what we, as humans, are and how we address those deep philosophical questions that are at the core of our being; questions about meaning, ethics and value – since it suggests that there is a God's eye view of the world from which such questions can be empirically solved. Heidegger believed the legacy of Descartes meant there has been a real impoverishment of diversity in the way we understand the world. The dominance of the technological attitude, and its reductionist approach moves us away from engaging with the richness of diversity in experience. We focus on physical entities (res extensa) to the detriment of engaging with spiritual entities (res cogitans), that is, we are limited in the way we conceptualise and make sense of the world if we see it purely as a scientist sees her specimens in the laboratory.

Heidegger asks us to see ourselves as an intrinsic part of the world that does not stand apart from it but is intimately connected to it. This is a view that is becoming increasingly accepted as can be seen in the growth of ecological approaches to issues, whether in environmentalism or sport and exercise science and coaching. Ecological approaches see the world not as the traditional detached, observer scientist would see it, but instead recognises the complexity, inter-relationship and non-distinctiveness of phenomena, and this includes our own existence in the world (see, for example, Næss, 1986, 1987).

Andy

My thoughts on *dualism* are an extension of my response to the technological attitude. The reflective work in my research reinforced for me that my experience was embodied, personal and contextual. I do not believe that I can be apart from the world therefore I cannot be a detached observer of my own actions. Consequently, I cannot, nor should not, attempt to reflect by simply trying to stand apart from the world. In addition, the Cartesian view contributes to us trying to compartmentalise problems in practice so that we can use the technological attitude to resolve them. By consistently standing apart from the world and breaking it in to component parts we run the risk of losing the essence of our holistic, complex experiences.

Unfortunately, when you examine commonly used reflective frameworks you could argue that many have been created based on a Cartesian view of the world. Even if not created from this view, practitioners may assume a Cartesian view in applying them. In rejecting a Cartesian view of the world, I am not suggesting that there is no value in attempting to look at our practice from the outside. I still see huge value in quietly, and with as little emotion as possible, seeking to understand different parts of my experience. Yet, in attempting to adopt the position of neutral observer I must accept that this position is unattainable and that my reflective observations are neither objective nor value-free. Consequently, this can no longer be the only way that I seek to access, interpret, and express understanding of my practice.

I believe I must seek additional complementary ways to engage with the richness of an experience. I need to actively seek to understand the *essence* of an experience engaging with issues like value, meaning, or the inherent spirituality in a moment as well as its physical elements. The vignette in Table 5.1 is a reflection that sought to capture the essence of an experience. By accepting the embodied nature of the experience and reporting on the physical feelings of the moment I did not try to stand apart from it. By doing this it opened a route to exploring deeper meaning in the experience.

"Being" and the "Unsayable"

Emily

Perhaps the most critical concept we need to address is that of *being*. Heidegger challenges us to consider the nature of being and what it means for our relationship with the world. As a way of resisting the technological attitude, Heidegger asks us to refocus our perspective on the question of being (or, in the case of human existence, what it is to be human[3]). In this, he wishes to return our attention towards the actual phenomenological raw-feel of experience rather than a detached, objective, scientistic conception of reality.

Heidegger argued that when faced with the beauty of something like a tree in bloom or a vivid rainbow stretching across the breadth of the sky, we do not, and should not, regard it as would a scientist but instead simply appreciate and enjoy the moment of being with it and as part of our presence. For Heidegger, *knowing* the world comes second to *existing* within it. He urges us to disregard the traditional scientistic method of answering the question, "What is it to be human?" according to necessary and sufficient conditions and replace it with a richer exploration of what it is to be an authentic human being. In relation to reflective practice, we need to move away from the question of, "How can I become more effective in solving this particular problem?" to, "How can I become more authentic as a being in my own right?" In this context "authentic" would refer to being able to recognise one's place and situation within the world. Such a view resonates with Eastern philosophies and religions that advocate meditation, contemplation, and a desire to become one with the world. It is a form of life that is incommensurate with the objective, sterile, scientific method that is advocated by Western approaches. As we adjust our attitude towards seeing the world, this results in not only seeing the world in a different way but in essence, seeing a different world.

This is a perspective also promoted by Wittgenstein (1978, p. 325) when he wrote, "Not empiricism, and yet realism in philosophy; that is the hardest thing." The use of the term "realism" here is arguably not to mean the truth, in a positivist sense, but rather acknowledge that empiricism only presents limited, and limiting, pictures of the world. Wittgenstein (1968, p. 127) urged us to resist theory and avoid abstracting phenomena away from their context.[4] For Wittgenstein, realism is essentially about the attitude one holds towards the world, one which recognises that science is unable to answer questions about ethics and value and that we can only gesture at moral truths rather than define or theorise them. Our reflective practices, therefore, need to deal with the holistic, complex, and profound nature of *being* as much as break down experience into component parts. Reflective practice, if done well, allows us to change our own attitude, and to change the attitude of others.

One of our challenges in being in the world, and reflecting in it, is to be able to express our relation to it without losing the essence of what we experience. In this regard, language can be a significant limitation especially when we constrain ourselves to writing in the forms considered acceptable within a scientistic view of the world. In responding to this problem Wittgenstein repeatedly talked about the *unsayable* when referring to matters of ethics and aesthetics (i.e., what is important and valuable in living a life). If we are to be true to our understanding of being in the world there are thoughts that we cannot express in a reductionist way. If we try to express these thoughts, they lose that which is most profound. Whilst Wittgenstein recognises that there is no direct way to say the "unsayable" he suggested that there are things that can contain those things that cannot be said. For example, narrative works are ways in which such things can be communicated: "It can communicate some ineffable truth about life while talking about the growth of a sprig into a hawthorn bush" (Edwards, 1982, p. 51). It is exactly for this reason that Wittgenstein recommended reading novels and literature over philosophical theory because literature (and arguably, this includes any narrative work, including [auto]biography) do not try to utter the unutterable yet still importantly hold on to important ethical reminders that serve to alter our attitude. Toulmin (2001, p. 123) captures this in saying:

> Convincing narratives have a kind of weight that mathematical formulas do not. They allow us to revive moral argumentation in disciplines that, since the eighteenth century, had aimed at value neutrality; in the process, they bridge the gulf between Science and Literature.

Andy

In my autoethnographic work it was the confrontation of *being* and how I presented reflections on being that caused the greatest challenge and the greatest learning. First, by becoming more aware of the concept of the *unsayable* I began to understand the influence of language on my practice and reflections. I also noted how the language of my performance world was the language of instrumental rationality. As Tekavc et al. (2015) noted, the performance world clothed itself in the language of business and economics. In high performance, achievement of an end-result was the only purpose, so we spoke of targets, audits, KPIs, return on investment, "what it takes to win" modelling and other quasi-business concepts. Consequently, as the language of my practice world centred around these forms of rhetoric, so had my reflections. Combined with an underpinning technological attitude the language I had been using in my reflections had moved them away from the aesthetic towards the transactional and instrumental. By engaging with the works of Heidegger and Wittgenstein I came to realise that I needed to respond more holistically to being in the world. My understanding of my practice was limited by the language I used.

I also came to see the importance in recognising the embodied nature of experience. Botelho (2020), in drawing upon the idea of body phenomenology, recognised that our physical responses to situations inform us of things. When we smile involuntarily it is not a conscious response but a non-verbal reaction to experience. A response that is neither verbal nor accessible to introspection but nevertheless tells us something about the experience. We experience the world through our bodies which determines what we perceive through the limitations of our senses. As such we must recognise that we experience the world in a holistic way and that not every aspect of our practice will be available for conscious scrutiny (Cushion & Partington, 2016). However, when we accept the embodied essence of experience then we must also accept that parts of our practice will always be unsayable within the limitations of instrumental language and a technological attitude.

Through my autoethnography I realised that my reflective practice must evolve to meet the challenge of being in the world. To meet this challenge, I had to step closer to more creative presentations of my reflections. In Table 5.2, I have shown a second reflective vignette from my autoethnography. This vignette is more aesthetic and is an example of how expressing myself differently allowed me to create a deeper understanding of my being in the world of my professional practice.[5] Table 5.2 shows my attempt to holistically express reflections about being on a longitudinal performance journey. To express something of this longitudinal experience I found that my writing needed to become both metaphorical and allegorical rather than literal. This writing style allowed me to better capture thoughts that I simply could not convey in technological language. It allowed me to get closer to the unsayable in my experience and develop a deeper understanding of my being in the world. The vignette might not make sense to some readers whilst others might feel it resonates with their experiences. Its value is not in what it conveys for others but how the metaphors create meaning for me.

The vignette conveys for me something of my understanding of the interaction of personal motivation, the lure of the end goal, and the positive nature of personal experience whilst recognising the inevitable sacrifice and loss that comes with choices made. By expressing my thoughts in this way, I felt better able to start to question how I, and others, drew meaning from those experiences. Additional value from writing in the style of this vignette emerged through the process of drafting and re-drafting the story. As a scientist, I initially found it hard to write creatively but with each successive draft presentation the process became easier and, more importantly, I gained new insight into my experience. I found that the process of writing creatively became an integral part of my reflective process. The writing was not simply a presentation of the output from a separate

Table 5.2 Vignette Capturing Reflections Around Purpose in Professional Practice

It's like looking at a series of islands stretching out into the sea. The island you want to get to is a hazy outline on a distant horizon and in between there are all these other islands. Some big, some small, all different . . . and to reach across the sea into the haze you have to visit each island in turn. Sometimes you can rest on an island for a while but most times you land, explore the island, and have to press on towards the next in the chain.

And the sea of life flows around the islands . . . at times the crossings are smooth, the voyage is gentle, relaxed, easy, fun . . . but then there are the storms that can spring out of nowhere . . . unexpected currents or tides that try and push you off course . . . or the wind dies, and you become becalmed, unable to move forwards.

So what may have seemed like a simple crossing between islands can become anything but . . . it becomes a battle, a contest . . . between you and the sea or you and the boat or you and yourself. It's not something to be enjoyed, it's something to be endured . . . but you keep moving forwards because it's the only way to reach that distant island sitting in the haze.

And every now and then another boat sails across your path and you see friends and family on its deck, and you want to go on their journey . . . you want to see what they are going to see, be a part of their experience but you can't. Or its your employer and they want you to be on their journey and a part of their 'team' but you can't commit. And you know at this moment in time you can't follow anyone else because once you step off this boat you can't get back on. You'd have to wait for another boat that's sailing to that distant, hazy island but another one might never come along or if it does there is no room onboard for you. So, you stand and watch as other boats pass by and sail away from you.

And then there's the issue of the crew. When you start you know that not everyone you see around you will be there at the end. People will be lost along the way . . . at any time someone can succumb to injury, can fail to perform . . . and the boat can't carry passengers . . . only crew, only people who can make it go faster or at least stay in a straight line . . . so the weak get cast adrift as the boat sails on.

And as the boat sails on all the while you practice, you train, you perform, you learn, and change comes slowly, incrementally. Collectively and individually, you keep looking for the small gains in performance, the 'inches' that can make the difference between winning and losing.

So why be on this boat, why go on this journey . . . well, it's simple really.

There is a Siren sitting on that final island and it's her song draws you on. It's a song that's about testing yourself, expressing yourself, about triumph, about the elation that comes with victory. So many things that you want to experience, and you know that the only way to experience them is to be on this boat and on this journey . . . and yet . . .

cognitive process. Writing and thinking were symbiotically linked in creating the final reflection. This reinforced for me how the presentational form you use to portray your reflection plays an active part in creating the reflection.

Moving forward I now believe we must step towards artistic and aesthetic forms of presentation and engage with the symbolic as well as the literal in our reflective practices. If I had allowed myself to remain rooted in language that was instrumentally focused and technological in nature, I could not have expressed what I understood of my performance experience. I could not have come closer to engaging with the unsayable element in my professional practice.

Conclusion

Reflective practice in sport has, understandably, largely focused on developing reflection through the use of systematic and structured reflective frameworks. There are many benefits to such approaches, which draw heavily on a natural science, reductionist approach to critical thinking. However, there are limitations and weaknesses inherent in the *technological attitude* that too often influences our thinking and our practice. These limitations have been discussed by 20th century philosophers such as Heidegger and Wittgenstein who challenged the dominance of this technological attitude. They suggested critical questions about life and experience cannot be considered as abstract questions that can be answered by turning to a formula or theory as directed by science.

Andy's autoethnographic journey highlighted that there is much to be gained from moving away from the technological attitude and an unquestioningly adopting a Cartesian view of the world. In reflective processes we need to allow ourselves to engage with a sense of being in the world in a holistic and embodied way because not all experience can, or should, be broken into constituent parts. Reflective practice needs to support us to engage with deep philosophical questions relating to meaning, ethics, value and ultimately what it is to live a good life. These are personal questions that we need to ask ourselves as individuals knowing whilst being comfortable that we are unlikely to find neat, unambiguous answers. This is what Wittgenstein meant when he said, "What is ragged must be left ragged" (Phillips, 1992, p. 270).

By exploring deeper philosophical questions about what it is to be human and what it is to live a worthwhile life, and to recognise the importance of *being* in the world, rather than just deconstructing it, then the *unsayable* becomes clearer. When we allow ourselves to recognise our embodied and holistic experience of the world then the limitations of our language in describing that experience comes to the fore. To counter this we have to learn to engage with more aesthetic ways for expressing thoughts and ideas. We must learn to work with artistic and literary devices such as metaphor and allegory to better reflect what we know but do not have the language to say directly.

In conclusion, the experience of Andy's autoethnographic research process has led us to believe it is time to re-think reflective practice. Current structured practices, whilst of value, may be limiting reflection as much as they are stimulating it. We hope that this chapter has stimulated readers to reconsider what it means to reflect and how a technological attitude may be limiting their understanding of their experience. We would like to encourage practitioners to explore their *being* in the world and how they may use more aesthetic forms of expression to access the unsayable in their experiences and thus facilitate a more meaningful reflective process.

Notes

1 Heidegger uses the term *Gestell* which means "enframing" (i.e., a way of conceptualising the world).
2 Heidegger's term is *Bestand*.
3 Heidegger uses the term *Dasein* to indicate the specific beingness of human being, as opposed to being (existence) in general.
4 In this Wittgenstein warns us that we should be careful to resist reifying his own observations into abstract theories as it is incredibly easy to attempt to formulate philosophical theories from Wittgenstein's writings even though it is exactly what he wanted to avoid. However, some academics have given up this battle and have simply rejected his anti-theoretical stance to be discarded as an unjustified anti-scientific prejudice (see Pleasants, 1999).
5 In presenting my vignettes as creative pieces I am conscious that in autoethnography there are now many researchers engaging in performative methodologies that are far more creative using poetry, music and drama to express reflective thoughts.

6 Barriers to Reflective Practice and Opportunities for Progress in the Sport and Exercise Sciences and Allied Disciplines

Spaces and Places in Between

Jo Trelfa and Hamish Telfer

Introduction

Rewards and failures are both immediate and powerful in the world of performance. Sport performance is no different and it is where coaches (and other support staff) are judged through the performance of those whom they work with. Explaining, disclosing, and accounting for their (coaches) methodologies, approaches and skills is risky, subjective, and introspective. Thus, the idea of reflective practice as a means of interrogating practice for the better is similarly problematic, particularly because sport performance and coaching itself is a messy, risky business. New, amateur or elite, sports performance and coaching is fluid and situational (Cassidy et al., 2015), deeply individual (with regards to processing, co-ordination, physiology, conditioning and skill; e.g., Faubert, 2013; Vaughan et al., 2021) whilst also relational (Jones et al., 2016; Vaughan et al., 2021) and uncertain and ambiguous (Abbott et al., 2005; Cassidy et al., 2020) such that outcomes are always "unpredictable" (Thue Bjørndal & Tore Ronglan, 2021). Even so, in this chapter we suggest that sports performance and coaching is wrapped around by *neoliberal body work*, that is, discourse and practice concerned with a "single social formation, centred on the self-responsible, committed and productive individual" (Martschukat, 2021, p. 2) who expresses success by "mastering its own body" (ibid). Thus, performance and coaching are couched in the explicit and tacit message that we "can achieve anything we aspire to have" (Martschukat, 2021, p. 5). *Neoliberalism* is often used weakly as a "catch-all" to refer to anything pejoratively (Einar Thorsen, 2010, p. 188). More clearly defined, it can be constructed variously as a new positive paradigm, a natural continuum of liberalism, or a "great reversal" (Einar Thorsen, 2010, p. 196) of freedom of individuals for the good of all to merely benefitting the privileged few. In our (authors) use of neoliberalism, we are referring to a reversal of liberalist practices through self-regulation to protect the interests of some by whatever means necessary.

DOI: 10.4324/9781003198758-8

Sport is, of course, overtly outcome oriented, involving predicted outcomes as well as outcomes of a more incidental nature (Mallett, 2010, p. 128). Coaching practice focuses on the means to those outcomes, referred to as process. The processes are a contested area in dialogue between coaches and coach educators and it is in this arena that reflective practice, as a lens, purports to illuminate practice and behaviour as well as open-up a critique that can stimulate and motivate coaching practice development, but also sow self-doubt. However, outcomes still invariably claim a higher value. As a consequence, the balance mechanisms in coaching practice are disturbed such that articulation of process relates only to the cues expected, related to a particular and individual lexicon of intention based on levels of coach expertise (Lyle & Cushion, 2010) and implicit or explicit compliance with the conventional norms of the day. Therefore, the outcomes are used as justification for the processes, hollowing out the value of reflective practice. The challenge for us as authors is to seek great credence for a reflective practice that focuses on the less obvious, less visible, often times hidden practices instead.

We, the authors of this chapter, define reflective practice as a rigorous approach of inquiry about practice, but also a lived, rich experience of noticing and attending to it as coaches (and sport and exercise scientists) seek to engage, innovate and challenge all the while wrestling with that need for compliance to accepted "norms". This nuanced balance between "what is the norm?" and "what could possibly be" is the basis of our motivation for exploring reflection within practice. Despite our definition, our contention within this chapter is that in its typical forms, reflective practice is merely part of the neoliberal apparatus described above. Although the *nature* of sport performance and coaching outlined at the outset of this introduction is well established, now shown to be tilted towards outcomes, we suggest that the practices of reflective practice in this context are also problematic, further compounding the situation. Stemming, as they are, from the original history and traditions of reflective practice, it too frames inquiry into practice toward outcomes (i.e., "if you reflect, in these ways, you achieve anything you aspire to have"). Processes, forms, and outcomes of reflective practice are controlled, censored, and managed into careful stories through critical thinking after the event, leaving a gap between them and the "liquidity of knowledge" (Nelson, 2013, p. 60), the managed story, and the messy, unpredictable, sensate, fast-moving nature of practice.

By drawing on the primary research of Jo Trelfa in the social professions (Trelfa, 2020), applied to sport and coaching by Hamish Telfer, in this chapter we argue that reflective practices fix and solidify uncertain practice through routines and results that serve only to return status quo (Trelfa, 2020). We offer ways forward through reflective practices that engage with the messy, risky business of sports performance and coaching, and in this endeavour, we find that the transdisciplinarity of the social professions and sport proves to be, "Fertile ground . . . for fundamental changes in the approaches we use to enhance learning and development of human creativity both on and off the field of sport" (Vaughan et al., 2019, np). We conclude that reflection-in-action is the *fertile ground* for spaces and places between the barriers to reflective practice of neoliberal body work and controlled narratives. We begin by considering risk, the knotty thread that runs throughout our chapter.

Risk and Risk Work

Risk is generally understood as weighing up the possibility of harm in relation to gains and prevention of significant damage (Gigerenzer, 2014). We extend that lens to consider the impact of practice decisions in the context of risk aversion and blame culture, the extent to which individuals, teams and organisations articulate and account for those decisions as they assess and manage risk. Indeed, it is in this broader frame that sport and coaching regulations, standards, and controls sit. As Vamplew (2007, p. 1) explained:

> Sport today is a rule-governed practice: constitutive rules, both prescriptive and proscriptive, define required equipment and facilities as well as setting the formal rules of play; auxiliary rules specify and control eligibility: and regulatory rules place restraints on behaviour independent of the sport itself.

The purpose of those rules is to assist in the risky business of coaching and sport and exercise science (SES) development. Coaches, lecturers and trainers (we recognise their differences but, for expediency in this chapter, from here on referred to as coaches) draw on the rules in the process of "risk work" (Whittaker & Taylor, 2017, p. 375). Combined with the established habitualised and repetitive routines of reflective practice, coaches articulate and explain what they did and why at the multiple junctions of hindsight based on a cognitive, rational process that we have previously explicated as faulty (Trelfa & Telfer, 2014). That process sits within awareness of boundaries created by rules, weighed up with potential consequences of their discourses about their practice, which influences the nature, transparency and honesty of their decisions and the reporting of or accounting for those decisions. Additionally weaving into this risk work are values. The articulation and explanation of practice involves the contested nature of *which* and *whose* values, and the extent of coaches' thinking that some are more acceptable, and at times popular, than others. *Reflective practice becomes "risk work".*

Risk, Risk Work, and Neoliberalism

The landscape for this risk work in the context of coaching is "motivational challenge and effort" (Ives et al., 2020, np) in the support and promotion of sport performance. Ives et al. (ibid) point to various research evidencing coaches' "use of highly intense, effortful, and stressful practices" – reward, punishment, as well as competition in this regard. However, our contention is that the effect of neoliberal body work wrapping around this has a particular impact. The "single social formation, centred on the self-responsible, committed and productive individual" (Martschukat, 2021, p. 2) in the context of reflective practice for coaches becomes protection of one's practice from scrutiny. Further, for students, participants in sport, and athletes, it becomes a desire to limit the risk of not performing or achieving as they intend, wish, or hope. Here reflective practice risks driving "a crisis of agency, representation, and resistance" with coaches reinforcing this status quo, their reflective practice an "incubator" for neoliberalism (Giroux, 2019, pp. 38–39). Of course, the expressed hope, even intention, of reflective practice, is declared as a process to challenge and question taken-for-granted assumptions and practices – but clearly this is risky. Telling controlled, censored, managed stories is safer.

Sport performance becomes writ large with self-improvement, productivity, and vitality by "work on the body" through "struggle and strength" (Martschukat, 2021, p. 110). Additionally, "activating oneself, exploiting one's opportunities, and enhancing one's potential" produces "productive, willing, capable" individual reflective coaches and participants who "rack up exceptional achievements" (ibid), in contrast to "lazy, fat, inflexible bodies incapable of taking responsibility" for themselves (Martschukat, 2021, pp. 138–140). It therefore follows that we suggest the defining barrier to reflective practice and opportunities for progress in the SES and allied disciplines to be that of coaches, students, participants, and athletes seeking practices that build certainty of productive attainment, whilst (sometimes) privately recognising that practice and performance are unpredictable, emergent, and unintentional, guided by experiential knowledge that is difficult to explain or justify. *The barrier to reflective practice is "risk".*

Reflective Practice and Risk

The very nature of pushing limits and exploring boundaries, at any level of sport, involves uncertainty. Practice and performance develop, intentionally or otherwise, through the creation of space to try, that is to explore and take risks. It involves "freedom to improvise and alter how the game is played whilst it is in progress" *whilst also obeying the rule book* (Vamplew, 2007, p. 843). The consequences of this going wrong, however, are sorely felt and can be severe; the stakes are high, the realisation for the individual that they have not or cannot achieve what was aspired to have, and for the coach that they are, or not perceived as, the expert they hope to be. It requires cognisance of risk, and therefore coaches and those judging or charged with an overview of practitioner competence and outcome (e.g., supervisors, reviewers), are gatekeepers with regard to skills deployed, direction of approach, and decisions made. The effect of this overview, in the context of regulation, narrows the acceptability of taking risks. Conservatism creeps into applied practice and the practice of reflection downplays boundary exploration in order to make practice accounts more acceptable to the gatekeepers. For example, coaches with a degree of experience and who operate within what may be called high-performance usually push boundaries and experiment with levels of physical loadings on performers or through movement boundaries never attempted before. Yet, by its very nature, this is risky, open to judgement by others and, at the very least initially, potentially open to high levels of failure.

It opens them up to high levels of potentially negative judgement. It is safer, therefore, to play safe!

Based on the pragmatism of John Dewey, Schön described reflective practice as "a dialogue of thinking and doing through which one becomes more skilful" (Schön, 1983, p. 31). In an uncertain world, one can gain control of self and situations through learning and thinking critically. Whilst Dewey (1933) focussed on only this (when writing about reflection), Schön extended by application to professional practice; practitioners engage with perplexing situations to find solutions. Thus, the term *practice* in reflective practice both describes *how*, and enables a practitioner *to*, control the "messy, indeterminate situations" in professional settings so that they can be effective (Schön, 1987, p. 4). In this sense it is obvious why reflective practice has become so popular in SES and coaching, a "promised land" of salvation from otherwise messy and indeterminate contexts (Papastephanou & Angeli, 2007, p. 604).

Explicating reflective practice, Schön (1983) distinguished between *reflection-on* and *reflection-in* action. Reflection-on-action refers to how, "In the relative tranquillity of a post-mortem, [coaches] think back on a project they have undertaken, a situation they have lived through, and they explore the understandings they have brought to their handling of the case" (p. 61). Reflection-in-action refers to the process whereby coaches "think about doing something while doing it" (Schön, 1983, p. 54) in "a stretch of time within which it is still possible to make a difference to the outcomes of action" (Schön, 1995, np). Together "knowledge of performance" (Vaughan et al., 2021, np) is produced, with reflection-on-action determined through tools and means by which coaches and sport and exercise scientists link their understanding of what they did and why with regulations and other drivers to construct a story about their actions (Trelfa, 2020). Despite these tools and means being problematic, the focus of our earlier work (Trelfa & Telfer, 2014), Schön's writing in the 1980's, followed by ever-blossoming literature based on it ever since, pays substantial attention to theorising and honing only reflection-on-action. The effect has been to firmly establish a developmental perspective to mainstream understanding of reflective practice, one that devotes attention to increasingly finer detail about the nature of suitable activities that foster the control of practitioner thought and situation.

To exemplify, we have clarified that sport is risky, and the problem with reflecting on a risky activity or environment is that by its very nature there is uncertainty about the variables and effects of that engagement. What is reflected *on* in these circumstances will be more to do with what can be grasped; measurable probabilities shaped by what they must account *for* (purpose of reflective practice and audience for the reflective account). It will also take into consideration the significance of risk to all those involved, more pronounced in higher risk compared to lower risk concern. Into this mix is the *impact* of activities, that is, those that are assumed or appear to hold a demonstrable benefit (whatever that may be); reflections afterward on that engagement are more likely to justify action and intention to "get at" those potential rewards. Thus, our assertion of reflective practice as risk work can be understood: engaging in a risky process of risk management to being able to justify one action over another to "get it right" even when "right" is uncertain, an escalation compounded by neoliberal discourse (i.e., that by "mastering one's own body" we can achieve anything we aspire to have; Martschukat, 2021, p. 5).

Reflection-on-Action

If a barrier to reflection, when focused on reflection-on-practice, is risk work, perhaps the way forward lies in reflection-in-action. Indeed, Schön (1983) defines reflection-in-action as "*central* to the art through which practitioners sometimes cope with the troublesome divergent situations of practice" [*emphasis added*] (p. 62). Yet, Schön immediately confuses this with reflection-*on*-action. When describing "action-present", that is the "zone of time in which action can still make a difference", he offers this to be minutes, which of course equates with *in-action*, but then refers to days, weeks, even months, obviously the timeframe of reflection-*on*-action. He then follows that with what he declares to be *an illustration* of a practitioner reflecting-in-practice, but does so in these (gendered) terms:

> He may reflect *on* the tacit norms and appreciations which underlie a judgement, or *on* the strategies and theories implicit in a pattern of behaviour. He may reflect *on* the feeling for a situation which has led him to adopt a particular course of action, *on* the way in which he has framed the problem he is trying to solve, or *on* the role he has constructed for himself within a larger institutional context [*sic*] [*emphasis added*]. (*ibid*).

So, when describing reflection-*in*-action, Schön exemplifies reflection-*on*-action. Indeed, when referring explicitly to sport, specifically that of baseball, Schön writes of pitchers talking about "finding the groove" of practice *in* their game. He first states that he does not wholly understand what finding the groove means, surprising given his original definition of reflection-in-action, Schön (1983, p. 55) then offers that they "are talking about a particular kind of reflection", a line of analysis that sounds promising, but then lists the possibilities of "that kind of reflection" as, "Reflection on their patterns of action, *on* the situations in which they are performing, and *on* the know-how implicit in their performance [*emphasis added*]" (p. 55). Later in the same text he returns again to baseball pitchers, this time contending that "*even* if" reflection-in-action is "feasible" [*emphasis added*], inferring that it may not be, he posits that it could be "dangerous" because reflection-in-action can "interfere with the smooth flow of action"; practitioners become "paralyse[d]" by what was "unconscious [being] brought to consciousness" (p. 277).

It is little wonder, then, when based on his early work, that mainstream reflective practice has only theorised and honed reflection-on-practice. But, what, then, are we left with, if reflection-on-action is problematic and reflection-in-action is "incoherent and illogical" (Gilroy, 1993, p. 139)? How do we move forward with this seemingly insurmountable barrier to reflective practice?

Reflection-in-Action

The undergraduate and postgraduate participants from the social professions[1] in Jo's (author) research from 2013 to 2016 (Trelfa, 2020) expressed the same conundrum, describing how the integral practices concerned with reflection-on-practice that were so central to their professional training did not support or address their "hot action" (Eraut, 1994, p. 53) of rich, complex, multi-layered, uncertain, and unpredictable work. To articulate this in Schönian terms, although some aspects of practice can be met through the "high ground" (Schön, 1987, p. 3) of technique, guidelines, and procedures, it is in the "swampy lowlands" (ibid) where issues and decisions are messy, risky, and confusing, where blueprints and formulae do not apply, and where practitioners rely on in-the-moment practice artistry. In fact, reflection-in-action is "core" (Finlay, 2008, p. 3) to the "artful practice" of professionals (Schön, 1983, p. 19), this being characterised as the "art of implementation and improvisation" (Schön, 1987, p. 13). Moreover, rather than this artistry of professional practice being required in the occasional, or even frequent, confusing swampy lowland *situation* as Schön suggests, Jo's research participants described making complex decisions and taking action in contexts that are inherently fluid, confusing, and messy *all the time*. Thus, they exemplify professional practice as complex action within a "stream-of-consciousness flow" (Lyle, 2002, p. 212).

Expressing the qualities and experience of this reflection-in-action, Jo's research participants described it variously as (here in their own words), "A felt sense of significant and prescient knowing in the moment"; "A coalescence"; "A gelling together in a flash through a process involving metaphorical and literal peripheral vision"; and "Noticing, capturing, and interrupting practice in the moment by moving focus in and out at the same time as trusting the experience of that process". This reflection-in-action thus requires connection with self, a receptive mind, connection with others, context, space, and place. It involves letting go of preconceptions, stereotypes, judgements in the moment, or tracking the shape and effect of them on behaviours and interactions, identifying what shaped them in that way and then managing the shape differently.

Moment, both expressed and featuring in Jo's participants' experiences of reflection-in-action, was deemed by them to be extremely pertinent. The participants described how, in the flow of their practice, moments do not happen *to* them; they make them. In their words, moments of reflection-in-action are "fleeting junctures in which they pay attention to it now", that is, to whatever they attend to right in the moment. In addition, by recognising *moment* in this way the participants also acknowledged times in their professional practice of *not moments*. These "not moments" were understood and discussed in different ways: (a) as *not* reflecting, and this being healthy and appropriate in some practice circumstances, which significantly they realised was never discussed during their professional training; and (b) in terms of deliberately doing something else during which, insights that are related to the *actual* moment emerge. Again, the participants noted that appreciation and discussion of the nature of, and grounds for, such creative incubation did not feature in their training. Finally, Jo's participants also acknowledged how they did not always create moments of reflection-in-action, this *despite* their training. Further, notwithstanding all the deliberate and cognitive emphasis on reflective practice, they wanted to become more effective in that creation, and more effective *in* those moments of reflection when they are created.

The qualities and experiences of reflection-in-action, reported by Jo's participants, contrasted markedly with their fixed, certain stories of reflection-on-action. In that differentiation, they exemplify practice that Fish (1998) described as "mysterious and ineffable" based on "the kind of knowledge that is endemic in doing" (p. 93). Less amorphous, O'Sullivan (2005, p. 222) referred to *reflective judgement*, "the ability to base sound judgements on deep understandings in conditions of uncertainty". Further, Nelson's (2013, p. 60) "liquid knowledge" elegantly recognises "human subjectivity" bound up in "the production of knowledge"; knowledge in experience of being in the moment, which cannot be "understood through measurement".

Reflection-in-action is the least theorised element of Schön's work, a fact that has perpetuated in mainstream literature and practices on and in reflective practice. Attempts to address this have, for the most part been ineffective (Newman, 1999). Consequently, it is little surprise that when reflection-in-action *is* considered, it is perceived and approached as *inferior* to reflection-on-action (see Mezirow, 1991; Zeichner & Liston, 1996), a hierarchy reinforced even in Schön's (1987) own "ladder of reflection" (p. 114). Thus, emphasis and focus remain at the presupposition that:

> One can "get at" the understanding and competence of the practitioner through the act of representation . . . Tacit, embodied understanding and competence are presumed to preserve their nature through the process of representation and therefore not bound in any significant sense to situated embodied action as such. (Dohn, 2011, p. 678)

Through her research (Trelfa, 2020), Jo posited that confusion concerning the "psychological realities" (Eraut, 1994, p. 147) of reflection-in-action compared to reflection-on-action have stalled its exploration. Further, arguments based on ideas that *only* experts can reflect-in-action are shown to be ground in problematic notions of relationships between *on* and *in* practice as well as being rooted in Schön's pragmatism and developmental stance to reflective practice (Trelfa, 2020). Indeed, Schön's own focus on providing his new epistemology of practice is also at issue. Epistemology being "how human beings come to have knowledge of the world around them" (Blaikie, 2007, p. 18), presupposes first a world, and second one's knowledge of it. So, no matter how a new epistemology is articulated it will inherently involve a gap between a situation and how one makes sense of it, maintaining thinking (knowledge) over being. Therefore, a Schönian

1980s-inspired theory of reflective practice rooted in epistemology cannot differ significantly from any other established approach to problem solving in professional practice contexts.

In *The Reflective Practitioner*, Schön (1983, p. 69) wrote that it might be possible to develop understanding of "reflection-in-action [as] rigorous in its own right", suggesting that "the art of practice in uncertainty and uniqueness" may potentially hold the key. Here, then, emphasis on reflection-in-action, not problem solving, and the nature of social reality rather than knowing (i.e., ontology rather than epistemology), holds promise. However, tied as he was by his epistemological, developmental and pragmatist endeavour, he did not follow through (Trelfa, 2020). Jo's research revealed that recognising, honouring, and dwelling in one's embodied and bodied knowing is central to professional practice, reflective practice, and specifically reflection-in-action. This said, embodied and bodied knowing is complex, or, as Sweet (2010, p. 187) puts it, it is "something of a tease". Embodied and bodied knowing as part of professional practice has been met with apprehension and it "continues to be marginalised, perhaps feared" (Probyn, 1991, p. 108). If acknowledging body in professional practice is bucking the trend, we can assume that focus on reflection-in-action will be too. It will be met with resistance, but if body cannot be considered in SES and coaching then something is seriously remiss! Perhaps here this work can *lead* the field of understanding about reflective practice.

"Gaze", "Glance", and "Leaving Go"

Jo's research is instructive. The participants in her research described the qualitative differences between reflection-on-action and reflection-in-action as *Gaze* and *Glance*. *Gaze* is a vehicle through which to describe the process of selecting an event, interaction, or happening, after its happening. As described by the research participants, and here in their own words, "What is gazed on is selected because it is big, dramatic or small, but either way the event is the trigger"; and, "[Gaze is] staring at it to pull something/s about it apart and in detail, wondering if you could/should have acted differently, thus breaking what existed as a complex dynamic whole into small fixed and static pieces for analysis". This (gaze) is written down, a typical requirement of professional training, and then, as the research participants described in their own words, they "layer it up" by "bringing in experiences and thoughts that have occurred" to the "gazer" since the selected event, doing this so that they can better report their practice and make certain that they perform themselves in "familiar, acceptable and expected ways as required".

In contrast, *Glance* is a vehicle through which to deepen understanding of the experience and qualities of reflection-in-action. Again, in the words of Jo's research participants, Glance has the quality of "a click brought on through a pause, interruption, a freezing of time but fleetingly in the moment". It (glance) is "quick, paying attention, and a bringing of attention fleetingly to embodied knowing". Glance is a skill and an art of "noticing, interrupting, attending, tuning in, tracking, trusting the experience/process of having no path", a sensate experience of "capturing, of getting at the whole of a moment in the moment". Unlike the deliberated cognitive rationality of Gaze, Glance is both embodied and involves memory in the body. Through the experiences of her research participants, Jo describes how the skill and art of Glance can be developed through improvisation, awareness, presence, and embodied knowing. Here, then, through Jo's research, Glance is a *new portal* (Meyer & Land, 2003) that enables reflection-in-practice, its significance, and its theorisation, previously absent from mainstream theory and practice on reflective practice.

Whilst Jo's research participants' predominant experience of Gaze, as it is shaped by the requirements of their professional training, was negative, they considered that it *could* be positive if a practitioner understands that their account of practice is an activity of controlled fiction, and follows that with a second activity where one deliberately returns to that account to identify where and how within it they have adopted domesticating discourses. This becomes an overt avenue of reflection *on oneself as a reflective writer*, and from this, as the participants described it, one may learn "something different". Here, then, where the Gaze of reflection-on-action pins down and fossilises knowledge, the fleeting quality and interruption of Glance is playful and invites creative and imaginative engagement free from constricting concerns with risk. Jo's exposition provides detail grounded in her research of facilitating Glance.

Leaving Go was the term Jo's participants gave to refer to the "not moments" of reflection, whether involvement in a tangibly different activity to the one they were engaged in or not reflecting as a healthy response to some situations. In the words of the participants, they described the former as "mind wandering" and "absorption" that "flushes through and washes or freshens the brain/mind". Leaving Go is not about deliberately setting about engaging in something different for this to occur, or merely getting distracted, but, in the words of the research participants, "they know it has happened because by not working on something, something works". They discussed their experience of "something works" in terms of "something clicks, a block is cleared" and "seeing is clearer". This exposition finds connection with mind-wandering studies in neuroscience (e.g., Baird et al., 2012; Smallwood & Andrews-Hanna, 2013), and illumination during incubation described in Bachelard's (1960/1969) *reverie* and Csikszentmihalyi's (1996) *aha* moments that are critical to creativity. Leaving Go can thus be understood as crucial in reflective practice *alongside* Gaze and Glance, in essence a third dimension to add to reflection-on and reflection-in action. As well as being important in its own right, Leaving Go supports the creativity of Glance (for further depth and detail, see Trelfa, 2020).

Reflection-in-Action: Catalyst to Progress in SES and Allied Disciplines

The defining barrier to reflective practice and opportunities for progress in SES, coaching, and allied disciplines is risk, and established understanding (theories and practices) of reflective practice concentrate on minimising risk to assert control of self and situation via reflection-on-action. Reflection-in-action is the least theorised element of writing and practice and, where it has been considered, confusion has meant that it remains inferior and neglected. Jo's research, however, revealed reflection-in-action to be central to effective professional practice, applied in this chapter to SES and coaching. *Gaze, Glance,* and *Leaving Go* offer an exciting, fresh contribution to conceptualising and practicing reflective practice differently.

By this argument, we are not suggesting that Glance will suddenly transform "fear of the near" (Probyn, 1991, p. 108) linked to reflection-in-action. However, as Csikszentmihalyi (1975) and Abuhamdeh (2020) observed, optimal performance is associated with task involvement. Optimal is not necessarily referring to elite or high levels of expertise but engaging at any optimal level whatever that may be. Previously, it was considered that in such contexts, reflection was problematic – or, circling back to Schön's (1983, p. 277) own argument, "dangerous". Total task concentration is seen to require the loss of reflective self-consciousness and yet that is critical to be able to engage in professional artistry. The challenge here is the temporal distortion of time. The concept and practice of Glance offers an important contribution to this conundrum expressed in reflective practice theory, dissolving that barrier to exploring and understanding reflection-in-action as part of reflective practice.

By our argument we are also not suggesting that the creativity offered through Gaze, Glance and Leaving Go is easy. Risk, as explained above, is an individual perception and creativity will still be measured in this regard. Moreover, as we now know, creativity in sport is discouraged by those who seek to manage practice when it might potentially undermine desired outcome. However, reflection-on-action understood as Gaze, reflection-in-action as Glance, and the addition of Leaving Go, together in a fresh conceptualisation of reflective practice, offers spaces and places in between the taken-for-granted barriers, and in this analysis the following three key themes stand clear (Trelfa, 2020). First, reflection-in-action requires its own specialist lexis and shared understanding. Without this, coaches and SES practitioners will be unable or less able to recognise, identify, acknowledge, and articulate their embodied and bodied knowing. Gaze, Glance, and Leaving Go, with their experiential descriptions assist here. Second, without methods that privilege bodily knowing that are at least comparable to the models and methods that favour Western preoccupation with visible, cognitive reflection-on-practice, it will remain invisible. Third, without theory to underpin all this, focus will drift back into the historically theoretically weightier cognitive realm as soon as possible, if not start and end there in entirety, and reflection-in-action will remain neglected.

There is a further consequence to this exposition. Whilst length of career experience can imbue practitioners with confidence when engaging in SES and coaching practice, and it could be argued that new practitioners might reflect using different constructs more to do with fear of failure and trying to do good practice without fully appreciating why. Such an approach adds weight to the challenge above against the argument that *only* experts, in contrast to novice practitioners, can engage in reflection-in-action. A very new practitioner bringing limited time-length experience to the role can still be, indeed, will be, aware of, and respond from, their senses and feelings, their bodily knowing, and this *all* the time. Facilitation of reflection-in-action can imbue confidence in and validation for all their bodily and embodied knowing.

When all is said and done, do we want coaches and SES practitioners who can account for their practice in controlled, censored, and managed ways or inhabit the risky spaces and places in between?

Note

1 "Social professions" refers to practitioners whose professional role is to work with those "regarded as in need of support, advocacy, informal education, or control" and do so "within a shared set of values stressing a commitment to individual and social change, respect for diversity and difference and a practice that is participatory and empowering" (Banks & Nøhr, 2003, p. 8).

Section 3

Pedagogical and Applied Issues

7 Issues in Education, Professional Training, and Development in the Sport and Exercise Sciences and Allied Disciplines

Brendan Cropley and Kate Williams

Introduction: The Emergence of Reflective Practice within Education and Training Pathways

The evolution of the Sport and Exercise Sciences (SES) and Allied Disciplines (AD) has gathered considerable momentum due to the ongoing globalisation and commercialisation of sport and exercise (Le Meur & Torres-Ronda, 2019). With performers at all levels becoming increasingly dependent on a range of innovative medical and scientific support (cf. Wagstaff et al., 2015), there has been a progressive expectation placed on those working in the different disciplines associated with these fields for the provision of high-quality, professional service delivery. Indeed, there has been a rising need for practitioners to be accountable for ensuring their relevance and that their work is considered useful by the end-user (Winter & Collins, 2016).

In attempts to regulate the quality of practice in these fields through the promotion of evidence-based practice and the development of ethical standards, a range of governing organisations (e.g., British Association of Sport & Exercise Sciences [BASES]; Exercise & Sports Science Australia [ESSA]; National Strength & Conditioning Association [NSCA]) have formulated accreditation/certification pathways designed to accompany or follow on from the completion of higher education degree programmes. The aim of these pathways has been to enable those working in the SES disciplines to demonstrate that they possess the knowledge and skills to practice safely and competently. While not universal, there has, however, been a growing recognition that professional training pathways across these fields have often fallen short in helping neophyte practitioners develop the forms of *knowing* and *doing* required for *effective service delivery* (Bartlett & Drust, 2021; Stevens et al., 2018). This critique has stemmed from the belief that education and training providers overly emphasise the theoretical (professional) knowledge and technical skills required to execute a professional activity *competently* at the expense of developing the integrated knowledge, abilities, behaviours and strategies, attitudes, beliefs, values, and personal characteristics that allow for effective service delivery (i.e., practice that results in positive client outcomes as a direct result of the value that the practitioner adds; Cropley et al., 2010a).

DOI: 10.4324/9781003198758-10

To address the gap in knowing and doing, education and training providers in the SES and AD have adopted approaches that seek to immerse the learner/trainee in applied practice while supporting their neophyte experiences through formal frameworks of supervision and mentoring. Coupled with these programmes of supervised experience, education and training providers have increasingly advocated *reflective practice* (RP) as a mechanism to support a process of systematic learning from these experiences (see HCPC, 2019). Certainly, there is an emerging evidence base in the SES and AD to suggest that RP offers a genuine approach for fostering positive change in practitioners' professional actions and for improving the effectiveness of service delivery (Cropley, Hanton et al., 2020; Picknell, Cropley et al., 2022). As such, while not entirely common, RP has been formally embedded into many training providers' competency frameworks, as well as becoming a common feature of many SES and AD undergraduate and postgraduate degree programmes (as bespoke modules, aspects of modules, and/or a method of assessment). The integration of RP into training providers' pathways has, however, been done so to different degrees. For example, some training providers see the attitudes and skills of/for RP as key practitioner competencies and so trainees must demonstrate their developing ability to engage in RP and learn critically from their experiences (e.g., BASES, see Huntley et al., 2019). Conversely, other providers simply expect practitioners to engage in RP on their practicum experiences as a mechanism to facilitate ongoing monitoring (e.g., NSCA; see Kuklick & Gearity, 2015).

Despite these developments, several issues concerning the nature, integration, and pedagogy of RP within the SES and AD remain, particularly with how it is understood and utilised on education and training pathways. For example, RP is often aligned to social science disciplines (e.g., sport and exercise psychology) more so than those favouring positivistic frameworks for practice (e.g., physiology, biomechanics; Doncaster, 2018). There is perhaps still a need, therefore, to convince those working across different disciplines as to the utility of RP for helping practitioners to understand how they might navigate the challenges of their roles and provide an effective service. Further, the requirements and demands associated with education and professional training result in the perception that individuals are better served by being engaged in practical action rather than in critically reflective thought (Huntley et al., 2019). Consequently, the quality of engagement in RP may become stunted. Finally, it can be argued that a lack of individual and organisational understanding of how to make RP meaningful and critical in a way that elicits effective learning and improvements to service delivery remains (Cropley, Hanton et al., 2020).

Through this chapter, we aim to discuss three main issues associated with the integration of RP into education and training pathways in the SES and AD; namely: the *quality of RP engagement*; the use of *RP as a form of assessment*; and the need to *develop the skills and attitudes for critical RP*. We also aim to offer a series of opportunities that individuals and organisations have for overcoming these issues in a way that supports more meaningful integration of RP into such pathways. First, however, in attempts to locate the importance of RP as a mechanism to facilitate individuals' personal and professional growth through their education and training experiences in *all* disciplines, we discuss the nature of practice itself. Specifically, we consider the way that education and training providers, particularly within certain disciplines, may relegate the forms of knowing practitioners require to navigate applied service delivery, which in sport is characterised by complexity. Some of this discussion will be presented in the form of extracts from a conversation that we, the authors, had about the position and importance placed on RP within SES and AD education and training programmes (Kate is a Graduate Sport Therapist and Musculoskeletal Clinician; Brendan is a British Association of Sport & Exercise Sciences Accredited Sport Scientist). In attending to these aims, we hope to raise into the reader's consciousness and encourage reflection on some of the issues that could arguably be affecting trainee practitioners' RP and thus potentially impeding their development as safe, competent, and effective professionals.

Understanding Applied Practice Across Disciplines as a Complex, Dynamic Process

Brendan: "So the role [of a Sport Therapist] appears to overlap with and be underpinned by a medical, scientific knowledge and skill base linked to a range of sport science disciplines?"

Kate: "Yes, although that's where our [professional practice tutors and supervisors] problems start. Students and trainees have the perception that they are 'body mechanics,' working with easily definable issues that have specific solutions. They come into training programmes expecting to engage in applied practice through a 'recipe book' approach and that this technical knowledge will allow them to be competent and effective. However, they overlook that they're actually working with human beings, which requires them [practitioners] to exhibit interpersonal, soft skills that potentially have a bigger impact on the effectiveness of their practice than the treatment itself."

Brendan: "I wonder whether those perceptions about the nature of applied practice and the expectations that trainee practitioners have about what they need to know and do to be effective creates a blind spot to the actual contexts in which they hope to work in? I notice many trainees across the sport and exercise sciences almost being fearful of not having sufficient professional knowledge, the technical knowledge you mentioned, associated with the discipline they work in and consequently overlook the wider attributes they need to be able to operate within the context of sport."

Kate: "Absolutely, we [practice supervisors] understand the professional and ethical requirements for being deemed as 'competent' and continuing to practice in a way that is congruent with these requirements. Yet, we need to be better at helping our learners, our trainees, to understand that 'being liked' [by a client or within an organisation], that being able to 'fit in' is almost a prerequisite to positive clinical and patient reported outcomes."

Across a range of industries, particularly those in which job roles are characterised by intricate social systems and interactions (e.g., education, nursing, social work), it has become increasingly accepted that applied professional practice is complex, messy, and contested (Pentland et al., 2018). This is due, in part, to the: dynamic environments in which individuals operate; need to work with others (e.g., clients, colleagues) on an individual level; multiple relationships that must be formed and maintained despite individuals potentially having conflicting agendas; challenging interplay between different forms of knowledge and personal factors (e.g., experience, values, philosophy) that orientate applied practice; need to translate complex information into dynamic environments; internal and external expectations placed on individuals to act effectively and achieve success; need for efficient in-situ decision-making; and need to ensure professionalism through the maintenance of industry-specific regulations and standards (Cropley et al., 2018; Fullagar et al., 2019).

Irrespective of specific discipline (e.g., exercise physiology, sport therapy, sport psychology, strength and conditioning), professional practice in the SES and AD is no different. In actuality, it could be argued that the level of complexity experienced by practitioners in the SES and AD is augmented by the varied nature of their roles and the diverse contexts in which they work that all contain nuanced organisational, personal, social, cultural, and micro-political features to which the practitioner must adapt (Le Meur & Torres-Ronda, 2019). Indeed, it is suggested that applied practice in SES is complicated by the different needs of clients and associated stakeholders, and the "complex and fast-moving environment that sport is," which, without appropriate application, can render service delivery as sub-optimal (Bartlett & Drust, 2021, p. 1580).

Navigating the Complexity: Challenging Traditional Approaches to Knowing and Doing

Understanding applied professional practice in the SES and AD as complex and contested[1] challenges the traditional assumptions held in these fields about the utility of professional (e.g., theoretical, scientific) knowledge, which comprises much of the content of education and training programmes, for facilitating practice that is effective (Szedlak, Callary et al., 2019). Specifically, it is argued that the neat application of theory-to-practice in the SES and AD is problematic (Bartlett & Drust, 2021; Winter & Collins, 2016). Within such a theory-to-practice (or positivistic) framework, practitioners are seen as instrumental problem solvers who exact solutions by applying theory and techniques derived from systematic scientific knowledge with the expectation that a particular solution will always solve a particular problem (Schön, 1987[2]).

For many trainee practitioners, this positivistic form of knowing offers stability because it provides an approach to practice that is uncomplicated, as solutions to practice-based problems are considered as universal and enduring (Cropley et al., 2018). However, while such an approach might be suitable for easily recognisable problems, given the complexity inherent within applied SES and AD practice, situations and issues are rarely simple in definition and resolution. For example, Morton (2014, p. 124) previously indicated that his work as an applied sport physiologist and nutritionist should be "straightforward" (e.g., translating research into performance enhance interventions) but "given the many cultural, organisational, financial, and political factors that occur in the context of professional sport" it is rarely so. The positivistic approach to practice also arguably fails to consider the impact of the individual (e.g., practitioner, client, athlete, team) on intervention design, implementation, and management. Yet, the personal and educational background, values, beliefs, and philosophy of the practitioner, for example, will have a significant bearing on how scientific knowledge is interpreted and how this may (or may not) be used to enact applied practice (McEwan et al., 2019). It is unlikely, therefore, that the scientific knowledge base within a discipline could ever be comprehensive and encompassing enough to address all practice-based problems (Winter & Collins, 2016).

To counteract issues with the technical-rational, positivistic approach to practice, Schön (1983) proposed that practitioners need to connect a form of knowing and doing that: (a) is responsive to individuals' needs; (b) delivers procedural expertise; and (c) demonstrates more than the mechanical application of tools and techniques. Schön referred to this as *knowledge-in-action* (or craft knowledge), which he considered as core to the artistry of professional practice, and others suggesting that it should be seen as "the most substantive form of knowledge" properly constituting the body of knowledge of a practice discipline (Johns, 1995, p. 25). To elaborate, knowledge-in-action is thought to be a union of social norms, values, prejudices, experiences, empirical (professional) knowledge, aesthetical knowledge, personal knowledge, and ethical knowledge (see Anderson et al., 2004). Practice is then constructed out of the assimilation and interplay of these different sources of knowledge – an individual's *knowing-in-action* – allowing the practitioner to manage and adapt to the dynamic and context specific nature of their work. Accordingly, knowing-in-action is a view that professional practice is no longer to be understood as a mechanical application of scientifically based rules. Instead, it locates the practitioner at the centre of effective service delivery as it facilitates an understanding of the function of personally tailored theories about what does and does not work for an individual in consideration of the context of their practice (Alfano & Collins, 2020).

Much of an individual's knowing-in-action is often difficult to make verbally explicit but it manifests itself in a practitioner's behaviours (Schön, 1987). To understand, construct, and augment this form of knowing and doing, therefore, individuals must actively engage in a process of experiential learning, extrapolating the knowledge embedded within the experience itself through a process of RP (Cropley et al., 2018). This process involves an individual actively exploring the self (e.g., values, decisions, thoughts, emotions behaviours), their interactions with the world around them (including their utility), and making sense of transformation, which generates a rich and detailed knowledge base derived from practice (i.e., knowledge-in-action; Ghaye, 2010). This makes RP fundamentally important within the education and training of neophyte practitioners in the SES and AD because it is the conduit through which individuals *actually learn about doing* practice in the complex and contested environments that epitomise sport and exercise (Doncaster, 2018; Huntley et al., 2019).

Navigating the Complexity: A Call to Action

If professional practice cannot be effectively enacted through a technical-rational approach, then SES and AD education/training providers (as well as the assessors, supervisors who guide learners/trainees, and the learners themselves) need to embrace the different forms of knowing that are constructed through what might be classified as non-traditional means. This requires an acceptance across all disciplines that the knowledge generated out of a lived experience through RP can be, and often is, equally as important for guiding effective service delivery as the forms of knowledge developed through positivistic means (Malone et al., 2019). Typically, this has been difficult for some to accept, particularly by those studying and training in disciplines rooted in positivism. For example, accounts by Morton (2014) and Doncaster (2018) attest to locating the self within their own practice as disconcerting given that personal detachment and objectivity are widely encouraged to avoid bias in research and practice (in physiology and nutrition). However, such contentions are established in models of *evidence-based practice*, which indicate that practice should be predicated on a triangulation of professional knowledge, patient preferences, and practitioner expertise, where the hierarchy of forms of knowledge is flattened in recognition of the collective (together we might see this as knowledge-in-action; Scott & McSherry, 2008). It is imperative, therefore, that all involved in the education and training process of SES and AD practitioners, recalibrate their epistemological stance (e.g., from dualistic to relative assumptions) and the prominence given to developing a commitment to meaningful RP. In doing so, learners/trainees can be better prepared to develop the forms knowing that contribute to what is required for them to enact professional practice and to be able to navigate the complexity inherent within it (Bartlett & Drust, 2021).

Reflective Practice in SES and AD Education and Training: Issues and Opportunities

The Quality of Reflective Practice Engagement

Kate: "The reflections I see as an educator and supervisor are often really descriptive accounts of what the learner did during their placement experiences. The reflections don't really offer insights into them [the practitioner] or their decision-making process or how the context of practice shaped those decisions."

Brendan: "I hear this a lot and certainly in the sport coaching literature researchers are arguing that coaches only reflect at that descriptive level. I've found with those who I've supervised that by scaffolding their reflections at the start and working with them to develop an understanding of what RP is actually about and for, supervisees are able to much more quickly develop those more critical reflective habits . . . working through the reflective process in a shared approach helps the supervisee to engage more meaningfully."

Kate: "I've noticed something similar, because when you discuss the experience with the learner and perhaps probe a little deeper with the questions that they might not be willing to ask themselves, the learner engages in a much more thoughtful conversation that I hope leads to better learning."

While many SES and AD education/training providers have (at least) begun to embed RP into their curricula, there remains a need for the careful consideration of how they develop a culture in which purposeful and meaningful RP are nurtured (Huntley et al., 2019). This is because, without appropriate insight it is not likely that individuals will be able to transform their experiences into the forms of knowing required to understand how they might better navigate the complexity of applied practice effectively. Indeed, researchers have argued that integrating RP into professional development programmes simply as a means of "ongoing monitoring" potentially stifles an individual's exploration of their own practice and the context in which it occurs (Mantzourani et al., 2019, p. 1476). Further, RP is essentially an introspective endeavour, requiring intrinsic motivation to engage in the process constructively. Where the requirements of education and training programmes are for individuals to merely demonstrate that they have reflected on their practice (to any extent), it is possible that an individual's motivation to reflect is reduced, which "may turn a meaningful exercise into a redundant ritual" (Gathu, 2022, p. 5).

In such conditions, it is possible that learners/trainees perceive the education and/or training provider as paying lip-service to RP, which in turn shapes their own perceptions and subsequent engagement in the process. The way in which RP is perceived as either a 'task to be done' or as a fundamental part of an individual's developmental journey and as a key aspect of what it means to be a professional practitioner, will also be influenced by the attitudes of the learner's/trainee's educators and/or supervisors, and the culture of the organisations and specific sector in which they work. Certainly, the educator or supervisor can simply support an individual to do what is necessary to 'get through' a qualification, or if modelled correctly, can facilitate the reflective capacity required for effective experiential learning and professional development (cf. Gathu, 2022).

Where the importance of RP is inadequately promoted, it is likely that learners/trainees engage in modes of thinking (e.g., description, evaluation) that seldom uncover the critical insights required to: initiate experiential learning; augment critical thinking and self-discovery; offer a gateway through which insights and meanings regarding the self and practice can develop; and facilitate personal and professional growth.[3] This is particularly compounded where education/training providers prescribe approaches to RP that do little to provide the facility for learners/trainees to elicit meaningful reflective insight. Instead, such approaches may dilute the level of engagement that individuals are likely to have with the process, often turning reflection into a simple tick-box exercise (Heeneman & de Grave, 2017). Although it is understood that different *levels*[4] of RP exist, each potentially beneficial depending on the purpose of/for the reflection, like others (e.g., Knowles & Gilbourne, 2010), we (authors) argue that learning is perhaps most powerful when reflection is meaningful and critical. This position is in support of Moon's (2004) assertions, which indicated that levels of reflection akin to performance reviews are only likely to elicit surface level learning through sense making, whereas critical RP is thought to lead to deeper learning that results in transformative outcomes. Thus, critical levels of reflection that alter the process from trivial to significant are necessary to achieve the cognitive and behavioural adaptations to enhance service delivery effectiveness (e.g., Cropley, Hanton et al., 2020).

If SES and AD education/training providers are to truly embrace RP, they must begin to create the conditions required for learners and trainees to both commit to consistently more meaningful engagement in RP and to explore the philosophical underpinnings of what it means to be a *reflective practitioner* (e.g., those who understand the position and potential of RP; are motivated to adopt an all-encompassing attitude to practice and personal and professional development; and locate the self at the centre of effective service delivery; Anderson et al., 2004). This may require education/training providers to reconsider how RP is integrated into their programmes and how it is promoted and facilitated in learners/trainees. Further, education/training providers must address the current systems they adopt that possibly constrain the forms of RP that can support personal and professional growth to move away from accepting a level of engagement akin to descriptive, performance evaluation.

Reflective Practice as a Method of Assessment

Kate: "The learners [Sport Therapy] have to do 250 hours of applied supervised experience . . . those hours are all practice-based . . . and the assessment is always reflection, but we prescribe quite an outdated framework to support learners' assessed reflections."

Brendan: "OK, so there is a formal requirement for RP and the learners have to submit those reflections as part of their final grade . . . as part of the assessment of whether they're deemed competent or not?"

Kate: "That's right, but this is difficult because everyone has conversations about how to grade reflections – what does a pass and fail look like and how do you consider different learners' reflections where one might consider a really trivial incident and one might consider a more critical incident?"

Brendan: "I totally agree. The whole 'RP as assessment' issue bothers me because I can see value in asking trainees to submit the outcomes of their reflective practices to demonstrate a level of accountability to their learning and development, but it is difficult, based on how an individual might present these outcomes to make a formal assessment of the individual's ability to practice. Also, we have to be careful that assessing RP in this way doesn't just breed compliance where trainees engage in less meaningful, safer reflection to meet the requirements of the programme."

Where RP has been integrated into SES and AD undergraduate and postgraduate degree modules, learners are often required, as part of the assessment for modules that include some form of work-related/practicum experience to reflect on their experiences as a way of demonstrating their learning and development. Similarly, neophyte practitioners undertaking professional training pathways in these fields are often expected to "submit" reflections on their work-related/practicum experiences to reviewers/assessors as a form of monitoring. In many professional training pathways, these reviewers/assessors, who are often not familiar with the trainee or their situation, are then asked to render judgement on the quality of their reflections. The outcome of this judgement can either support or hinder an individual's progression depending on whether the reflection is deemed as "suitable." Despite many SES and AD education/training providers adopting such approaches, the assessment of reflection continues to be a contentious point (Kirk, 2019; Trelfa & Telfer, 2014).

Utilising reflection as a form of assessment may fundamentally undermine the philosophical and practical position of RP. RP is a process through which individuals can, through their own experiences, develop a greater understanding of the self and of the forms of knowing and doing that facilitate more effective (or consistent) practice. An individual's reflections are, therefore, personally and emotionally laden, significant and meaningful to the individual, often making it "difficult for others to see or feel their relevance" (Trelfa & Telfer, 2014, p. 51). Summative assessment of the product of an individual's RP against standardised criteria, therefore, is likely to restrict an individual to the extent that the process of reflection becomes a technical-rational activity that exerts a level of control (Tummons, 2011). For instance, the learner/trainee becomes concerned with the criteria against which they are to be assessed, and how they construct their reflections to meet those criteria. In doing so, they present what they think is necessary rather than experiencing RP as something of intrinsic worth and value (Cropley et al., 2018). Further, learners and trainees may construct their reflections in a way to avoid producing a more reflexive account (e.g., examination of one's own feelings, reactions, and motives and how these influenced what they did or thought in a situation) of an experience so that they do not position themselves as vulnerable or open themselves up for criticism. Trelfa and Telfer (2014) suggested that the assessment process impinges on what individuals reflect on and creates a potential ethical issue as the assessor/reviewer intrudes into the individual's personal and emotional accounts, which suppresses honest self-disclosure. Researchers have detailed how this has resulted in neophytes fabricating, exaggerating, and/or censoring reflective accounts that form evidence toward a qualification (cf. Gathu, 2022; Trelfa & Telfer, 2014).

Assessments of RP are typically manifest through written reflective accounts, often guided by a recommended framework. While engaging in RP through written portfolios or journals is well established (Knowles & Gilbourne, 2010), the prescriptive nature of written reflective assessment exercises can put those who are less comfortable with the practicalities of reflective writing and associated skills at a disadvantage. For some, reflective writing is an unfamiliar and uncomfortable process, which in some cases contradicts the requirements of more traditional forms of written assessment (particularly in education), which has the effect of limiting the scope or criticality of what individuals feel able to write (Tummons, 2011). Dictating a written approach can also limit the creativity that learners and trainees may bring to bear on their RP. While written approaches might be easier to standardise and grade for assessment purposes, they represent only a small portion of the reflective modalities through which individuals (in a solitary or collaborative fashion) can engage in purposeful, meaningful reflection (e.g., shared conversation; audio; visual sociology). Isolating learners'/trainees' reflective experiences to written approaches that seek to meet the requirements of the assessment and/or the expectations of the assessor/reviewer potentially stunts their progression as reflective practitioners. For instance, the purpose *of* the reflection (e.g., the "thing" to be explored and its meaning to the individual) should dictate the approach rather than the purpose *for* the reflection (e.g., assessment), meaning that neophytes should be supported to explore the efficacy of a range of modalities and given the freedom to engage in the approach they deem appropriate in that moment (Huntley et al., 2019).

Finally, if the assessment of RP is to be considered valid and useful, then those assessing/reviewing reflective accounts need to understand what RP "looks like" and this needs to be aligned with learner/trainee perceptions. This is potentially difficult due to the lack of conceptual agreement regarding RP, and subsequently, the challenge associated with setting criteria against which a diverse, complex, individualistic process is assessed (Marshall, 2019). From a research perspective, reflective accounts have previously been assessed against criteria linked to levels of reflection, with greater kudos afforded to those accounts deemed as more critical (e.g., Cropley, Hanton et al., 2020). However, this approach overlooks the significance of learning and development some individuals may take from their reflections classified as lower in level. It also assumes that because the reflection is well-written the learning gained by the individual is indeed transformative and meaningful. Thus, clarity over what is being assessed is vital (e.g., is the assessment focused on the content and/or presentation of the written account, or on the extent of personal and professional growth through the individual experiences through RP?).

Despite the arguments raised here, there is an acceptance of the need for the examination of practice on professional training pathways as a way of developing individuals who are responsible for challenging and developing what they do and as a way of ensuring professionalism (Winter & Collins, 2016). We (authors) also agree that, across their education and development journeys, learners and trainees should be accountable for developing the necessary skills and attitudes to become reflective practitioners. SES and AD education/training providers must consider, therefore, how they adopt appropriate foci and processes when engaging learners and trainees with RP as a form of assessment or monitoring (cf. Gathu, 2022). For example, by encouraging neophytes to interrogate their experiences through aptly designed *formative assessments* that embrace a variety of reflective modalities, with criteria focused on individual growth, individuals can receive ongoing feedback and support to promote improvement in the quality of their RP over time (Cropley, Hanton et al., 2020; Knowles et al., 2001).

Developing the Skills and Attitudes for Critical Reflective Practice

Kate: "How do we train them [learners] to be better at RP – I'm not sure we teach learners or trainees in other disciplines how to engage in RP. We expect them to do it [RP] but we don't really focus on supporting their understanding of the process or how it might improve them and their practices."

Brendan: "I know that some organisations, like BASES, run specific workshops designed to help trainees to better understand RP, what it might look like, and how they can engage in it. However, I'm not sure that this is the norm across those who accredit or certify practitioners in the sport and exercise sciences. I also think that the systems for qualification might stunt the development of the attributes required for really critical RP as trainees often only need to demonstrate engagement in RP, irrespective of the quality of the learning experience."

Kate: "There's certainly scope for better education and training and perhaps we need to consider where and how RP features on undergraduate degree programmes so that those who progress onto professional training pathways have already begun to develop those skills needed for better reflection."

It appears that many SES and AD education/training providers make the assumption that those undertaking their programmes already have the ability required to engage in RP in a meaningful and critical way prior to commencing on the course. Few education/training providers, for example, formally teach, or seek to develop, an individual's reflective capacity. Yet, as we have discussed, there is often an expectation that learners and trainees are able to reflect at a level (e.g., critical) deemed necessary to pass an assessment or progress on their professional development journeys (Huntley et al., 2019). This is despite consistent agreement that RP is a highly skilled, meta-cognitive process that needs to be trained and nurtured (Knowles & Gilbourne, 2010; Mantzourani et al., 2019).

If neophytes are not appropriately guided to understand RP and develop their ability to engage in the process effectively, it is likely that their experiential learning (and subsequent personal and professional development) will be limited (Gathu, 2022). Certainly, to achieve the transformative outcomes associated with RP, the process requires more than retrospection, rationalisation, and evaluation. Instead, it requires a purposeful exploration of the whole-self so that meanings behind thoughts, feelings, and actions can be uncovered (Cropley et al., 2018). At times, the process can be challenging and requires the individual to exhibit certain *skills* (e.g., problem-solving; introspection; critical thinking) and *attitudes* (e.g., open-mindedness; whole-heartedness), which can be fostered through interventions that promote systematic engagement in RP (Marshall et al., 2021). Thus, education/training providers must consider how they educate and support the development of individual's reflective capacities if they expect meaningful engagement in the process. Indeed, researchers have reported that by developing participating practitioners' abilities to reflect more critically they observed positive developments in their service delivery, with participants reporting the development of the knowledge and capabilities required to better manage the demands associated with their roles (Cropley, Hanton et al., 2020).

Similarly, to develop and nurture the skills and attitudes required for RP in neophytes, the training of suitably knowledgeable, competent, and experienced educators, supervisors, and assessors needs consideration. In programmes that do include RP as educational content, researchers have argued that a lack of tutor confidence in, and commitment to, the teaching of RP can result in poor and staged learner reflections (Platt, 2014). Further, educators who are not trained are less able to facilitate RP in others and more likely to extol indifference to the process, which adversely impacts the value that learners place on RP (Gathu, 2022). These issues may be particularly prevalent in SES and AD, where supervisors of neophyte practitioners, who have had no formal education or training in RP, are expected to support and enable their supervisees' reflective capacities to the extent that the process aids their progression towards professional accreditation/certification.

The problem here is that certain modalities and functions of RP may be advocated by educators/supervisors without due consideration of how these might stifle individuals' engagement. For example, an implicit fixation on the use of reflective frameworks may be endorsed without due consideration for how frameworks can be malleable and adaptable so as not to overly constrain critical thought (Huntley et al., 2019). Further, encouraging individuals to reflect on problems, issues, and/or difficulties, which can result in deficit-based thinking (e.g., fault finding) is widely over emphasised (Dixon et al., 2013). While such frames were traditionally suggested as core to instigating RP, reflecting on problems should not be done at the expense of explicitly reflecting on successful aspects of an individual's life and work. Within education and training programmes, the promotion of *strengths-based* RP can result in many positive, transformative outcomes that enable an individual to engage in appreciative action by understanding how they create more opportunities to use their strengths within the context of their work (Dixon et al., 2013). Educators/supervisors are, therefore, urged to: promote exploration of RP in a way that is meaningful to the individual; encourage flexibility in reflective modality (including shared approaches that facilitate development through collaboration); endorse a balance between appreciative and problem-based RP; be expressive about their own RP as a form of modelling; and work with individuals to understand their RP, its impact, and how it might be made better.

Reflective Practice in SES and AD Education and Training: Summary and Opportunities

In this chapter, we have presented a case for RP to be firmly established in the education and training of learners and neophytes in SES and AD, and more widely for it to become a fundamental part of who practitioners are and what they do. This case is built on the premise that professional practice in these fields is ultimately complex and contested. Thus, to develop the forms of knowing and doing required to effectively navigate the contexts in which practitioners operate, individuals have to engage in experiential learning through a process of meaningful and critical RP. We have also presented three key issues that may have an adverse effect on individual's understanding of, and engagement in, RP across their education and training journeys.

Within our discussion we have alluded to several considerations and opportunities for education/training providers that we hope raises reflection and discussion. Importantly, while we have intentionally focused these on education/training providers in this chapter, we recognise that learners/trainees and educators/supervisors/assessors also have a significant responsibility to explore the potential significance of RP for professional practice. Certainly, if all stakeholders truly believe that RP offers a genuine approach to promoting the personal and professional growth required to enhance service delivery effectiveness, the issues we have raised should be considered. To succour this, we conclude this chapter with a summary of opportunities for learners, educators, supervisors, and organisations within the SES and AD that may help them to further address the issues presented in this chapter (see Table 7.1).

Table 7.1 Reflective Practice in SES and AD Education and Training: Opportunities

Area	Opportunity	Support
Quality of engagement	Learners/trainees must move beyond descriptive accounts of practice by placing themselves at the centre of the process – seeking to critically explore the self, their interactions with the world around them (including their utility), and making sense of opportunities for transformation (e.g., improved or corroboration of knowledge, evolution of personal theory).	Ghaye (2010); Moon (2004)
Quality of engagement	Educators/supervisors must work with individuals to create the trust and safety required for learners/trainees to share, be open and whole-hearted, and truly reflexive in their RP without fear of judgement.	Gathu (2022)
Quality of engagement	New and innovative approaches to RP that help to cultivate learning and facilitate lasting and consistent engagement should be embraced. No one modality is more suitable than another – the quality of the approach lies in the significance and impact of the learning outcome.	Huntley et al. (2019)

(*Continued*)

Table 7.1 (Continued)

Area	Opportunity	Support
Assessment	Those responsible for judging an individual's RP need to be trained and supported to understand what "good" RP might look like. Consensus is also required between the judge and the person "submitting" reflections regarding the purpose of the process. Criteria should also be flexible enough to allow learners/trainees engage in personally selected reflective modalities.	Tummons (2011)
Developing skills and attitudes	Education/training providers must consider how RP is developed and nurtured from the start of individuals' educational journeys. Critical dialogue, which considers how pedagogically the necessary skills and attitudes required for effective experiential learning through RP can be facilitated, is required. Further, educators/supervisors should be trained to help them better model RP and facilitate RP in others.	Cropley, Hanton et al. (2020); Huntley et al. (2019)
Developing skills and attitudes	Accepting the value of publishing and disseminating experienced practitioners' reflective accounts across all SES disciplines (and those allied to the field) can help to convince learners/trainees of the importance of RP and the potential it has for personal and professional growth.	Knowles et al. (2012)
Quality of engagement; developing skills and attitudes	If an environment of trust, honesty, and confidentiality can be created, shared (group) reflection that promotes interaction where learners/trainees can support and check/challenge each other should be valued. Such approaches can develop a culture of RP and elicit more critical insight and meaningful learning.	Cropley et al. (2018); Ghaye (2010)
Quality of engagement; developing skills and attitudes	Learners/trainees should move away from seeing reflective practice as "something to be done" to a focus on what it means to be a reflective practitioner and their commitment to engaging in a process that is meaningful and critical. This should be supported by the culture created by education/training providers. Further, RP should be appreciative in nature. It should afford learners/trainees the mechanism to value what they do, explore their strengths, and create opportunities to use these more often.	Dixon et al. (2013); Huntley et al. (2019)

Area	Opportunity	Support
Quality of engagement; developing skills and attitudes	Education/training providers and those who work/study on their programmes should reconsider their epistemological stance regarding the types of knowledge that should be valued for effective applied service delivery. In doing so, explicit emphasis should be placed on supporting learners/trainees to develop and explore their knowledge-in-action.	Bartlett and Drust (2021); Cropley et al. (2010b)
Assessment; developing skills and attitudes	There should be a movement away from the prescription on a particular reflective modality in both assessment and monitoring. Instead, learners/trainees should be given the freedom to experiment with a range of approaches that are selected to suit the purpose of the reflection.	Gathu (2022); Tummons (2011)
Assessment; quality of engagement	Assessment of RP should be formative in nature, affording the learner/trainee ongoing feedback on their RP to promote the improvement of the depth and quality of their RP, and their progression as a reflective practitioner, over time.	Gathu (2022); Trelfa and Telfer (2014)

Notes

1 Applied SES and AD service delivery is contested for several reasons, such as the individuation process in which practitioners develop their approaches to practice in accord with their personalities and worldviews, and then evolve them through experimentation (Tod et al., 2017). Thus, universally accepted best practice becomes difficult to locate as often this is bound in the individual and the context in which they are working.

2 Schön (1987) referred to this as *technical rationality* which holds the premise that practice is separated from theory and thus devalues the knowledge that practitioners develop about and through their work.

3 We (authors) contend that collectively these outcomes represent a process of RP that is *meaningful*.

4 Several authors have considered the typology of reflective levels that largely range from *technical* (e.g., descriptive, surface level insights focused on competency-based development) to *critical* (e.g., transformative insights focused on questioning habitual practices, thoughts and feelings, and exploration of the meaning of self and practice to elicit deep learning and meaningful change) reflection (see Anderson et al., 2004).

8 Facilitating Multicultural Reflective Practice During Supervision

Tegan Adams and Alison Pope-Rhodius

Introduction

To us (chapter authors), reflective practice (RP) is the process of critically thinking through one's actions deliberately, and consciously evaluating the impact of who we are, our goals, what we did, how it went, and how we plan to move forward. This process helps supervisors to continue to learn, adapt, and can aid in our growth. Further, RP can be beneficial for everyone in our field including trainee practitioners, however, the knowledge of these benefits may not always lead to action and result in consistent practice. RP is a well-known concept in our field (see Knowles et al., 2014a), however, encouraging RP from a multicultural perspective has received little attention.

Within our practice, one of our goals is to help our trainees develop the life-long habit of reflecting. We know that it is not enough to simply ask them to participate in the process while they are in training, so we ask our trainees to experience the value of reflecting and incorporate reflection as part of their own ethical practice. Since 2020, we have been developing supervisor training in our new master's programme, and in doing so, we have realised how much we need to help supervisors establish their own RPs so that they can, in turn, help their trainees. How to facilitate RP in others is the focus of this chapter. In addition, we will describe how we help our trainees develop the knowledge and skills to reflect and the values to incorporate into their work from a multicultural perspective (i.e., using what we are calling Multicultural RP [MRP][1]).

To set the scene, as we illustrate our experiences and offer advice, we would like to introduce ourselves. Tegan (TA, pronouns: she/her) is a sport and clinical psychologist by training, licensed in California, and certified as a Certified Mental Performance Consultant (CMPC) through the Association for Applied Sport Psychology (AASP). She is a white, cisgender, straight woman, who grew up in the Pacific Northwest and now lives in Northern California. She is an affiliate faculty member of the Sport and Performance Psychology Department at Holy Names University (HNU) and has over ten years of experience teaching and supervising trainees. She is the official meta-supervisor (supervisor of supervisors; Barney & Andersen, 2014) for the programme and instrumental in facilitating

DOI: 10.4324/9781003198758-11

RP in our supervisory team. As first author, her voice is the primary one in terms of her reflections and advice on MRP.

Alison (APR, pronouns: she/her) is a Professor and the Programme Director of the same department at HNU. She is a white, cisgender, British-American, straight woman originally from Northwest England and now lives in Northern California. She has been teaching and supervising for over 20 years. She studied and trained for applied work in the UK and is also certified as a CMPC through AASP. She has presented and written about RP before (e.g., Rhodius, 2012; Rhodius & Huntley, 2014), however, multicultural aspects did not feature as strongly in the earlier writings and became more prominent later as she continued to grow in her cultural awareness (Rhodius & Park, 2016).

Interestingly, APR did not receive any type of diversity training in multicultural issues in her own doctoral education over 20 years ago, and she has since grown her knowledge through professional development opportunities. However, TA did complete extensive training in this area in her clinical doctorate and so she guides our HNU programme on this aspect. It is the value of striving to be culturally humble and culturally responsive that has become a focus for our programme. We not only want our students to be trained from a multicultural perspective, but also our supervisors. "The multicultural perspective is an ideological orientation that values the recognition and inclusion of diverse ethnic and cultural groups as sources of identity and culture that are favourable to society, because they promote positive intergroup relations and social equality" (Urbiola et al., 2018, p. 608). We believe that the multicultural perspective is fundamental to the way in which supervisors facilitate RP in ourselves and in others.

We are writing this chapter whilst housed in an applied programme that focuses on training practitioners. Our programme's mission is focused on educating and training students to become ethical, professional, and culturally competent practitioners. We have programme learning outcomes (PLOs) around ethics and professionalism, theory and research, mental skills, emotional and cultural intelligence. Our values also appear on every syllabus in the graduate programme, which reflects the importance that we place on it:

> We value diversity, equity, and inclusion, and strive to take an anti-racist and anti-oppressive approach in the classroom. We work to both be culturally humble professors and help develop cultural humility in our trainee-practitioners. We encourage students to join us in the ongoing work of social justice and advocacy.

We also ask all our teaching faculty to include a section about themselves in their syllabus that shares some personal insight, rather than just what they do or the content of the class. We ask that they include their own cultural background (e.g., race, ethnicity, nationality, pronouns), and some also choose to indicate their gender identity. We believe this, in addition to diversifying the required readings (Donovan, 2021), helps the instructor create an inclusive, diverse, and equitable environment in which to learn and is the starting point for all students to feel comfortable showing up as themselves and feeling safe to learn (Ahadi & Guerrero, 2020).

Since this programme's start in 2020, we have offered diversity training every semester to our teaching faculty and our placement supervisors. In addition, we now require our academic diversity course for the students during the first semester of the programme, thus underlining the importance of it as a foundational aspect of the students' training with us. We understand the significance of, and want the emphasis on, multicultural awareness to begin at the start of the programme, to be integrated throughout, supported using MRP, and not be limited to one disconnected and standalone diversity course experience.

Going on a Reflective Practice Journey

I (TA) first began my journey with RP in a sport psychology master's programme at John F. Kennedy University (JFKU). In this programme, I was provided with a solid foundation, and what I learned there has influenced all my clinical work. However, it was not until the linked clinical doctorate programme there that I first learned about reflecting from a multicultural perspective. Once I learned this, my perspective completely changed.

The doctoral programme and reflective process began with an incredibly deep self-awareness process, whereby we learned about ourselves as cultural beings. This was especially important for me as a white woman who held significant privilege. The process included recognising each of my different identities, how I saw myself, understood myself, and how I moved through the world in other peoples' eyes. The experience is often different for people of colour, who have had experiences related to race and ethnicity, that, at least for me, as a white person, had not. The education and training centred on understanding our privilege, our biases, and assumptions. While it can be uncomfortable to acknowledge biases and assumptions we hold about other people – based on ethnicity, race, socio-economic status, and other identities visible and invisible – we must acknowledge that we are all taught messages about other people, conscious and unconscious, and our brain works to quickly categorise. As a result, we need to bring these biases and assumptions about other people to the conscious forefront of our awareness so we can actively work to minimise discrimination, and engage in the ongoing, lifelong work of anti-racism and anti-oppression. Put simply, we as supervisors must develop an ability to recognise our own baggage and blind spots, learning how to reflect individually, and developing more comfort with having challenges and sometimes uncomfortable conversations with others. I find it helpful to differentiate between safety and comfort. We do not always feel comfortable when we are growing, but we need to be safe to do so.

Reflection with peers became much more useful in the doctoral programme as we practiced it more often. We spent the entire first year of our doctoral training with a small group of peers, eight to ten people, and met weekly for three hours. This practice continued each year, but with a new cohort of peers at the start of each academic year. Peers can offer one another a new and distinct perspective to reflect on, and these perspectives may be easier to accept than from supervisors who are in power-laden positions. The facilitators in my doctorate programme taught us how to effectively engage in dialogue, helped us to reflect on our own experiences, and they modelled difficult dialogues in the groups as well. Most importantly, by continuing their own MRP, the facilitators showed us that it is an ongoing and evolving process. The facilitators' modelling only deepened "buy-in" to the process.

Building awareness and understanding about our feelings is a critical step. This can be done with a list of questions, or open-ended journaling, or through conversations. However, we need to be honest and transparent with ourselves first about these feelings. Unhelpful consequences result when we misinterpret our feelings (Drigas & Papoutsi, 2018). Even if we do not know what we are feeling, or (what often occurs) we are feeling multiple things at once, breaking down our own reactions and various feelings can be such a useful process. It is the foundation for the work we do. However, I often ask questions to my supervisees such as "what do you think about that?" as a starting place since it is usually easier for people to recognise their thinking. However, it is crucial to move towards recognising and naming our feelings and the impact of our feelings because it decreases the emotional stress response (Lieberman et al., 2007). It is also vital to acknowledge that our own feelings about the process are based on who we are: our culture (in terms of ethnicity, race, gender, ability, as well as our family culture), our genetic psychological make-up, our biases, and automatic assumptions.

While not all programmes have devoted so much time to this MRP aspect of education and training, we strongly encourage this, and here at HNU we are moving to include more of this in our curriculum. We also prioritise training our supervisors to engage in this work and to incorporate and support their trainees in this process. Reflecting is a paramount skill, because we want trainees to recognise and experience the value of peer support for consultation purposes when they are no longer required to be in supervision (Rhodius & Sugarman, 2014). For some this occurs after graduation or, for others, after they have obtained the number of supervised hours to sit for, for example, the CMPC exam that is based in the USA.

Professional Relationship-Building as a Foundation for Multicultural Reflective Practice

Building a professional relationship with a trainee is the foundation for effective supervision. Guidance, collaboration, and trust, from a non-judgmental perspective, are found to be paramount (Foltz et al., 2015). We believe that to build a professional working relationship effectively we need to incorporate multicultural awareness, cultural sensitivity and responsiveness, and values of anti-bias, anti-racism, and anti-oppression as a framework from which we work.

While all supervision experiences and relationships will vary, we as meta-supervisors need our supervisors to understand themselves and their own characteristics, biases, and assumptions to form healthy working relationships with our trainees. There is a "perceived lack of attention paid to multicultural issues in sport psychology supervision, which represents an area for improvement in the field" (Foltz et al., 2015, p. 460). This needs to change in the sport and performance psychology field (and more widely across the sport and exercise sciences); supervisors need to do better, and one important way to start is how we train the next generation of practitioners. Building self-awareness, and knowing our own biases and assumptions, and practicing these dialogues with our trainees is a good start. Prioritising on-going training with our supervisors, as well as engaging in this often-challenging RP ourselves, is how we plan to influence the field. Supervisors also need to help our trainees practice conversations about the impact of culture, racism, and oppression, because these conversations can be anxiety provoking, feel risky, and damage relationships if done without care – yet even more damage can be done if these dialogues are not had at all.

In supervision, I (TA) bring my authentic self when I am forming a professional relationship with trainees, and try to show up as myself, with all my imperfections, as well as experience, and strengths. I ask my trainees in the beginning meetings about who they are, what identities are salient to them, share about myself and my background, explore the impact of our intersecting identities, and what helps them to have a positive supervision experience. This is the most meaningful part of the work for me, and always fuels me as I help build my trainees' skill sets, help them understand themselves better, and feel confident in what they are bringing as well as identifying ways they want to grow. When I support supervisors in the meta-supervisor role, I in fact do the same. I appreciate how critical it is for me to know myself, my areas of growth, and my biases and assumptions that may come up about my trainees, supervisors, and the clients they are developing professional relationships with during their work.

Facilitating a Multicultural Perspective in Reflective Practice

Facilitating a multicultural perspective in RP includes reflecting on *who we are*, not just on *what* we did or *how* we did something. We supervisors and practitioners are the tool, and we need to reflect and recognise ourselves from a cultural perspective so we can effectively engage in professional working relationships where we value how culture influences interactions, understanding, and effectiveness. How we facilitate reflection in others needs to be grounded in a cultural perspective as well. Therefore, modelling our own reflection about how we engage in a professional relationship matters. We might think there is a specific way to utilise RP, however, there are many other ways to engage in reflection. People from varying cultural perspectives will understand their needs differently and will find diverse approaches to incorporating RP into their work. Openness to this will be critical in connecting with people who come from differing backgrounds, have different beliefs, and individualised ways of engaging in the world. We will run into considerable trouble if we come from a place where we believe we know the way, and our way is the right way to engage in RP. If we hold on to this perspective, it may mean we are unable to develop trust with our trainee or get the trainee's "buy-in." In my experience, when we do not have a healthy working relationship with our trainee, they are less likely to share honestly about challenges or growth areas, all to the detriment of the clients.

The foundation of this process is beginning to know ourselves as cultural beings. Especially, for myself (TA), as a white, cisgender, straight woman, I hold a lot of privileges that were unearned, and I had to learn to unpack these privileges, notice and name them, and recognise the way trainees and clients, and others experience me. Sometimes this involves reflecting internally, verbally with others, and sometimes reflections on paper. This unpacking and noticing are on-going. Some of this is about me, and some not, but it is my responsibility to acknowledge the impact I have on others, and how my beliefs influence how I handle interactions, my professional relationship building, and even how I define success. Opportunities for growth in my trainees may be impacted if I do not address race and culture because it leads to misunderstanding and mistrust (Colistra & Brown-Rice, 2011).

Often as supervisors we may have preferences about how we want our trainees to try a new technique. I (TA) find it useful to share a certain way of implementing a technique when the trainee is early in their learning, with the caveat that this technique is based upon *my perspective and experience*. I then engage the trainees in a dialogue about how this approach feels to them, what they think about it, and what they are drawn to initially. I am open to dialogue about what methods they prefer and encourage them to try a new technique as an experiment, even if they decide later that it is not their preferred approach to reflection. This also regularly shows up in my work as a meta-supervisor, given the supervisors I am supporting sometimes have years of experience supervising. By focusing on connecting with them first, hearing from them about their perspective, valuing their strengths, and encouraging them to engage in MRP, they are better enabled to model this with their trainees. Connecting with them looks different depending on the person, but casual conversation to get to know each other is helpful, as well as building confidence by asking about strengths and providing feedback on what they think is going well.

I bring a developmental approach to my work with trainees and find this to be helpful in recognising there is much to learn for everyone, and it is most useful and empowering to help trainees from the place they currently are at. I work by focusing on building trust and showing warmth, while providing supportive confrontation to the trainees to increase self-awareness and competence, while providing structured support as needed (Poncy, 2020). Connecting a developmental approach to RP to me means that we start with where the trainee is at, including what they think about RP, their experience with RP, and identifying how to help build the skill from their current starting point.

I try to focus on a strength-based perspective (Wade & Jones, 2014) focused on where the trainee is heading as opposed to what they should avoid. I aim to support the person in developing their own self-awareness, and my understanding of their own preferences, tastes, and style will really help in this approach. If a trainee begins to understand themselves better, and feels like their perspective is valued, it is easier for them to be vulnerable, take risks, and have the confidence to make some minor changes, which lead to greater confidence and growth.

Teaching Trainees Reflective Practice and Helping to Identify the Best Fit

How do we create an environment where RP is useful? Many of our trainees at first struggle to make the time in their busy and demanding schedules to carve out time for reflection. Creating an environment where RP is accepted, and valued, can take time and we want and need trust for reviewing their reflections. The way we respond as supervisors is critical to trainees' ability to continue to show up and take risks in the relationship by being honest with their feelings and thoughts regarding their work, and what happened. We owe this effort to the people we support, since they are the ones impacted by our well-being and ability to reflect on ourselves and our work, and to continue to grow and deepen our skill.

Recognising our preferences and the privileges associated with distinct types of reflection tools is useful. For example, unless we are providing audio or video recording technology, we should recognise potential limits to our trainees' ability to purchase or utilise such tools. Video journaling (Parikh et al., 2012) or audio journaling as a method RP can be an effective and efficient way to complete reflections. These formats work particularly well immediately following telehealth appointments or audio recording sessions when trainees can easily reflect via these mediums. The structure can be free form, as is often utilised when handwriting or typing out reflections. It is often most effective to have the space for general processing time, as well as an opportunity to answer set RP questions. People's brains need time to reflect and make sense of what is happening and what we think and feel about a situation.

Utilising a list of MRP questions can help supervisors achieve a clearer result. This might include heightening a supervisor's ability to appropriately assess, and additionally notice, discuss, and help the trainee engage in reflection regarding differences between clients. If the reflective process is the same every time, then supervisors can determine how much content there was as well as the experience and differences in the experience. According to Keegan, (2016) "one key reason for using structure in RP is to facilitate the demonstration of competence – either the subject of the reflections or the reflections themselves – so that a supervisor or assessor can access them" (p. 233). For example, it might be easier to notice when it was exceedingly difficult to reflect or acknowledge mistakes. How do we as supervisors know if it is effective? Asking our trainees about their experience with the reflective process and assessing over time to determine ways they are demonstrating growth, change, and improved or deepened reflection.

Possible Multicultural Reflective Practice Questions to Consider as a Supervisor

- Questions about oneself
  - Who am I/what are my salient identities?
  - What are my cultural perspectives?
  - What is the impact on the trainee?

- Questions about the trainee
  - Who is the trainee/what are their salient identities?
  - What are their cultural perspectives?
  - What is their impact on me?

- Questions about the supervision process and outcome
  - What were your goals?
  - What happened?
  - What influenced decision making?
  - What went well?
  - Growth areas?

- Questions regarding the future and taking learning to the next supervision meeting
  - Goals and intentions for next time?

At times reflection-in-action can be helpful, though this comes in time and with experience, and encouraging reflection-on-action is a good starting point (Schön, 1983). Reflection-in-action can help an individual change course or acknowledge something in real-time. Reflecting-on-action is how we typically think about RP. We need enough experience to know when reflection-in-action is not effective and takes us out of the moment and leads us to perform less effectively. How do we know when RP is effective? We do not always know. However, we often reflect on and know if our work is *not* effective. While we do not want to assume all challenges with clients or our trainees are about us, we should do our best to identify what could have gone wrong, and or what we could do better next time. Additionally, understanding and processing how we might approach a conversation in real-time and working together to identify what is working or not working can be a key step in the process.

Modelling Multicultural Reflective Practice

We (authors) want trainees to develop authentic interest in reflection and not just "perform" it for us. This takes effort and we believe that the part that has made the biggest difference is to model reflection ourselves. As supervisors we need to model MRP regarding our own work with clients if we are currently practicing, and most importantly, regarding our supervision with the trainee. Additionally, utilising the concept of "Meta-Reflection," which involves reflecting with curiosity about our own process and upon one's own ability to reflect regarding our feelings, how it is going, and is it helping to build insight (Keegan, 2016). In my (TA) experience, when we bring ourselves into the room in terms of our professional relationship and vulnerably share about our own professional strengths and areas of growth, including RP, we are more likely to build healthy working relationships, that are based on trust. Transparency prompts trainees to also want to be vulnerable.

We also want to encourage MRP to ensure the quality of care that is being provided to clients. I go through a similar process reflecting on my supervision process. I try to first notice my own cultural perspective, notice who I am in the room and in the professional relationship and how I show up in that relationship (meaning my intersecting identities as well as my power and privilege). Since there are various norms, perspectives, values, and diversity in worldviews, we need to increase our sensitivity to multicultural issues to effectively work together (Jain & Aggarwal, 2020). I think about and attempt to see my trainees and all their intersecting identities. Those that are different, and those that are like my own. We often assume people who look like us also think like us or are similar, which is an assumption we can and should recognise through our RP. I work to evaluate how my relationship with each trainee is working, how I am creating space for them as humans, and how I am bringing in and noticing my own challenges and ways of improving. I identify steps and intentions for our next meeting. I often make small notes for myself as well if I am concerned about an issue I might forget, or if I do not want to avoid bringing up something that might be more challenging to discuss. I also try to notice any parallel processes that may be happening between the trainee and myself as supervisor, as well as the trainee and their client.

Handling Challenges or Resistance in Trainees

It takes a significant amount of effort, and therefore time, to engage in the reflective process. Utilising our own RP as supervisors, we must honestly acknowledge our own resistance that may surface about using MRP. Resistance can result from concerns such as: ego, defensiveness, and blind spots. If supervisors can honestly reflect on our own work with clients, as well as our work with trainees, we are more likely to manage concerns and help our trainees develop effective RPs that happen automatically and are a regular part of the work.

Trying to notice what went wrong, or what could be improved, considering what gets in the way of oneself, identifying when reflection is hard to incorporate, and looking back to when the process of RP began in one's own life is worthwhile. The question for many practitioners is about the necessity of making it a formal practice, when they believe they engage in reflection already (Keegan, 2016). The benefit of having more formal practice is to ensure we are putting in the time and energy to reflect, to notice our errors, and identify ways we can move forward more effectively. We need to be honest with ourselves about this.

I (TA) notice in my own process that there are times when it is easy to reflect, usually this is when there is not something I am particularly sensitive about regarding my skills and strengths. It is also extremely useful to reflect when I am feeling emotional or particularly upset about something, but this can take me more time to process, and answering a specific list of questions may be difficult. It may require more patience over time for the questions to be fully answered. Knowing myself and identifying what can get in my way is the first step.

The next step is to build MRP as a habit, where it becomes a natural step in one's process and not something to be avoided. This usually means that we have practiced it enough that it becomes automatically integrated, and not so dreadful that the trainee struggles to engage with the important process. Additionally, we want to understand the resistance, if there is any, and to be curious about it. Ask our trainees "why?" with curiosity and not judgment, as "why" usually feels critical. I shift this and I ask myself with curiosity and compassion, "Hmm, why am I feeling this way? What is going on with me? Is there anything that I need to address here?" We need to attempt to engage the trainee in MRP during supervision sessions to practice and understand what is going on for the trainee. I try to learn whether there has been an unpleasant experience in the past, or a poor relationship with a supervisor that is impacting the trainee's willingness to try RP. I may ask, "What is your experience with RP in the past?," "What has supervision been like for you in the past? What has gone well? What has been difficult?" Sometimes trainees want to focus on the client only, and so I try to show how an increased understanding of oneself benefits the trainee and the client. I also take this as an opportunity to check my "own stuff," and, again, try to recognise my impact on the trainee, starting with a reflection about who I am, how my cultural beliefs are impacting me and the professional relationship and focusing on connection and relationship building with the trainee.

Future Directions

Future directions for research on MRP and facilitating RP in others need to include: multicultural awareness; working towards being culturally responsive practitioners and supervisors; and being committed to the lifelong process of cultural competence and cultural humility, which is not an end point, but an ongoing goal. The goal of MRP is to bring the unknown into awareness, so by modelling, relationship building, recognising, and working with resistance, finding the appropriate format that fits with our trainees' cultural perspective and preference, we can effectively facilitate this process in others. If we work personally and professionally towards anti-oppression, anti-racism, recognising our own biases, working to take necessary steps to be inclusive, identify when we misstep, and acknowledge our impact on others, then we are closer to facilitating MRP in others. We welcome you all, from varying backgrounds and experiences, consider MRP and look forward to learning more about how you utilise this approach in your own work. Please reach out to us with any questions, share how you utilise this in your own work, and with the trainees you support and supervise.

Takeaways

MRP Questions (Figure 8.1): Supervisors are recommended to provide this to their trainees to facilitate MRP and are encouraged to utilise this practice for themselves as well since we think it is important that we also model it and engage in the process ourselves. We believe that including a multicultural perspective is paramount as we engage as supervisors and with our trainees. The questions ask you to consider, and then share, your own identities and their impact on those you are working with individually and in supervision.

Multicultural Reflective Practice Questions to Answer (Use this template or answer questions on video or an audio recording)	
QUESTIONS	**REFLECTIVE NOTES**
Who Are You? (What is your vantage point?)	
What are your salient identities? (race/ethnicity, gender, sexual orientation, religion, disability status, age/generation)	
What are your privileges?	
What might your impact on your client be?	
Who holds the power?	
What were your goals?	
What happened?	
What influenced your decision-making?	
What went well?	
What could go better?	
Goals for next time?	
Will you review with your supervisor and/or with peers in group supervision?	

Figure 8.1 Multicultural Reflective Practice Question Framework

Acknowledgements

We would like to thank Ray Libman, Juan Garcia, Meetika Srivastava for their help with the research on this topic. We would also like to thank Daniery Rosario for his insightful feedback and suggestions. Finally, we want to thank the supervisors we have worked with over the years; they have helped to keep motivation high regarding improving our standards, which will, in turn, aid the development of the trainees in our field.

Note

1 Multicultural Critical Reflective Practice (MCRP) has been cited in Crum and Hendrick's (2014) work in museum studies, which draws upon Brookfield's (1998) work regarding critical reflective practice, but the term MRP is new.

9 The Reflective Sport System

Christopher R. D. Wagstaff, Matthew Miller,
and Alessandro Quartiroli

Introduction

In sport, individuals function in highly complex and challenging environments and must regularly refresh their knowledge and skills to solve complex problems (Mann et al., 2009). In some professions (e.g., healthcare, education, and psychology) reflective practice is regarded by many as an essential component of professional competence (Finlay, 2008). Indeed, across a growing number of professions there exist formal requirements for healthcare practitioners to provide evidence of reflective practice as part of licensing and revalidation processes. Therefore, preparing professionals to be reflective remains fundamental to the developing and sustaining ethical, competent, and effective practice. Further, in sport, such professionals typically operate in complex, dynamic, and interdependent systems and, therefore, reflective practice might be reconceptualised, undertaken, and promoted as a shared and collective endeavour.

Originating from Aristotle's notion of practical wisdom, the contemporary Western understanding of reflective practice originated from the work of Dewey (1859–1952) in fields of psychology and pedagogy. Dewey allied reflection to the kind of thinking that consists of serious thought, is active and deliberate in nature, and involves sequences of interconnected ideas that take account of underlying beliefs and knowledge (Cropley et al., 2010b). In practice, reflective thinking primarily addresses practical problems, allowing for doubt and uncertainty before viable solutions can be reached. And yet such practice is rarely undertaken in isolation but in collaboration with others. To elaborate, in sport systems, athletes, coaches, science and medicine professionals, and administrators work together to toward shared goals. It follows that while better-informed practitioners might use their knowledge and experience to frame complex problems more effectively in professional *their* own practice (cf. Mann et al., 2009), those who undertake and share their learning with colleagues might help develop a more effective *system*.

Reflective practice came to prominence in the United Kingdom in the early 1990s primarily within nurse education and practice and has remained a foundational component of care systems since. Within the growing body of evidence in the nursing literature, researchers have reported numerous benefits associated with reflective practice, including: the development of a form of knowledge rooted

DOI: 10.4324/9781003198758-12

in practice and recognition of nurse expertise (Argyris & Schön, 1974; Johns, 2017); the modification and improvement of clinical practices (Boyd & Fales, 1983; Reid, 1993); the possibility of bridging the gap between theory and practice (Schön, 1983); and finally, the development of a new learning tool (Conway, 1994; Driscoll & Teh, 2001; Walsh et al., 2002). Further to the value attached to reflection in other domains, in the sport context emphasis has been increasingly placed on the effective practices of service providers, with sport psychology consultants recognising the need to demonstrate professional competence and be accountable for the effectiveness of their service delivery (Cropley, Hanton et al., 2020; Martindale & Collins, 2007). Indeed, reflective practice can improve learning and promote professional and personal development (Andersen, 2000; Anderson et al., 2004; Cropley et al., 2007), aid self-examination and uncover more effective ways of "being" (e.g., Andersen, 2005; Holt & Strean, 2001; Tonn & Harmison, 2004), as well as assist practitioners to examine and justify their professional practice philosophy and service delivery model, to personally monitor and evaluate their practice, and improve their professional effectiveness and impact (see Anderson et al., 2002; Cropley, Hanton et al., 2020).

In a recent review of the literature, which explored the reflective accounts of sport psychology practitioners, Wadsworth et al. (2021) highlighted common themes that provide focus to their reflective practice among trainee practitioners, newly qualified practitioners, and experienced practitioners. Briefly, the trainee practitioners reflected on: their attempts to integrate within sporting environments (Christensen & Aoyagi, 2014); adopting multiple roles within these environments (Collins et al., 2013); experiencing inauthenticity and incongruence (Holt & Strean, 2001); and feelings of self-doubt and pressure (Woodcock et al., 2008). Newly qualified practitioners also reflected on their experiences of self-doubt, related to their perceived level of competence (Cropley et al., 2007), but in contrast to the trainee practitioners, also chose to reflect on: their lack of contact time with athletes (Rowley et al., 2012); the importance of practitioner self-care (Jackson, 2006); conflicts between self-promotion and sound ethical practice (Lindsay & Thomas, 2014); and becoming more aware of the connection between their beliefs and their applied research (McGregor & Winter, 2017). Experienced practitioners reflected on themselves (i.e., developing a congruent professional identity; Anderson, 2014), but also described how they as individuals were able to effectively integrate within the culture in which they were situated to support the needs of both individuals and organisations (Brooks, 2007; Fifer et al., 2008; Tod, 2014). It follows that if practitioners can gain a shared understanding from their own and others' motives, decision-making, learnings, perspectives, and practice, they can better make sense of these experiences and situate themselves and their practice within the complex system in which they operate.

The Emergence of Complex Elite Sport Systems

Elite sports organisations are comprised of a network of individuals and groups who transact with each other to perform functions essential to the development and performance of that organisation. Fletcher and Wagstaff (2009) argued that a "twilight zone" (p. 428) has existed between sport management and sport psychology, which encompasses the organisational culture and climate of sport, together with how personnel and the environment are led, and how individuals and stakeholder groups interact within and with the broader organisation. Researchers exploring this twilight zone do so under the banner of organisational sport psychology to gain the knowledge and understanding that facilitates the development of "optimally functioning sport organisations" (Wagstaff, 2019, p. 1). The prominence of organisational sport psychology is characterised by complex social environments where a diverse range of performance staff (e.g., athletes, coaches, managers, support staff, and administrators) interact in the pursuit of development, preparation, and performance. Moreover, sustained success in sport is not solely dependent on the talent of an individual athlete or group of athletes but how a system of stakeholders (e.g., performance staff and administrators) can work effectively together to ensure athletes are optimally prepared to perform at competitions (Wagstaff, 2019).

Organisational sport psychology researchers and practitioners have acknowledged the importance of the *team behind the team* in elite sport (e.g., Arnold et al., 2019; Wagstaff et al., 2015; Mechbach et al., 2022). Indeed, it is now common for elite sport teams to comprise of sports medicine personnel (e.g., doctors, physiotherapists, soft tissue therapists), sports scientists (e.g., psychologists, physiologists, nutritionists, performance analysts, strength and conditioning coaches), and various other support staff and individuals working for the organisation (e.g., performance lifestyle advisors, performance knowledge and innovation specialists, engineers). The prominent and pivotal role played by these interdisciplinary teams, in performance settings has led researchers to examine their experiences of interdisciplinary work (Reid et al., 2004), organisational change (Hings et al., 2018; Wagstaff et al., 2015, 2016), stress (e.g., Arnold et al., 2019; Larner et al., 2017), and precarious employment (e.g., Gilmore et al., 2018), as well as the recruitment and development of such teams (Mechbach et al., 2022). What is clear from the extant literature and practice is that a cohesive and healthy performance team is pivotal for the sport organisation thriving. What occurs to us is that, if the ethical, competent, and effective performance of these practitioners is predicated on reflective practice, to what extent should reflective practice be a shared endeavour?

The shift towards *scientisation* and *medicalisation* of sport prompts us, the authors, to speculate on ways to best support and advance the work of performance teams, by supporting reflection and supervision across these stakeholder groups. Specifically, while we have hitherto referred to interdisciplinary teams, we perceive opportunities to translate knowledge and practice strengths between the "performance team" (i.e., coaches and athletes) and the "team behind the team" (i.e., science, medicine, and technology). Indeed, in our experience, in the best functioning sport organisations these "team" are subgroups only in role and responsibility with teams within a given organisation having a high degree of connectedness and integration of working practices. As such, for the purpose of brevity, we refer to the "systems" in this chapter as a combination of coaches, athletes, support staff, senior leaders, and administrator stakeholder who regularly interact and have both direct and indirect influences on performance outcomes within an elite sport organisation.

Taking the emergence of reflective practice and the complex, intertwined nature of elite sport systems, we hypothesise that advancing collective reflection would benefit individuals in these contexts. In doing so, we offer two bodies of literature to advance this argument. Specifically, we propose *communities of practice* and *reflective practice groups* as bodies of work that might offer a foundation and rationale to extend reflective practice beyond the individual level shifting toward to become a mechanism for promoting safe and effective practice within elite sport systems.

Communities of Practice

Over the past three decades, scholars (e.g., Berman et al., 2002; Lubit, 2001) have highlighted the salience of knowledge as a source of competitive advantage in professional life, with these scholars seeking ways to leverage knowledge in everyday practice. While traditional knowledge management approaches attempt to capture existing knowledge within formal systems (e.g., databases), systematically addressing the kind of "dynamic knowing" that has the potential to make a significant impact in practice requires the participation of people who are fully engaged in the process of creating, refining, communicating, and using knowledge (Wenger, 1998). We perceive that this dynamic knowledge can be facilitated and augmented by shared reflection processes and might be informed by communities of practice.

The concept of communities of practice (CoPs) was coined by cognitive anthropologist Jean Lave and educational theorist Etienne Wenger (see Lave & Wenger, 1991) and represents a multi-purpose concept that considers learning as a social system formed by groups of people who engage regularly in a shared domain of human endeavour (Wenger, 2009). A CoP refers to "a group of people who share a common concern, set of problems or passion about a topic and who deepen their knowledge and expertise in this area by interacting on an ongoing basis" (Wenger et al., 2002, p. 4). Wenger (1998) argued that CoPs have three characteristics that distinguish them from other groups: (a) mutual engagement; (b) a joint enterprise; and (c) a shared repertoire. Accordingly, the shared repertoire of a community of practice comprises the knowledge base and practices of the community and serves as a "common conceptual framework for action" (Bain et al., 2009, p. 336) or schema for the community (Marshall, 1995). From a practical perspective, within CoPs, feedback is the foundation of regular critical reflection and enables ongoing monitoring of understanding in the given domain and thereby expanding the knowledge of the community and contributing to its future development (Daniel et al., 2013). In considering feedback, the community endeavours to draw on the collective experience of individuals as well as theory and new information, to critique current practice, and advance knowledge and practice. Trede (2010) referred to this professional engagement in critical discussion as *critical transformative dialogue*.

CoPs consist of two levels, including a CoPs scale and a systems scale. A CoP scale is defined by three dimensions: (a) the domain; (b) the community; and (c) the practice. *The domain* – a CoP is characterised by a shared domain of interest. Membership therefore entails a commitment to the domain, and a shared competence that distinguishes members from other people. *The community* – members engage in joint activities and discussions, support each other, and share information. Relationships are developed to enhance learning across the community. *The practice* – members of CoPs are practitioners, who through their membership, develop a shared repertoire of resources, including experiences, stories, tools, and ways of addressing complex work-place problems, in short, a shared practice.

An overarching belief, which is integral to the functionality of CoPs, is *the identity*. The identity of CoP members reflects the complex relationship between the learning environment (i.e., place of work or study) and the person. The extent to which a learner aligns (or not) with the culture and utility of the CoP is mediated by the learner themselves and is always in a state of change. Consequently, a learner's identity adds an element of dynamism to the formation of, and continued use of a CoPs, as each member finds, and reaffirms their place in a community. It follows that the effective facilitation, openness to vulnerability, and identity of the individual practitioner and group will influence the potential success of the community of practice for promoting meaningful reflection within a sport system.

In addition to the CoP scale, CoPs also encompass a systems scale. From a systems scale perspective, a CoP can be viewed both as a simple social learning system, and a complex social learning system comprised of numerous interrelated CoPs. As such, CoPs are not isolated entities but are part of the broader social systems (e.g., organisations, communities, and cities) that characterise the contemporary workplace, and therefore, these broader social systems, together with their interrelated activities form *landscapes of practice*. According to Blackmore (2010) there are three different modes of identity that positions learning in the landscape: *engagement* (e.g., participating in activities, working individually or as part of a team); *imagination* (e.g., forming an image of the learning environment that helps us to understand how we belong or not); and *alignment* (e.g., orientation with the context – ensuring that learning activities are planned and organised, and intentions are clearly communicated).

In practice, CoPs vary in size and might be small (e.g., 2–3 members), exceptionally large (e.g., 150–200 members), or consist of a core group with many peripheral members. Some CoPs are situated within or in close proximity to an organisation, and some include members from various organisations which extend across the globe (Wenger, 1998). While some communities meet face-to-face others function online (see Table 9.1).

To better understand the learning that takes place outside-of-the-classroom, during the last two decades, an emerging line of research in sport coaching has explored how the concept of CoPs can support coaching pedagogy

Table 9.1 Framing Questions for How an Elite Sport System Community of Practice Might Develop Their Practice (adapted from Wenger, 2009)

Frame	Question
Problem solving	"Can we work on this client intervention plan and share some ideas; I need some help"
Requests for information	"Where can I find the client's individual development plan?"
Seeking experience	"Has anyone worked with a client who has similar challenges?"
Reusing assets	"I have a case formulation template I normally use; I can send it to you, and you can easily tweak it for this new client"
Coordination and synergy	"As an interdisciplinary team, can we combine our knowledge of this client and formulate an intervention plan?"
Discussing developments	"What progress do you think the client has made during the last 12 months? Have the interventions been effective?"
Documentation projects	"Over the past few years, we have encountered similar challenges, lets write a best practice model to inform our work"
Visits	"Can I come and observe you work? I'd like to learn from your practice"
Mapping knowledge and identifying gaps	"What do we know about and what are we missing to better support this individual?"

(e.g., Galipeu & Trudel, 2005; Culver & Trudel, 2006, 2008; Lemyre et al., 2007). Central to these research investigations has been the key role of peer collaboration in the learning process. Participation in CoPs provide coaches and support staff one such opportunity for learning; we believe this process can be extended beyond groups of coaches and instead integrate professionals from a variety of disciplines that collaborate toward shared understanding, processes, and goals.

Interdisciplinary collaboration is critical to maximise the potential for success for elite athletes. The term interdisciplinary describes a group of professionals from several different disciplines who work together as a collective and with the same athlete(s), team(s), or organisation. Consequently, an interdisciplinary community of practice has the potential to support both self-management and self-renewal in response to the ever-changing internal and external environment within sport systems. In this sense, ongoing feedback and critical reflection become crucial processes within these CoPs. This offers a vital confluence for reflective practice and the complex dynamics that characterise elite sport systems. Moreover, the CoP frame might provide a mechanism to create discourse around tacit knowledge, and, via a constellation of interconnected CoPs, it can create, revise, and share knowledge based on situated learning across a sport system. It is perhaps not surprising that we believe such activities could greatly benefit the practices of interdisciplinary teams working in sport systems as a mechanism to frame reflective practice. As such, we also welcome the development of reflective practice among a range of stakeholders in sport, including athletes, coaches, science and medicine practitioners, and administrators as demonstrated across other chapters of this book.

Reflective Practice Groups

Individuals in sport systems are often challenged to make time-sensitive decisions in highly complex and demanding contexts, with many uncontrolled and unknown factors. Nevertheless, making difficult decisions is based on more than just technical, rational, or academic knowledge (Schön, 1983) and reflective practice can guard against practitioners becoming overly simplistic and technique driven in their application of knowledge (Johns, 2017).

Reflective practice groups (RGs) are a prominent method for facilitating personal and professional development within the training of competent reflective scientist-practitioners in the clinical psychology field (Binks et al., 2013). RGs are facilitated groups in which trainee clinical psychologists have an opportunity to explore and discuss their experiences of training, their clinical work and themselves (Binks et al., 2013). They are unique in terms of being deliberately established to explore the social self and self in relation to others, to gain an experience of others' positions, and to learn about group dynamics (Kiff et al., 2010).

These groups offer system-wide and individual benefits through opportunities for greater shared understanding and enhanced group dynamics, while serving personal advancement by aiding "reflection-on-action," reflection about "impact on others," along with reflection 'about self' (Knight et al., 2010). Central to these benefits is personal and professional development through extension of the "capability to reflect critically and systematically on the work-self interface" (Gillmer & Markus, 2003, p. 23). Although only a limited body of work exists examining the utility of RGs, in a survey study, Gillmer and Marckus reported that RGs were the most favoured medium for teaching personal and professional development among participants on UK clinical psychology training programmes.

A small body of research now exists in which scholars have investigated the experience and personal and professional development outcomes of attending unstructured, facilitated, reflective practice groups within counselling and psychology training (e.g., Binks et al., 2013; Knight et al., 2010; Nathan & Poulsen, 2004; Robson & Robson, 2008). Collectively, this work shows that participants of RGs perceive a range of benefits, including experiencing the client position, learning about group process, reflecting on their impact on others, learning about the potential impact of personal issues on client work, and improved practice skills (Nathan & Poulsen, 2004). What is also apparent from this body of work is that some individuals can be challenged by the ambiguous nature of these groups, that participants' openness can be inhibited by current and potential future relationships with other members of the group, and that participants' experience of the group as a safe space is necessary before they will demonstrate vulnerability through self-disclosure (Binks et al., 2013; Nathan & Poulsen, 2004; Robson & Robson, 2008). Knight et al. (2010), in a survey of former trainee psychologists, reported that participants associated both value and distress to their RG experience. Most of these former trainee psychologists (71%) found these groups to have immense value for their training. Yet, interestingly, 38% of the "highly-valuing" participants and 55% of the "low valuing" participants also found their experience in these groups to be distressing. In a later phenomenological interview study, Binks et al. (2013) concluded that distress was an inherent feature of RGs for participants and that exploring distress was essential for learning and beneficial to trainees' self-understanding and practice development. This was further supported by studies in which counselling and psychology students reported that experiencing their own vulnerability within the groups was beneficial in helping them to better connect therapeutically with clients (see Ieva et al., 2009; Nathan & Poulsen, 2004). An examination of the use of RGs and the veracity of such observations within elite sport systems is yet to be developed and it would be highly beneficial.

Drawing from RG facilitators in the nursing context, Murrell (1998) found that participants felt it was their responsibility to foster trust and safety through the management of group dynamics and that this helped contribute to participant learning at emotional and theoretical levels. Such findings were supported and extended by Binks et al. (2013) who found facilitators to perceive their role to manage destructive group dynamics and foster trust and relative safety within the group, while also containing their own powerful affective responses and regulating feelings of professional scrutiny by participants. Binks et al. also noted that some facilitators felt that the unstructured space within the group supported greater freedoms in learning, while others regarded this as a source of anxiety for trainees. Regardless, it would appear to be important that facilitators clearly communicate the philosophy underpinning the group at its formation. Taken collectively, such observations point to the importance of competent and careful RG facilitation, perhaps by an individual with psychological training, given the potential for participants to be traumatised by overly distressing experiences (cf. Binks et al., 2013).

Conclusion

Reflective practice has been well established as a professional necessity and aid for practitioners across a variety of disciplines and professions, including sport-related professions. Concurrently, within elite sport domains we have witnessed the development of interdisciplinary science and medicine teams and systems that support performance and well-being with, through, and for performance staff (i.e., coaches and athletes). The confluence of these developments prompts us to speculate on ways to best support and advance work in elite sport systems given the interdependence of stakeholders for effective, ethical, and competent practice. In this chapter we have argued that there is potential value in supporting reflective practice and supervision across stakeholder groups – that is, beyond individual professionals – with the aim of promoting reflective teams and systems. To realise these opportunities, we have drawn on the notions of *communities of practice* and *reflective practice groups* as foundations for extending reflective practice beyond the individual practitioner and across elite sport systems. While reflective practice is primarily an individual pursuit, we believe that the complex interdependence that characterises performance problems and solutions in elite sport necessitates a shift towards a shared responsibility and support for critical reflective practice. Such a shift might support connection among individuals as well as individual and reciprocal support to personal and professional development and care. What is now needed is for programmes of work to be undertaken by researcher-practitioners in collaboration with elite sport systems to better understand the utility of such initiatives to promote performance and well-being in such environments. Nevertheless, until such programmes of work are complete, we offer some initial practice suggestions for those seeking to develop CoPs or RGs in their sport system. We believe that a range of perspectives will be valuable to CoPs and RGs and therefore encourage systems to seek membership and contribution from a range of stakeholders. To ensure appropriate facilitation, careful planning and introduction to potential participants is needed at the outset of such endeavours. Specifically, CoP and RG facilitators in sport must consider issues of power and status, group size, the way the group is formed and how ground rules are established. Moreover, further considerations include how work is to be boundaried, to what extent membership is organised into cohorts or intentionally cross-pollinated, and the extent to which communities and groups might impacted by the high turnover that is inherent in sport systems and how to mitigate against the negative effects of this. It follows that facilitators who do not have a consistent presence might struggle to influence how a CoP or RG functions or develops over time. Indeed, adroit facilitation is needed to safeguard well-being and psychological safety while promoting optimal outcomes from collective reflective practice, through appropriate challenge and support, considerations of confidentiality, and robust action planning outside of meetings.

10 Think Aloud as a Reflection In- and On-Action Tool

Amy Whitehead

Introduction

Traditionally, reflective methods focus on 'looking back' at an event or experience and questioning both that of the positive and negative as well as areas for subsequent development. Within the discipline of sport coach education, some have argued that the field has suffered from focusing on a type of reflection that links retrospection and review to projection, which differs very little from the concept of performance evaluation (Cushion, 2018). The view of projection refers to sport coaches considering 'so what am I going to do next time?' without really considering potential implications of their proposed actions (Cropley et al., 2015; Dixon et al., 2013). Furthermore, what is most commonplace about these methods is that they occur sometime after the event, episode, or experience. This timeframe leads to a potential memory gap between what occurs during practice and how the experience is remembered. In addition, what is less known is how *reflection-in-action* or indeed *in situ* occurs or can occur and what mechanisms can be used to promote this. One method that can support such reflection is known as Think Aloud (TA; Whitehead, Cropley et al., 2016). TA involves a person verbalising their thoughts, the rationale for having those thoughts (where possible), and then reflecting on those thought processes as they occur within an experience, event, or performance (e.g., a coach using TA: "OK, they're [players] not communicating at all. I wanna know why. Is there something I can do to help them communicate or not?"; Stephenson et al., 2020, p. 16). This process is supported by an individual wearing a clip microphone and Dictaphone as a method of recording 'evidence' of their TA, which can then be used for further reflection at an appropriate time.

The TA method has been demonstrated as having utility across various disciplines (e.g., nursing, Banning, 2008; sport coaching, Whitehead, Cropley et al., 2016; police training, Pais & Felgueiras, 2016). Therefore, this chapter aims to provide readers from the sport and exercises sciences and allied disciplines with an understanding of why reflection-in-action or in-situ needs to be considered to prevent the memory gap that occurs during reflection-on-action, potentially supporting a more dynamic and productive approach to reflection. The chapter will

DOI: 10.4324/9781003198758-13

also consider why reflection-in-action is often neglected and offer some practical recommendations for practitioners working across the sport and exercise sciences and allied disciplines, in their quest to develop as reflective practitioners.

Why We Should Consider Reflecting 'In Situ'

When reflecting it is vital that practitioners consider 'what' they are reflecting on and 'why' they are reflecting on it, or the aspect of it (e.g., behaviour, episode, thought). Perhaps more importantly, practitioners need to be clear that what they are reflecting on is a true representation of the event or the experience as it occurred. Human memory is not perfect, and as humans we may choose to lose or keep certain memories. While many researchers have explored the differences as to how practitioners (or humans in general) experience and remember an event, according to Kahneman and Riis (2005), "Experiences are fleeting [whereas] memories are what we get to keep from our experience" (p. 286). Therefore, how we remember an event can be vastly different from how we experienced it. This phenomenon is known as the *memory-experience gap* and is defined as a discrepancy between the average of experienced emotions and the overall evaluation of the experience, which is usually more intense than the averaged emotions. This gap has been demonstrated in people's ratings of various experiences, ranging from vacations (e.g., Kemp et al., 2008; Wirtz et al., 2003) to episodes of pain (e.g., Broderick et al., 2006; Stone et al., 2004). The memory-experience gap may also be common in sport. For example, a soccer team may be playing well, but then concede a goal in the very last minute, the final emotions experienced by the team's coach at the end of the game may, therefore, supersede the *average* emotions and experiences occurring during the game and result in a memory-experience gap. In turn, this may impact on how she or he may reflect and report back to their players.

Outside of the sports domain, early research by Kahneman (2000) into the pleasure and pain people experience in different moments found that retrospective evaluations were strongly associated with the worst pain experienced during a given event. These memories were also strongly associated with the pain experienced at the end of the event, which was labelled the *peak end rule* (Kahneman, 2000). This rule has been studied extensively with the negative subjective experience of pain (physical and/or emotional), both in experimental settings and in the context of medical procedures such as colonoscopy and lithotripsy (e.g., Redelmeier et al., 2003). What is also evident from this research is that memory experience gaps were more pronounced from the unpleasant emotions, in that people remember being angrier, sadder, and more tense overall than they report during their actual experience (Miron-Shatz et al., 2009). A potential reason for this type of 'remembering' is that if these memories/emotions convey a sense of danger or distress, which emphasises the unpleasant emotions in memory, it could serve as a warning function for future behaviour (Miron-Shatz et al., 2009).

In an attempt to explain the memory-experience gap, female participants in Miron-Shatz et al.'s (2009) research were asked to rate their day overall in a retrospectively evaluative frame of mind. The participants recalled more unpleasant and pleasant emotions than they reported feeling during the individual episodes. Interestingly, a larger discrepancy for the unpleasant emotions than pleasant was also found. This suggests that separate processes are used for committing positive and negative events to memory. Indeed, it is thought that when unpleasant emotions are involved, caution is favoured over accuracy, which could then influence how reflection-on these experiences occurs, the outcome of which may not be fully representative of what was occurring during the in-situ event. Thus, in application to the context of reflection and what we, as sport and exercise science practitioners, reflect on, these insights raise the following questions: what do we reflect on – the experience or the memory?; and, how does the peak end rule affect what we reflect on? In other words, are our reflections-on-action just reflections on our memories and how we felt at the end of that particular experience? If this is the case, what might we be missing out on during the retrospective process of reflection-on-action?

The differences between data captured during performance (using TA) and retrospectively (using interviews) identified in Miron-Shatz et al.'s (2009) research have also been reported within the sport literature. Tenenbaum and Elran (2003) examined the congruence between actual and retrospective reports for pre- and post-emotional states that were collected one hour before the event, and 30 minutes and 72 hours after the event. The results revealed that thoughts and feelings openly expressed after 72 hours were not fully congruent with thoughts and feelings reported in real-time. Further, Whitehead et al. (2015) used TA to capture the concurrent thoughts of participants during golf performance and then conducted interviews with the participants immediately, 24 hours, and 48 hours after performance. Whitehead et al. (2015) did not measure specific emotional responses, as in Miron-Shatz et al.'s (2009) study, however when a comparison of the data was conducted there appeared to be large discrepancies between what was verbalised during performance, using the TA method and what was reported at the post-performance interviews, with only a 40% similarity between data reported. Although not significantly different, more verbalisations were reported that related to emotions during the post-performance interviews (up to 24 hours), which could support the concept of the memory-experience gap in that these emotions may have been remembered more vividly in comparison to how they were experienced during the actual performance. Collectively the research presented here provides evidence that retrospective memories of thoughts and feelings may be vastly different from the thoughts and feelings that occur during specific days, events, and experiences. Therefore, it is important to consider how reflection can happen to capture thoughts and feelings as close to the experience as possible to generate reflective insights that are based on real-time experiences rather than memories.

Think Aloud as a Method for Reflecting on the Experience

TA as an approach to reflective practice could offer an alternative mechanism to facilitate reflection within the experience as it occurs. The TA protocol was originally designed as a data collection tool (Ericsson & Simon, 1993) to understand cognition in participants whilst performing tasks such as chess (Gobet & Charness, 2006), Scrabble (Tuffiash et al., 2007), and algebra (Cook, 2006). However, TA is now widely used in occupational contexts, including medical practice (Ericsson, 2007), whereby doctors, nurses, and surgeons are required to verbalise their decision-making processes in-action (Banning, 2008). Over the last 20 years, sport psychology researchers have used TA with athletes to examine expert-novice differences (Whitehead et al., 2015), the impact of stressors on thought processes in practice and competition (Whitehead, Taylor et al., 2016), how judges make decisions in gymnastics (Lee et al., 2019), and coping responses (e.g., Swettenham et al., 2020; McGreary et al., 2020; Whitehead & Jackman, 2021). In this respect, therefore, TA was not designed to promote reflection *per se* and it has been argued that verbalising thought processes using Level 1 and/or 2 verbalisations should not promote reactivity or metacognition (i.e., thinking about thinking) during the performance of a task (Fox et al., 2011). TA Level 1 verbalisation simply refers to the vocalisation of inner speech where the individual does not need to make any effort to communicate his or her thoughts. TA Level 2 verbalisation refers to verbalisation that involves the verbal encoding and vocalization of an internal representation that is not originally in verbal code. For example, verbal encoding and vocalisation of scents, visual stimuli, or movement. With this level of verbalisation, only the information that is in the participant's focus is to be verbalised. TA Level 3 verbalisation requires the individual to explain his or her thoughts, ideas, hypotheses, or motives (Ericsson & Simon, 1993). Level 3 verbalisation may trigger an individual to become more aware of these thoughts, also known as reactivity (Double & Birney, 2019). This promotes metacognition, which in turn could facilitate a process of reflection-in-action or in situ. Additionally, by recording these verbalisations as they occur, an individual can capture real-time thoughts, feelings, and reflection during the experience. In turn, the information gathered within these recordings has the potential to promote further reflective practices in situ and on on-action.

Think Aloud Within a Clinical Setting

Much like the origins of reflective practice, the roots of TA as a method to facilitate reflection can be found within clinical and educare settings. Indeed, the emergence of the importance of both mechanisms stemmed from the argument that practitioners in these sectors must develop the ability to engage in clinical reasoning as a fundamental aspect of their roles. Fonteyn and Ritter (2008) argued that clinical reasoning can be defined as the cognitive processes and strategies used to understand the significance of patient data, as well as to identify and diagnose patient problems. The ability to make effective clinical decisions is important to achieve positive patient outcomes in health care and necessitates the effective use of clinical reasoning, and especially so for complex care situations. The clinical reasoning process is dependent on a critical thinking approach and is influenced by attitudes and philosophical perspectives (McCarthy, 2003).

To compare clinical decision making in expert and novice nurses working in an Intensive/Critical Care Unit through TA, Hoffman et al. (2009) asked nurses to concurrently verbalise their thought processes as they carried out care during the first two hours of each shift. Using this approach, Hoffman et al. (2009) were able to identify how experts collected nearly twice as many cues as their novice counterparts. For example, experts collected cues around (but not limited to) electrolyte measures, chest movement, and muscle strength that were not collected by novices. In addition, the expert nurses were able to cluster these cues together to identify a patient's status when making decisions. Finally, the experts were more efficient and proactive in collecting relevant cues to anticipate problems, which may have helped them to offer more appropriate and proactive patient care.

Forsberg et al. (2014) used TA to study clinical reasoning with experienced nurses and their interactions with virtual patients. Through use of a computer-based simulation of real-life clinical scenarios, the researchers were able to identify three categories that were important to the clinical reasoning and decision making of these experienced paediatric nurses. These three categories were: *hypothesis orientated*; *high specific competence*; and *experience*. Through analysis of the TA verbalisations via a content analysis, data showed that these nurses followed patterns among the signs, symptoms, physical examinations, and laboratory tests to create a hypothesis during this clinical reasoning. In addition, nurses' experience was evident through TA, as the participants verbalised how previous and similar cases had helped them in their deductive reasoning when forming their hypotheses. This perhaps supports the notion that, within nursing, when engaging in metacognitive processing, individuals will use both inductive and deductive logic to simultaneously assemble and evaluate patient information and supportive evidence before making judgements about nursing care (Simmons et al., 2003).

TA has been used more widely in the domains of nursing (e.g., Banning, 2008), medicine (e.g., Borleffs et al., 2003), and physiotherapy (e.g., Atkinson & Nixon-Cave, 2011) in the training and development of practitioners' clinical reasoning and decision making. TA has been identified as a unique method to augment reflection-in-action for either the trainee practitioner or their mentor in any given situation. Specifically, Borleffs et al. (2003) developed an approach to clinical reasoning, called Clinical Reasoning Theatre (CRT), which involves students observing a senior doctor with his or her patient, whilst engaging in TA. During CRT, students are able to listen to and observe the doctor's clinical reasoning skills, and to understand why he or she asks particular questions. On the flip side, having a novice clinician or practitioner engage in TA during a clinical encounter can facilitate the metacognitive process, which in turn may aid self-reflection and discovery (and subsequent addressing) of ineffective thought processes (Atkinson & Nixon-Cave, 2011). Similarly, Banning (2008) adopted the same method as an educational tool to develop and assess clinical reasoning in undergraduate nursing students with some success. Specifically, Banning (2008) adopted the *TA seminar* (Lee & Ryan-Wenger, 1997), whereby student nurses are encouraged to verbalise their thoughts as they problem solve a case study or interpret a statement. It is proposed that the process of TA allows nurses to "verbalise their thought processes and rationale for the types of questions that they ask during a history or physical examination for the diagnostic hypotheses that they consider" (Lee & Ryan-Wenger, 1997, p. 102). Banning (2008) found that this TA approach developed skills in problem-solving, heuristics, verbalised reasoning, and enhanced the experience of using and applying clinical reasoning strategies.

Like nursing and educare settings, within the sport and exercise sciences, individuals must engage in formal education followed by professional training throughout which they have to learn to reflect on their craft and regularly engage in the process to support their growth. The development of metacognition skills (Banning, 2008) and making thoughts visible (Atkinson & Nixon-Cave, 2011) through reflective practice are thought to be key to augmenting sport and exercise practitioner expertise. The next section will, therefore, provide details of how sport has borrowed from allied fields of medicine and educare.

Think Aloud Within Sport Coaching

Within sport coaching, Whitehead, Cropley et al. (2016) were the first to pilot the use of TA as a method for reflective practice. In this inaugural study, six rugby league coaches attended a workshop through which they were educated and trained on the use of TA. Once coaches deemed themselves comfortable with using TA, they then engaged in the process within their usual coaching environment. Coaches were then instructed to listen back to their TA audio and reflect on their in-situ TA verbalisations and reflections. Following this, coaches attended a second workshop whereby they shared their reflections of engaging in TA. This study involved the process of reflection-in-action, on-action, and shared reflection amongst the coaches with social validation interviews revealing that coaches felt the process of using TA had promoted their self-awareness, which in turn improved their communication with their athletes. Furthermore, coaches reported an improvement in the delivery of their sessions, where they were able to make changes more quickly during the session itself rather than waiting until after the session to reflect.

Developing this tool further within sport coaching, Stephenson et al. (2020) examined the experiences of one soccer coach as he engaged in four coaching sessions using TA. The coach (Dave) within this study also completed a reflective diary and engaged in a retrospective interview to provide an overall narrative account of his experiences of using TA. Dave reported becoming more aware of his coaching practices and, in turn, also reported an improvement in his communication with his players and in the pedagogy and design of his sessions. Dave also, however, experienced feelings of apprehension and distraction, which offered further practical guidelines for coaches when considering the use of TA. For example, engaging in the process of using TA was deemed a new skill within itself requiring the coach to both attend to the athletes and the act of coaching the session in addition to stepping back and verbalising their thoughts and reflections as they occur. Consequently, coaches might find it difficult at times to attend to *both* TA and their coaching sessions and thus it is important that they are trained appropriately and are aware that TA itself is a learning process.

Swettenham and Whitehead (2021) introduced eight coaches from an elite soccer academy within the UK to TA. Following an introductory workshop, whereby coaches were able to engage in the process of TA, coaches were interviewed to glean an understanding into their perceptions of TA as a tool to aid reflective practice. Participants revealed that TA has the potential to develop three types of knowledge (professional, interpersonal, intrapersonal) deemed as vital for effective coaching practice. More specifically, the coaches reported developing an increase in self-awareness, becoming more aware of their biases, and an overall improvement in their ability to reflect and the learning outcomes associated with this (intrapersonal knowledge). Participating coaches also reported developing their communication with their athletes and also their relationships with their fellow coaches by sharing the TA audio (interpersonal knowledge) as a form of critical friend support. Finally, coaches were able to articulate how TA supported them with session design and general engagement in more effective coaching processes (professional knowledge).

The common thread between these studies appears to be that of the perceived increase in level of self-awareness generated through the process of TA. By thinking about one's own thinking during a coaching session, coaches are able to bring some potentially ignored or implicit thoughts to the fore, which supports coaches in making sense of and questioning (as a way of ensuring or improving their efficacy) their thoughts, decisions, and actions as they occur.

Think Aloud as a Tool to Use with Reflection-on-Action

Within most (if not all) examples provided within this chapter, individuals will also engage in a process of reflection-on-action following completion of their TA processes. TA can be used to support reflection-on-action or meta-reflections, whereby practitioners will engage with their TA audio to support further stages of reflection, arguably allowing for deeper, more critical insights. For example, within Whitehead, Cropley et al.'s (2016) study, all coaches engaged in a reflective practice workshop, which involved open discussions about coaches' use of TA within their practice and what they had learnt from the experience. More specifically, coaches were given a set of questions to consider (see Figure 10.1) and encouraged to explore how they would further engage in TA within their practice on what specifically they might focus on during their next coaching session to improve their practice. Coaches within Whitehead, Cropley et al.'s (2016) study reported the benefit of these workshops, with one coach stating, "It's [TA] really made me think about myself, everything really in terms of the players and thinking about a game situation, thinking am I doing right to intervene with the players now should I just let them get on with it" (p. 275). Similarly, student nurses engaging in a TA seminar (Banning, 2008) were given opportunities to engage in reflection-on-action by discussing their TA audio and decision making with

Figure 10.1 Questions Asked to Coaches Following the Use of TA in Practice

other students or faculty members. The above example from Whitehead, Cropley et al. (2016) was inspired by this earlier work. Within Stephenson et al.'s (2020) research, the participating coach used a reflective diary to capture reflection-on-action from his coaching sessions but also to reflect on the processes of TA and how this impacted his role as a coach.

It is permissible to argue, therefore, that for TA to be most effective it should be supported by the retrospective process of reflection-on-action. To further support this approach (e.g., TA followed by reflection-on-action) the use of critical friends who are able to engage in critical questioning and reflection would seem efficacious. Indeed, such mechanisms allow the individual who is reflecting to address potential blind-spots, to assist memory recall, and to further add to the depth of the reflective process, which is suggested to lead to more positive learning and practice outcomes (Cropley et al., 2015).

Practical Implications for Practitioners Considering the Use of TA Within Their Practice

1. **TA as a mechanism for reflection within practice does have potential limitations that practitioners should consider prior to engagement.** Engaging in the TA method requires individuals to engage in an activity that may feel slightly obscure and cause feelings of self-consciousness. These feelings of self-consciousness may lead to distraction from the task at hand and in turn, negatively impact of performance of the task. For example, the coach within Stephenson et al.'s (2020) research explicitly stated how TA

did become a distraction and he became extremely focussed on his internal thoughts rather than the activity in front of him. Introducing a new task that requires a person to engage in TA in addition to them attending to the task itself may result in a slowing down of action. An individual new to TA is potentially at the cognitive stage of learning (Fitts & Posner, 1967) and adding in an additional novel cognitive activity like TA could be difficult. It is, therefore, extremely important for an individual new to TA to practice engaging in the process in a safe setting, before applying it directly in applied practice. For example, Whitehead, Cropley et al. (2016) took their partici-pant coaches through a series of training exercises and allowed each coach to trial the use of TA in a workshop setting.

2. **When introducing practitioners to TA and encouraging them to use it for the first time, it is important that they do not think it is being used as a form of surveillance.** As with traditional methods, especially within education and training settings, reflective practice can be seen as a way to determine if an individual is 'thinking correctly' in line with the expectations of that specific discipline or organisation (Cushion, 2018). An individual's reflective practices could, therefore, become dishonest or moulded into what they think is required. To try and navigate this issue, allowing practition-ers to use TA on their own and keep their recordings to themselves, even in the initial engagement in TA is an important consideration. However, it is important to note that within medical professions where practitioners (e.g., nurses) are dealing with often life-threatening situations, it is perhaps important that reflections on reasoning and decision making are made visible (Banning, 2008).

3. **To date, there is no concrete or universal approach in which TA should and could be used as a reflection tool.** Across different disciplines, TA has been used to make clinical decision making and reasoning visible and aid medical practitioners in their reflective practices, and also, as shown through this chapter, to support sport coaches' reflections during their coaching prac-tice and when in competitive environments. When TA has been used to support reflection, a process of reflection-on-action has also been included, where TA audio is listened to, which creates a scaffolding approach to reflec-tion. It is, therefore, recommended that practitioners using TA to support reflection in-situ should also listen back and engage in some form of reflec-tion-on-action or a meta-reflection (reflecting on their reflections in situ) as a way of ensuring that learning is made sense of and used in subsequent action. In doing so, practitioners can overcome the issues associated with the memory-experience gap that may be linked to reflection-on-action, whilst also revisiting their in-action/in situ TA and reflection to confirm the out-comes gleaned from this process.

Section 4

Applied Case Studies

11 The Four A's Framework for Service Delivery and Reflective Practice

Amanda J. Wilding

The Back Story

Since the age of 11, my self-identity has been as a runner. Even at that age, I would reflect on my races; but not dissecting every inch of the race as my peers did. This form of post-race reflective dissection always seemed to me to be pointless because the moment had passed, and no two races were ever the same. I was interested in analysing the strengths and weaknesses of my upcoming opposition and wondering, depending on what I knew of them, what could potentially happen in the race. My concern was – when would I unleash my sprint finish? I came to think of this as my *super strength*, as I noticed that those who executed the same race plan every time were predictable, and therefore beatable.

At this early age, for me reflection was about increasing my own self-awareness and the ability to execute my race plan until that last 250 meters. From that point, I would make a conscious in-the-moment decision when to 'go' – to sprint for the finish – and in that way to be unpredictable. This form of embodied knowing (whereby experience, knowledge, and reflection occur simultaneously to cause a particular in-the-moment action; Sodhi, 2008) had a massive impact upon my development and success as an athlete and, without realising it, this in-action decision-making would form the basis of my future practice as a sport and exercise psychologist. Getting to this point of embodied knowing, however, was not simple, fast, or straightforward. I had to fail in order to learn what was right for me.

Years later, during my initial training as a sport and exercise psychologist, reflection was an integral part of the development process, yet the emphasis upon reflection-on-action I found, once again, operationally pointless. I would never set out to have a poor session thus, in my desire to be an effective practitioner, in advance of the session I would contemplate numerous ways of running a task. Reflecting by myself post-session was limited as 'I didn't know what I didn't know', consequently, I found it provoked anxiety. For example, as a neophyte trainee sport and exercise psychologist, it was not uncommon for me to reflect to the point where it seemed nothing had gone well, and the poor client had gained nothing. Reflection was a tick-box exercise about what went well, what

DOI: 10.4324/9781003198758-15

went wrong, and how you would change it for the next time, but if I knew that I would have done it the first-time round.

My reflective practice in those early days occurred in two stages. Stage one was my emotionally charged reflective account of what had occurred in the session under the guise of on-action reflection. In reality, it was a narrative of my failings. At this stage, I would focus on what I had missed out, what I had said versus what I wanted to say and my attempts to rationalise that 'as long as one person in the room was inspired, that was enough for me'. To some extent this was representative of the timing of the reflection. Initially, I would undertake my retrospective reflections in the car on the way home when I was either still filled with adrenalin and excitement, or with dread and fear of the feedback. All this would lead me to focus on the one thing that went wrong as opposed to a balanced analysis of the overall session. Thus, my reflection comprised of negatively evaluating haphazard random memories of the session as they occurred, rather than a systematic process that considered how important each random thought actually was, rendering the activity ineffective.

Stage one was a negative rollercoaster of emotions, in contrast, stage two was the aftermath reflection. It was a more balanced review of my performance within the session and how this impacted upon the thoughts and behaviours of the attendees. This occurred a couple of days later when I could reinstate my 'frontal lobe', thus some logical thinking. Here, I would consider what different responses I could have given to questions, or alternative tasks that would have been more effective and how I could be a better practitioner next time. However, the outcome of this always brought me back to the same point. As with my race reflections years earlier, the session was in the past; those clients got what I thought was right prior to the session. I could consider my thoughts in the planning of the next session, but it would be a different client, the same client on a new subject, or a new client and a new subject.

Evidently, my reflective process contained elements of Gibb's (1988) reflective cycle (description, feelings, evaluation, analysis, conclusion, and action plans), which is designed to enable learning from an experience. However, my reflective process occurred in a different order with some stages occurring simultaneously. For example, the *feelings* (thoughts about the experience) phase occurred parallel to the *evaluation* phase, which initially only focuses on the negative aspects of a session. It was when I spoke to others, in my aftermath reflection that I described and analysed, allowing me to make sense of what happened. For me, action planning occurred as an independent element due to the next client or session being different. Hence, unlike previous models, my reflective process occurred in two stages with the first being negative and isolating, and the second being undertaken with someone else, either knowingly purposeful, or because they simply asked, 'How did it go?'. This second stage could be empowering and motivating when a new perspective was gained, but at other times continued being a negative cycle of emotional responses. There was never reason or prediction of which one would occur.

Despite such realisations, to meet the requirements of my training programme in relation to my personal growth, I was required to show what I had learnt and how I had grown from the experience of reflection. As a result, if truth be told, I often submitted ramblings of what I knew the reviewers wanted to hear regarding my changes for future practice. With the thought that no two sessions were ever the same, I knew that none of my planned changes would ever see the light of day. Thus, retrospective reflection on the hard science of what was delivered – and beating myself up about the soft skills relating to how I delivered – was not an effective process for me as a practitioner.

Whilst it might seem I am averse to retrospective reflection; without it I wouldn't have found a form of reflection that works for me. It was retrospective reflection that made me realise it was not uncommon for clients who had had a competition at the weekend to want to reflect on their performance and on what they could now do to move forwards psychologically. This would cause me to change my planned session. During my training, I explained to my reviewers how I would arrive at sessions with a plan of action and intended outcomes but how, more often than not, they would never go according to plan and how frustrating this was for me. They responded that I was too rigid and controlled with my sessions and I had to learn to react and respond in the moment. To pre-empt this, I started carrying around an A4 ring binder of worksheets and activities organised under psychological headings such as confidence, anxiety, pressure, and motivation, so I could always respond in a meaningful, evidence-based manner to anything the client presented to me during the session. When I reported such changes to my sessions the reviewers subsequently fed back that this was the part they liked about my practice (although I had to learn to lose the folder).

The feedback then hit me. I had recognised the need to be adaptive in sessions, as opposed to carrying on with what was planned, even when the client needed a different session. Having the folder was insurance against my perceived lack of knowledge and ability to think on the spot. But, with time and confidence, I grew to learn the fine line between following a rigid session plan, in order to achieve the overall intended outcomes of a session and knowing when to change sessions to meet the emotional requirements of the client. I now refer to this as understanding and recognising the contextual sensitivities of the session – in-action reflection.

The session that led me to understand this skillset my reviewers were trying to develop in me was during a group session with a team of under-23 male football players. I was trying to show them how distractions affected their performance to the point where they couldn't recover physically or mentally. The session worked too well; the players over indulged in the distractors to the point where the session fell apart. They were getting nothing from the session as they were too distracted, and I felt I had lost control of the group. I left the room and came back with a completely new task and focus. I made them sit and write down their goals for the next game, what they wanted to achieve and why in order to calm them down ready to move on to their next session. I came out crying and beating myself up for failing, the players got the better of me. I had to change my session plan and so I must be a bad practitioner as I didn't plan it correctly. It was only when talking to my manager, I realised I had actually achieved my desired outcome. I knew distractions were definitely the issue, but now I also knew the underlying cause was the pack mentality. I realised this was a mirror of what would happen on the pitch, but what I hadn't prepared for was when it went too far. Without realising, by leaving the room and starting a new task I had not planned for, I had managed to regroup and change the content of the session to ultimately bring control back, as opposed to pushing on with the session I had planned despite it not working. It was the shared reflection that made me realise my growth as a practitioner, rather than my usual independent reflection which would have demolished my confidence.

It was retrospective reflection with an external person that made the process worthwhile. I felt vulnerable telling my manager I had failed, but he stopped me going into my usual emotionally charged reflection and helped me to be logical and factual about the situation. When I told the players the session was a massive success, they thought I was crazy. But I had learnt that a critical friend was my best form of retrospective reflection. In addition, by leaving the room and coming back again, I had proved to myself I had the awareness, confidence, knowledge, and ability to manage and adapt sessions in the moment. But most importantly, I had learnt that this in-action reflection was how I was going to make myself a better practitioner. Suddenly, reflection wasn't something that occurred after the session, it was a continuous cycle of thoughts which impacted upon behaviours before during and after the session. I realised reflection was a process and not a tick-box exercise. The critical friend reflection activity became a regular occurrence between me and the rest of the sport psychology department at the club and in part led to the development of a service delivery framework (The Four A's), which comprises layers of reflective processes.

In 2018, I was made project lead on a piece of research that was being undertaken by the sport psychology department at the football club. The project's aim was to consolidate the practitioner's applied experiences into a framework (now called The Four A's), that was evolved out of practitioners' lived experience and underpinned by an evidence base. The desire was to develop a framework for practitioners by practitioners working in industry, so it represented, as closely as possible, the realities of practise as opposed to lab-based research which failed to consider the context-specific exogenous factors.

The Four A's Framework for Service Delivery

The Four A's framework was originally proposed by sport and exercise psychology practitioner Malcom Frame. He wanted a framework which guided him through his practice whilst taking account of his personal philosophy, but more importantly, the client's perception of themselves, the demands of the task, the environment of operation and how, in combination, these affect behaviours.

Furthermore, as Head of Department in the football club, he recognised the need for a framework that could be used collaboratively within his team in the pursuit of a shared vision. Therefore, it had to be adjustable to multiple people, tasks, and environments. A team of psychologists (myself, Amy Spencer, Ana Soares and Greg Clark) subsequently developed the Four A's into a framework that acknowledges multiple philosophies, periodised programmes and intended session outcomes. It enables these parameters to be scientifically aligned and yet differ in their application by individual practitioners all at the same time.

The Four A's (Figure 11.1) now provides me with a framework for planning, implementing, and reviewing my service delivery. The client's agreed intervention outcome and components are represented by the black and white wheels on Figure 11.1. Specifically, the outer black wheel represents the client's notion of optimal performance. What constitutes optimal performance, for the client, is established by:

1. Assessing the client's needs.
2. Accepting the parameters of the service delivery contract.
3. Establishing the extent to which the client and their support network is willing to adapt and negotiate barriers.
4. Applying new ideas to existing practices.

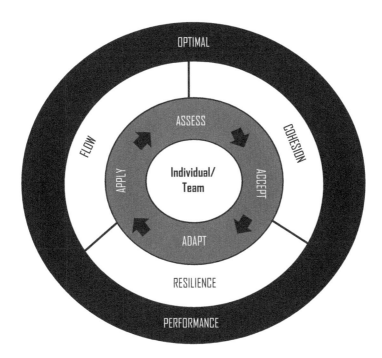

Figure 11.1 Example of the Four A's Conceptual Framework for Service Delivery

Essentially, optimal performance represents the primary psychological skill (construct) such as increased confidence, emotional intelligence, or arousal control. It should be changed to suit the requirements of each client and is, therefore, referred to as the key performance indicator (KPI), as it is the objective measure against which success will be determined. The construct must, therefore, be measurable through process, performance, and outcome goals (Figure 11.2).

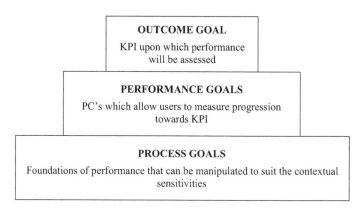

Figure 11.2 Goal Setting Pyramid for Establishing the Overarching Performance Outcome

Inside of this (the white wheel) sit the Performance Construct's (PCs), established by the client and me. These act as the scaffolding or secondary intervention elements that intertwine with the optimal performance construct, creating a complementary or multiple level intervention. The grey wheel holds the service delivery process which consists of four stages, each of which are referred to as a *Pass* to represent the movement through each of the A's (Assess, Accept, Adapt, and Apply), rather than getting psychologically stuck at one point. Each Pass is grounded in a philosophical paradigm which dictates the delivery content of the intervention package being applied.

The first two Passes (Assess and Accept), are conceptualised as cognitive orientated Passes whereby, concepts such as self-awareness and personal identity are explored by the client and developed into meaningful representations of behavioural intent (Henriksen et al., 2011). Their central focus is on understanding one's subjective reality and subsequent level of psychological literacy. This enables the development of case formulations and intervention goals.

Pass One: Assess

Like previous models (Boutcher & Rotella, 1987; Bull, 1991), Pass One forms the initial assessment part of the intervention programme. This involves collecting pertinent information via interviews, observations, and performance data. Only that which is relevant to the client's own development should be gathered.

According to Chow and Luzzeri (2019), self-evaluation when performed systematically increases self-awareness, meaning it allows for the adaptation of individual processes (thinking, feeling, and behaving). The purpose of this Pass is thus to increase the client's self-awareness of their lived experiences through self-reflection practices. To increase the client's self-awareness, key tools I use at this Pass are, active listening, paraphrasing, probing, and summarising to encourage the client to see themselves from a different perspective.

Due to clients often having perceptions and misconceptions of sport psychology, the second aspect of Pass One is to explore the origins and impacts of the client's barriers to use, which includes a process of revisiting past events to understand their current impact (psychodynamic approach). It is critical to discover the client's first point of knowledge and perception development, whether this was via mediated (peer reviewed) or unmediated sources of information, and the time lag between gathering such knowledge and working with them. This enables an understanding of where, when, and why barriers may have been formed, but also how changeable they may be.

To elicit the required information associated with this aspect of Pass One, I undertake a reflective recall interview with the client. Example topics discussed are:

1. Previous knowledge and experiences of sport psychology
2. Who is in their influential network
3. Barriers which have consciously developed.

We extract how these factors interact with cognitions, and therefore behaviours, to increase the likelihood of acceptance, adaptions and application occurring. Questions such as, 'Can you tell me about a time when you tried to use sport psychology?' and, 'Can you give me an example of a performance that didn't go as well as you hoped?' should be included. From such discussions the practitioner is then required to classify the client's barriers (conscious and subconscious) into intrapersonal (their own), interpersonal (being influenced by others) and structural (organisational issues) categories (Table 11.1). This process enables the practitioner to understand the antecedents to barriers (why the barrier has occurred), and therefore why they are now ready to negotiate them (to ensure I don't come up against the same issues, thus limiting the success of my intervention programme with the client).

Once this information is collected, I provide the client with a summary of information gathered. They go away and ensure they: (1) have shared all the information they believe is pertinent to a successful intervention programme; (2) check that the information I have captured has been done so in the intended (correct) manner; and (3) identify any changes in their self-awareness (*self-awareness evaluation*) through examining their thoughts, feelings, and emotions based on this reflective recall process and share them with me as the practitioner.

Whilst the client is undergoing this self-awareness evaluation (normally over the period of one week), as the practitioner, I also reflect upon the verbal and

Table 11.1 Example Classification and Negotiation of Client's Barriers

Barrier	Category	Impact	Antecedent	Negotiation
Receptivity towards sport psychology services.	Intrapersonal	Not open to new ideas.	Tried sport psychology when wasn't ready for it.	My decision to now use it. I want it.
My coach doesn't like sport psychology.	Interpersonal	Won't use it openly and share interventions with my coach.	Asked coach about controlling nerves and was told to just get on with it.	I think it will help me so will use it independently of my coach. It's my performance on the line.
My club don't have a sport psychologist.	Structural	Previously had limited access to a sport psychologist.	Didn't know if I could go outside the club.	I want to ensure I'm selected, so sourced my own practitioner.

non-verbal information collected which informs the subsequent intervention programme at Pass Three (adapt). From a practitioner's perspective, a key aspect of this initial Pass is encouraging case-based learning between psychologists. This can be achieved through peer review supervisions and best practice support networks. To achieve this, I have several colleagues as informal critical friend's whereby each of us brings a case study to a meeting and we discuss our findings from Pass One along with possible ways forward. This allows each of us to create an intervention beyond our own singular perspective, thus leading me to have a wider pool of ideas as we learn from each other, which I find helps me to identify blind spots in my own delivery.

These collaborative reflections between practitioners helped me to overcome my previous experiences of emotionally charged reflections. It allows me to describe and analyse the initial assessment to other people. Moreover, rather than planning future sessions based upon the need to overcome my own shortcomings highlighted by my on-action reflection, it allows me to better plan for the next stage based on the needs of the client.

Pass Two: Accept

Pass Two focuses on developing psychological acceptance, hence the client's ability to accept their existing cognitive processes at any given time and the practitioner accepting there is only so much they can do to change clients' thoughts and behaviours. Initially this Pass focuses on the results of the reflective recall interview. Interventions for negotiating barriers are established, but this Pass predominantly focuses on mindfulness practices based upon Western science as opposed to Eastern religions. Without undertaking such activities, the subsequent interventions have been found to be less effective as the client continues to consciously or subconsciously carry baggage which can prevent them from the act of acceptance.

Mindfulness encapsulates the notion of regulating one's emotional response through awareness of current thoughts and feelings. Western mindfulness was made the underpinning approach to Pass Two as, it enabled the client to have greater awareness of their thoughts and feelings in a given context and to accept them as opposed to trying to control them (Ong et al., 2020). Reflection in action is a key tool of this Pass as it ensures the user is present and aware of their personal resources and contextual sensitivities of the moment. Practitioners and clients alike must recognise the current situation, the task and the resources available, and sit with them (accept what cannot be changed. For example, accept that a referee's decision cannot be changed by shouting at them). To achieve this, mindfulness scripts, developed by Amy Spencer, (a practitioner trained in mindful sport performance enhancement protocols), were utilised to develop athletes' ability to show no self-judgment and increase a sense of well-being specifically in the sports setting.

These first two Passes are cognitive in nature as they involve raising, recognising, and recalling thought processes to ensure optimal cognitive functioning by the client. These are followed by two behavioural Passes (Adapt and Apply), which are underpinned by positive psychology and cognitive-behavioural approaches. The aim of these second two Passes is to develop the client's ability to perform optimally in any given environment through the manipulation of behaviours.

Pass Three: Adapt

Gardner and Moore (2019) note that mindfulness lessens the need for later response modulation strategies but does not fully eradicate the need for further interventions for all individuals. Thus, mindfulness in Pass Two alone may not be enough as an intervention to allow clients to optimise performance on a regular basis. Pass Three, therefore, focuses on an individual's ability to adapt to the task and/or environment. Adaptations could occur on multiple levels including physiological, psychological and behavioural. Based on the work of Weinberg and Gould (2019) the emphasis of Pass Three is thus placed on the acquisition process, which entails learning strategies and techniques. In this Pass, *cognitive interventions* (such as self-talk, self-affirmation statements, and imagery) are established along with *behavioural interventions* (e.g., breathing and progressive muscular relaxation) for performance enhancement. In addition, *positive psychology interventions* such as gratitude journaling, where the client self-reflects upon those incidences and people they are grateful for/too, are undertaken to enhance internal motivation. *Optimistic interventions*, including the client writing an account of their strengths and achievements to continuously reinforce their positives rather than weaknesses, are completed. Thus, the case formulation established in Pass One is operationalised in Pass Three.

Pass Four: Apply

The aim of Pass Four is to operationalise the self-awareness, reflection in action and interventions established in previous Passes, the purpose of which is to enhance or maintain optimal performance states. This can be achieved via manipulations of the environment, the task and/or individual/team (Renshaw & Chappell, 2010). The practitioner in this Pass is looking to ensure the client can apply the learnt skills in a variety of situations and circumstances (Araujo & Davids, 2009). In-action reflection should again be used to apply the right tool at the right time, whilst retrospective reflection facilitated by the practitioner should help the client identify new outcomes of actions. Such recognition of new thought processes and behavioural actions should lead to new cognitive assessments of the self, task, and environment, thus leading to a new cycle of development, meaning the process starts again.

Each Pass is designed to be flexible to the needs of each user but descriptive enough to ensure the end product of their delivery is measurable. It is predominantly the service delivery framework that is grounded in the notion of reflective practice, due to its cyclical design, which allows individuals within the process to account for their own constant development of cognitions and behaviours (perception to action). The reflective element of the framework aims to enable client's to ultimately self-govern their performance entities. Users of the framework must recognise the continuous flow of in-action decision-making due to the dynamic nature of sport as opposed to linear processes often represented in many current frameworks. It highlights firstly a constant need to assess levels of self-regulation in order to achieve optimal performance states through increased psychological literacy (Flett, 2015). Secondly, it examines the notion of psychological acceptance, to ensure clients are open to subjective reality in a non-judgemental way (Ong et al., 2020). Thirdly, interventions are devised to enable psychological adaptations to new experiences followed by an application Pass where all learnings from Passes One to Three are implemented to ensure users can optimise performance in any environment in which they are operating (Araujo & Davids, 2009).

Application of the Four A's Framework

In 2018, I was approached by an elite hockey player who was living between the South of England and Germany. Having previously played field hockey for England, Hannah was now playing in a German league. To fulfil the requirements of Pass One, an initial assessment was undertaken. Here, the athlete reported finding herself coming home from training in tears, feeling sick and not eating well. Yet she would always keep pushing herself to continue, while constantly questioning why she was putting herself through it. Hannah would feel anxious and nervous that she would make a mistake in training as this would usually result in being shouted at. She would always be checking the clock to see when training would be finished, and it would give her great satisfaction when she had finished (upon reflection this was her motivation to continue).

During the reflective recall interview, Hannah revealed she was aware of sport psychology from a young age. She was involved with some concepts but was not 'ready' for it (as referred to in Table 11.1). During the interview Hannah realised that at the time sport psychology did not work for her because she wasn't open to it. She didn't believe she really needed it. However, in the present day, following many late-night phone calls with her mum, they decided she needed some help and so they contacted me. Hannah reflected that ultimately, at this point, it was her decision, she wanted some guidance/assistance to continue her pathway to getting to the Olympics. She believed that was why this time she had a very successful experience with sport psychology, because it was her decision and something she wanted to do. For me, this confirmed that the reflective recall process was not only an important part of cognitive adoption but also is essential to breaking down clients' conscious or subconscious barriers.

Next, behavioural profiles of Hannah and her teammates were undertaken to better understand where her self-doubt originated. Additionally, we undertook a SWOT analysis to compare the impact of internal and external factors upon her current beliefs. These tasks allowed Hannah to increase her self-awareness. Of these, Hannah reported The DISC (dominant, influencer, steadiness, and compliance) personality test (Thomas International Ltd, 2020) as the most pertinent tool within this Pass, as it highlighted the behavioural styles of the coaching staff and teammates, thus helping her to recognise disconnect between her behavioural style and that of others.

The reflective recall interview was used to help Hannah recall times she perceived she was being shouted at. Her new awareness of others' behavioural style allowed her to now recognise a 'dominant behaviour style', in turn this changed her perception of the situation and therefore her cognitive response pattern. It allowed her to take personal emotions out of the situation and understand individuals' different communication styles. We then established reinforcement statements to remind her of their colour category (behavioural style in the DISC profile) such as 'she's not mean, just red'. Following the initial assessment, my notes and reflections, I created Hannah's case formulation which led to the identification of cognitive anxiety and PC's of arousal regulation, resilience and self-awareness. The case formulation based on Johnstone and Dallos' (2013) 5 P's, informed the subsequent intervention.

At Pass Two, in order to create a non-judgemental mental state, we discovered mindfulness was not enough to reduce the apprehension of making a mistake. I reflected on the use of a mindful approach and changed it to that of positive psychology which better suited my knowledge base. As a result, we created a super-strength profile through Lego play (the process of creating a tactile visual representation of her thoughts, feelings, behaviours, and barriers) which allowed Hannah to not only identify her strengths but also identify those factors which broke down her resilience. This allowed her to better understand her ideal arousal state and those factors which helped her move closer towards it and those which drew her away. This task was undertaken three times during the intervention in order to assess changes to her profile.

At Pass Three the cognitive-behavioural intervention package was consolidated. It was established based on Hannah's reflection that from a very young age, she caused herself much stress before training and England training camps, especially when packing her bag. She reported being 'enlightened' when I helped her realise that every little stressor took away a percentage of her best performance. Here, I gave Hannah a piece of paper and drew a circle to represent a pie chart that began with 100%. Those factors which took energy away from her performance were given a percentage. For example, the stress of packing her bag took 10% of her energy. Getting to the pitch and still having to apply tape, caused a potential performance drop of 20%. The list went on and before we knew it Hannah had increased her stress level to a point where performing was inevitably going to be difficult.

This was the first time I had done this task. The intended outcome of the session was to understand the role of stress, anxiety and arousal and it was an in-the-moment decision to draw all the factors that stressed Hannah out as a percentage, as she reflected upon them. This collaborative in-action reflection developed a new way of visually representing the impact of stress. Subsequently, performance routines to reduce stress and increase control, were put in place to replace the stressors.

Pass Four was a critical friend process. Sessions took place once a week, at least two days post-match, to enable emotion attachment to the performance to decrease. In these sessions we would review Hannah's use of the prescribed psychological methods. The review would start from the night before through to going to bed after a match. This gave us an overview of the whole performance which was broken down into blocks of performance. Hannah's cognitive state at each stage was discussed followed by a review of the utility of any tools utilised and those that could have been used and why. These were then depicted on the operational Four A's framework (Figure 11.3).

Benefits and Limitations of Applying the Four A's

For me, the Four A's Framework has provided a structure for creating a clear vision of what outcomes need to be delivered and in what order of priority. Integration of psychological approaches enables a wider range of psychological tools to be utilised, but with the freedom to do so in a way that suits my personality. However, I had to recognise my professional boundaries. For me, mindfulness was not an approach I was comfortable enough with to implement in a meaningful way. I believe this influenced Hannah's perception of its associated tools as she too reported it to have limited impact upon mental performance. This is where the collective practitioner sessions came to fruition as I was able to describe the sessions to others and evaluate what I was doing. Those trained in mindfulness then highlighted my blind spots and help me develop my practise. From a

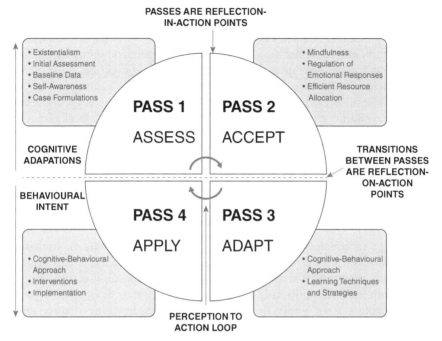

Figure 11.3 Operational Version of the Four A's Conceptual Framework for Service Delivery

practitioner perspective, this aspect of the framework raised my personal standards and love of reflection on-action. Within the framework, these collaborative on-action reflections now occur as a practitioner activity as the client transitions between Passes (as shown on Figure 11.3). The framework now operates with layers of reflection where everyone in the process reflects – client and practitioner alike. The type of reflection utilised is determined by the timing of use. In-action reflection is used during a psychology session to make it more appropriate/responsive to the client's needs. Reflection on-action is undertaken by the client and practitioner in between sessions and again for the practitioner as they transition the client between Passes.

The framework has thus proved to be an effective in-action reflective framework when working with clients. It helped Hannah to know herself as a player, where she can sit comfortably and what stretches her comfort zone. From this, she was able to be more reflective in sessions, provide me with more articulate information, rather than 'I don't know' answers to questions. From this, I could make more well-informed in-action reflections and thus effective adaptations to the sessions. Use of the framework has made me realise how both retrospective and in-action reflection are essential elements for clients and practitioners alike. Each Pass has a specific purpose, which gives me the freedom within each session to listen to the client, establish the theory associated with their language and create tools that reflect the client's narrative back at them so they can see themselves in a different light. It's given me a structure for explaining and justifying my skill set, tools, and subsequent application of these to others but without the need for rigid predetermined session plans.

From a client's perspective, I have found this approach facilitates their journey of discovery. Rather than psychoeducational sessions where each week one tool is taught and implemented, this process encourages clients to explore the constructs associated with each Pass and work out how it positively or negatively impacts their performance. For example, Hannah reported the Assess and Accept Passes as the most useful to her, as self-realisation allowed her to develop awareness of the antecedents of her performance barriers. Reflecting upon the creation of her super strength profile, Hannah stated:

> Using a stick man to represent my current beliefs surrounding my strengths allowed me to delve deeper into what was really happening. It encouraged positive thoughts around what constituted my personal strengths. Highlighting these strengths, helped reduce my nervousness before training and competition as the points could be referred back to. In a time of uncertainty prior to training, I decided to take this strategy a step further, upon reflection of my notes, I drew part of the stick man on my hand, this enabled me to look at this and remember all my strengths.

When I asked Hannah about the role of reflection, she said it stopped the emotionally charged negative thinking and allowed her to make balanced judgements about what was actually occurring. Commonly referred to as reflective thinking, it was this that allowed Hannah's positive thoughts to arise. Hannah's review of the Four A's also highlighted the importance of notetaking by the athlete. Creating her own logbook of the reflective recall interview and notes of the interventions meant Hannah could reflect upon the material in her own time and adapt the tools learnt to suit her needs in any situation – aftermath reflection.

Considerations for Effective Utilisation

If the framework is to be utilised effectively, several key considerations at the individual level must be addressed at the start of the service delivery process.

- Proposition questions need to be identified, so the parameters of operation are clearly framed. This ensures all those involved in the intervention programme have a shared vision of the task and resources available to them, as well as the limitations of practice within the environment in which they are operating.

- The framework is founded upon the integration of ideas which provides a holistic approach to service delivery. Feedback from key stakeholders such as other service delivery teams working with the athlete, should therefore be sought during each Pass. This allows the synthesis of key information and timely decisions that have widespread impact throughout the programme. It can minimise the chances for blind spots in delivery.
- Establishment of collective reflection. Practitioners are encouraged to operate as a formal or informal team, co-developing and sharing ideas for implementation at each Pass. The idea is to increase levels of support and morale between sport psychologists in order to, at the macro level, raise the professional standards of the industry, whilst at the micro level improving personal delivery through retrospective sharing of ideas and practices.

Recommendations for Others to Use the Four A's Framework

The Four A's framework is a cyclical continuous process, but one that ideally starts with 'Assess'. The initial assessment is the foundation of what is to come. A quality assessment goes beyond understanding the client's strengths, weaknesses, and ultimate goals. Of importance is understanding:

1. What is the client's motivation for coming to you at this point in time?
2. Was it their decision or one influenced by others?
3. What has their previous interaction with sport psychology been, and how long ago?
4. What are their expectations?

As a practitioner it is important to consider:

- The wider context of the sport, lifestyle, and social networks. It is these interpersonal and structural relationships that interact on both the conscious and subconscious level with a client, thus affecting their receptivity to you and your work.
- Your role in the relationship. Are you too invested due to your role within the sport? Will a lack of understanding of the sport help or hinder your ability to be effective? What bias do you bring to the table and therefore create blind spots? Critical friend discussions can help counteract the negative aspects of such questions as they offer you a mirror to see your own knowledge, boundaries, and skills.
- How much potential flexibility does the client display in terms of the time constraints versus perceived success of your delivery package?
- Where are the key pinch points of performance and how can you help adapt the client's viewpoint?
- How can you move clients away from a singular view of success and how to achieve it?

- Does the removal of philosophical paradigm rules from your practice allow you to be pragmatic to the needs of the client as opposed to true your own paradigm?
- Does the use of multiple paradigms prevent authentic practice?

Thus, it is highly recommended to ensure you have:

- A range of tools to both analyse the needs of your client from several perspectives and intervention methods which can be applied in a variety of ways.
- A critical friend to help you look at the situation from various perspectives.
- A comprehensive set of soft skills (e.g., active listening, empathy, and summarising).
- Let the client hear themselves through you, so they gain self-awareness and learn to see and hear themselves in a non-judgemental way.

Remember, in this framework you are there to help them discover their own blind spots, barriers, and constraints to performance success.

For you as the practitioner, the model can be used as a cycle of reflection. Using the same framework, you can reflect on yourself, the session, and its context, with a critical friend. This ensures balanced and productive development whereby you must accept things happen in sessions which sometimes make it a success and other times a failure. Subsequently, how can you adapt your knowledge, skills and interventions and apply them more effectively with a range of clients? This process of reflection allows acknowledgement, growth, and development as part of the journey. It doesn't mean what came before is worthless; it's just part of the upwards cycle of development.

Summary

The 'old way' of retrospective reflection didn't work for me as a practitioner. Being an ethnographic action researcher, I embed myself in the environment. Thus, as a practitioner, my postpositive philosophy allows me to recognise that biases exist in terms of me working with a client, but also their coming to sport psychology. Reflection-in-action thus allows me to continually assess how the client's values and beliefs merge and clash with mine, thus influencing the in-the-moment effectiveness of my work. Acknowledging, understanding, and responding to this allows me to account for these processes in real-time.

Reflection-in-action, for me, is therefore most effective as it directly influences success or failure of any given session. Reflection-on-action is more formulaic, a retrospective account of practical outcomes, which allow for emotional processing. Reflection-on-action is my own cathartic 'beat myself up' process. It wasn't as productive for me, in comparison to the reflection in situ, until I recognised its role and function. No two situations are ever the same, so emotionally charged reflection doesn't help me or the client. The Four A's is a framework that works for me in the moment of operation. I would be interested to know how you, the reader, have interpreted, tried and adapted the Four A's framework for your own practice.

12 Finding My "Dharma"

Critical Reflective Practice During a Mid-Career Transition from Academia to Applied Exercise Psychology

Paula Watson

Introduction

> "Life is guided by a changing understanding of and interpretation of my experience. It is always in process of becoming."
>
> (Rogers, 1961, 1990, p. 28)

When I was first approached to write this chapter, I responded with "I'd love to, but I'm not sure I do enough (formal) reflective practice". I regularly supported students to develop critical reflection skills and I enjoyed marking reflective narratives. I had also engaged in reflection during formal leadership and teaching courses, and completed written evaluations after most lectures (i.e., "what went well, what could I improve for next year"). But as far as I was concerned, "formal" reflective practice had not featured in my working life for the best part of 15 years.

My initial hesitancy was perhaps driven by a fear that I had never really done reflective practice "properly". Like many in the sport and exercise sciences, I had duly referenced Gibbs (1988) when mentioning reflective practice in academic papers. But had I ever read Gibbs' (1988) "Learning by Doing" book for myself? And had I ever made a priori use of Gibbs' cycle to guide my own reflective practice? I would be lying if I said I had. Furthermore, definitions of reflective practice were becoming increasingly complex (e.g., Knowles et al., 2014b), making it challenging to know whether my view of reflective practice was correct. Supposing I was one of the "unconsciously incompetent" practitioners who mistakenly believed their reflections were actually reflective practice (Cropley & Hanton, 2011).

Having reflected further on what reflective practice means to me, I soon got over my imposter syndrome and realised I have been reflecting more than I thought throughout my career. I may not have always engaged in reflective practice in the formal sense, but I constantly engage in reflective dialogue (be it in thought, in writing, or in conversation) driven by a curiosity to understand myself, others and the world around me. My initial introduction to reflective

DOI: 10.4324/9781003198758-16

practice was 18 years ago, when I learned to reflect as a means of building self-awareness and empathy during an M.Sc. client-centred counselling skills module. I am not sure whether I was not taught about Gibbs' (1988) Reflective Cycle or whether I actively disregarded it, but I quickly embraced reflection as a personal and creative process, grounded in authenticity. My reflection is mostly critical in nature (Anderson et al., 2004), involving a process of observing my inner and outer worlds, seeking to understand what is going on and why, and letting myself grow as a practitioner from what I learn.

I see parallels between the process through which reflection instigates change and humanistic psychology (thus explaining the importance of reflection within client-centred counselling). In humanistic psychology, understanding, self-acceptance and experiential learning are at the heart of personal development. In his 1961 book "On becoming a person" (Rogers, 1961, 1990), the psychologist Carl Rogers described how "truly" understanding ourselves or another person might be perceived as a risky process, as such deep understanding will invariably lead us to change. In critical reflective practice, it is the conscious effort to deeply understand our experiences (e.g., why we behave a certain way) that forms the foundation of transformational learning. This understanding may be achieved after a single reflection or multiple reflective episodes building on connected ideas over days, weeks, months or even longer. Through asking ourselves *why* we behave as we do, we are able to identify and challenge habitual processes, question their origin and explore alternative perspectives. This increased self-awareness may lead to affective change (e.g., a deeper sense of empathy for clients), new cognitive strategies (e.g., a conscious effort to be more mindful of the way we communicate), and/or practical actions (e.g., developing a clearer information sheet for clients). Thus, through enabling us to reach a deeper understanding of our experiences, critical reflection serves as an instigator for personal and professional growth.

In this chapter, I will reflect on the role critical reflection has played during my transition from academia to applied exercise psychology practice. After 17 years working in higher education, I recently gave notice to say I would be leaving academia on 31 August 2022. As I write this chapter, I am in the early days of that notice period. I have an applied exercise psychology company in place (https://madeuptomove.co.uk) and a few ideas brewing, but I am open-minded for what lies ahead. I will first share my story and the role reflective practice played in my decision to leave full-time academia, before outlining my approach to critical reflection in more depth, supported by examples from my early career to the present. The chapter is interspersed with excerpts from my written reflections (in handwritten, typed, and e-mail forms) as a means of illustrating how reflective writing contributed to my journey of self-discovery.

Finding My "Dharma"

> "Our heads might try to convince us that we've only ever made the best choices, but our true nature – our passion and purpose – isn't in our head, it's in our hearts."
>
> (Shetty, 2020, p. 117)

For most of my adult life, I have been passionate about both psychology and physical activity. After graduating from my M.Sc. Sport Psychology in 2004, my real desire was to find an applied role where I could support people in developing a healthy relationship with physical activity. In those days, there was little in the way of structured training pathways for exercise psychology, and after dabbling in a few (unsuccessful) job applications for community physical activity roles, I applied for a research role to develop a family-based child weight management programme at my local university. I remember thinking "I'll do it for the year and see how it goes". As it turned out the role was pretty applied in nature, and I found myself working with a team of amazing staff to run a successful child weight management service for families across Liverpool (GOALS, Watson et al., 2015). For 3+ years in this "practitioner-researcher" role I resisted well-meaning pressure that "I must do a PhD" and what I am missing is that "rubber stamp". But as I acclimatised to the academic environment, I soon started to see the value in research for myself. I completed my PhD in 2012 and became a lecturer in Exercise and Health Psychology the same year.

Fast-forward to October 2021, I'd published 30+ applied research papers in physical activity behaviour change, I'd recently been promoted to Reader, and was working three days in higher education and two days in applied practice (having switched to a part-time contract in June 2020). My overt narrative was "I loved what I did", but I rarely stopped to look beneath the surface at what this meant. Why would I? I was in a great job, working with a great team and still passionate about physical activity and psychology. Yet I was sensing a frustration brewing inside. Despite (or perhaps because of) enjoying many aspects of my work, I was spreading myself so thinly that I had little time to invest in the projects that mattered most to me.

During this time, I was reading "Think Like a Monk" by Jay Shetty (2020) who, having lived as a monk for three years in India, discovered his "dharma" was not to be a monk himself but to share the monks' wisdom with others. *Dharma* is a Sanskrit term that cannot be defined by a single English word, but Shetty suggests your "calling" is the closest our language comes. "When your natural talents and passion (your *varna*) connect with what the universe needs (*seva*) and become your purpose, you are living in your dharma" (Shetty, 2020, p. 94). Within the field of sport and exercise psychology, this might be likened to the process of individuation (McEwan et al., 2019), whereby the practitioner develops a fit between their self and the context they work in. With this comes a sense of meaning, authenticity, and fulfilment.

As I navigated the tricky maze towards understanding my own dharma, Shetty's (2020) writings became a trigger for critical reflection, self-insight and "ah ha" moments. I began to notice and listen to sensations in my body. I noticed the excited "buzz" I would feel in my stomach before and after psychology sessions with individual clients, or in visiting a physical activity session in the community. Reflecting with my clinical supervisor one day, she asked, "Why do you sound apologetic when you say you want to work with individual clients?" It dawned on me; I was worried about judgement from other people. I was fearful of breaking the rules of mid-career progression, where you were expected to move from depth to breadth, making a difference not through your own delivery but through strategic management and supervision of others. I was trying to live up to what I *thought* others thought of me, regardless of what they actually thought or of what I felt to be important (Shetty, 2020). It was not until I had this conversation with my supervisor that I realised the incongruence between my head and my heart (see excerpt 1 for post-conversation reflections). I was also beginning to realise how unviable it was to be both a high performing academic and to make the headway I was hoping for in applied practice.

Excerpt 1. Taken from e-mail to Supervisor, 16 September 2021

> Dear [supervisor]
> Just wanted to say a huge thank you for the time you took to listen and talk things through yesterday. You made some pertinent – and accurate – observations of my passion for applied work and it's helped me reflect how this has always been there . . . for as long as I can remember I've looked at clinical or sport psychologists thinking "I'd love to do that (tailored to an exercise/physical activity context)", but being held back by a misplaced belief that I'm not capable or qualified, or perhaps a fear of change/leaving the security of a career I have so much autonomy in and do really love aspects of. But our conversation made me reflect on this in a different light, and I believe I do have relevant skills, knowledge, and experience to work within an NHS weight management service for instance. I know I'm excited about that idea, as I couldn't sleep for my mind buzzing with possibilities about what a 5-year plan might look like if I take out the equation that the "secure employment" always has to come from academia! . . .

One Friday evening, the reality of my work situation hit me. Through tears I searched Google for "spreading myself too thin" and "how to help with overcommitment". The next day, I sat at my laptop, and I reflected. That 7-page document is now saved as my "Over-Commitment Treatment Plan", with a running header of "time to be honest with myself". I reflected on how I was feeling, what it was I "really wanted", and the fears that were holding me back. Afterwards I felt a clarity I had not experienced for ages, and I knew from that point something needed to change.

A couple of months later, I was inspired after watching an experienced sport psychologist present at a conference about his multi-level role in an elite sports organisation. I eagerly typed notes in my phone while I listened (excerpt 2). That night, I remember vividly not being able to sleep with excitement and ideas running through my head – how could I create a similar psychology role within a physical activity and health environment?

Excerpt 2. Taken from phone reflections, 30 November 2021

> This appeals. This resonates. Getting away from the computer. People-focused. Facilitating change. Relationships. Vision and creativity. Developing others.

Two days later, as I was cycling to work, my head caught up with my heart. I thought to myself, "I keep saying I've got all these ideas but it's time and capacity holding me back". And I explicitly remember, at the traffic lights, thinking, "Why don't I make myself that time?" It suddenly seemed so obvious, yet it had never dawned on me before. For the first time, I allowed myself to visualise what life would *actually* be like if I left academia and pursued my dharma in applied exercise psychology. From that moment, a lightness and sense of excitement came over me.

Critical Reflection as a Transformative Process (A Humanistic Model)

As I told my story in the preceding passage the transformative nature of the reflective process became evident (e.g., "I began to notice", "I realised", "I felt a clarity"). Multiple formal (e.g., written reflection, supervision) and informal (e.g., e-mail, phone notes) reflective processes contributed to my deeper understanding of self, which in turn instigated a process of change. Whilst the impact of reflection was on my practice, the triggers for reflection were diverse (e.g., bodily sensations, supervision, conference presentations), highlighting that reflection relevant to practice might be triggered by experiences from both within and outside the practice context (e.g., a reflection triggered by a podcast might influence how I later conduct a consultation with a client). In particular, shared reflection with a skilled individual (clinical supervisor) led to a "critical learning moment" that helped me better understand my underlying tendencies, why these were occurring and the effects they were having on my practice. To provide further insight into the role of critical reflection throughout my journey, I will first consider my early experiences of reflective practice, before outlining the humanistic model of reflection that underpins my approach (illustrated with examples from my recent career transition).

Early Experiences of Reflective Practice

Back in 2004 as an M.Sc. student, I engaged in critical, unstructured reflections in a handwritten journal that I still pull out today when teaching students, the "power" of reflective practice. I was doing a research study on obesity, and I wanted to learn what it felt like to live with obesity. I reflected on everything – from the research process to TV programmes, to everyday experiences (e.g., excerpts 3–4).

Excerpt 3. Taken from reflective journal, 13 April 2004

Coming back from London yesterday I was sitting next to a fat lady. I had half a seat for 4 hours. Initially, I thought "great, I can't really get much closer to her world than this". But as the journey went on my patience began to dwindle and I found myself getting increasingly annoyed with the lack of personal space . . . I wonder how she felt? Did she feel guilty/embarrassed taking up one and a half seats when I only had half? If so, she didn't show it . . . to think she must feel as uncomfortable as I felt that journey all the time – squashed, hot, overlapping others' personal space (if I had sat as close to a slim person who I did not know, we would have been quite aware of the intrusion of others' personal space, and somehow it would have been more awkward).

Excerpt 4. Taken from reflective journal, 12 May 2004

I've been working through my First Steps in Counselling Book and realised this journal is largely about exploring my own prejudices. When conjuring up a hypothetical counselling group in my mind I realised they were all white. And they were all slim. What does that say about me? Slim and white is obviously what I consider to be the norm. How might this affect my relationship with participants who are obese in an in-depth interview?

I discovered ill-founded beliefs and assumptions that had previously gone unchallenged, and, in line with Rogers' (1961, 1990) humanistic theory, I noticed how this process of discovery was leading my attitudes to change. I stopped believing obesity was the result of lazy individuals who ate too much and moved too little (which was the view I had unconsciously absorbed during my childhood). I began to understand the influence of social inequalities on health education, opportunity, and cultural norms, and I observed for myself the genetic disparities in metabolism and fitness (excerpt 5).

Excerpt 5. Taken from reflective journal, 16 July 2004

I've always, from experience, stood by the fact that activity is what matters [for weight maintenance], rather than exercise per se. But now I've met [participant], who is classified as obese, eats salads every day with a minimum intake and "never stops". She is a lively person and says she feels physically fit yet cannot lose the weight. She says people (including herself) cannot understand why she's fat . . . I could feel how frustrating this must be and felt almost guilty about my weight/health given all the crap I eat . . .

Eighteen years on, reflecting on the language and views I expressed in my early training is uncomfortable. Both I, and the world, have changed since then. With a growing recognition of issues that affect equity, diversity and inclusion, we are more aware of our unconscious biases and we better understand their environmental sources (e.g., my automatic imagery of people who are white and slim was most likely driven by the fact I had spent most of my life surrounded by people with these characteristics (Eberhardt, 2019). It is no longer acceptable to use non-person-centred language, and even in my private reflections "fat" would not come close to featuring within my descriptions of others. Reflecting on these historical journal entries does, however, highlight how powerful and permanent critical reflection can be when we open ourselves to the possibility of personal growth. Had I not reflected so honestly, I would not have learned the real meaning of empathy, and the importance of putting myself in the shoes of others. Thus, I experienced for myself the "curious paradox" of which Carl Rogers (1961, 1990) spoke, "When I accept myself as I am, then I change" (p. 19). I didn't know it at the time, but I was documenting critical turning points in my career that continue to influence the person and practitioner I am today.

Re-Igniting Reflection

Since returning to applied practice 18 months ago, I have re-ignited my love affair with reflection. As well as engaging in formal reflective practice through written journals, 1-to-1 coaching and clinical supervision, I've learned extensively through less formal, more "incidental" reflection, triggered by peer discussions, e-mail correspondence, supervising others, reading books and listening to podcasts. Whilst critical reflection requires conscious and active engagement (i.e., we need to be aware we are doing it and invest cognitive resource in the process), my experiences have led me to believe critical reflection may not always be "intentional". For example, some of my most pertinent reflections happen whilst cycling to work or talking to colleagues. Whilst I may not set out with the explicit intention to engage in reflective practice, it is the conscious and active processing of these reflective thoughts that invariably leads to change.

My reflection continues to be humanistic and "free-flowing", as I feel being overly prescriptive risks missing what matters or may block the critical depth needed for growth. The fact my reflection is unstructured, and often incidental, does not, however, mean it lacks purpose or direction. Regardless of whether I am reflecting formally or informally, my reflective practice is underpinned by three stages (see Figure 12.1):

1. **Take notice.** At the heart of reflective practice is the premise that: (a) experience is a rich source of knowledge; and (b) we need to stop and think about our experiences if we want to learn from them. This requires me to notice, or observe, what's going on inside and around me. My stimulus for reflection could be anything that sparks a feeling or thought in my mind related to my personal and professional development (e.g., a session with a client, a collection of thoughts, previous reflections, a podcast). It could be a nagging but unexplained emotion, or something as innocuous as walking past someone

on the street. When I embrace a reflective mindset and I am open to personal growth, I see opportunities everywhere.

2. **Be curious.** Once I've noticed something, I think more deeply about it (either alone or with others) to better understand what it means about me and my practice. Although I do not always consciously ask myself or write the question down, the overarching curiosity that drives my reflection is "What's going on here and *why?*" I might ask "Why am I feeling this way?" "Why did I behave that way?" or "How might my client have been feeling when we talked about X?" If I am reading a book or listening to a podcast, I might ask "How does this relate to my own situation?" I may return to the "take notice" stage and look for patterns or connections with my previous behaviours, e.g., "Are there any similarities between this event/thought/feeling and others I've noticed?", "Am I noticing any particular traits or tendencies in myself and how do I feel about these?"

3. **Allow yourself to change.** Once I've crafted some sense of the event, I find this invariably leads to new insights. For personal and professional growth however, I need to be open to change. This change might require pro-active actions (e.g., asking myself "What could I do to move forward?" or "What might I do differently next time?"), or change may happen more subtly over time (e.g., changes in attitude as a result of viewing a situation from another perspective). If change does not come readily, I might return to the "take notice" stage and ask myself "Has reflecting on this experience helped me see things differently or challenged my assumptions in any way?" I might write down actions to take forward or consider what I can learn from this experience to grow as a practitioner.

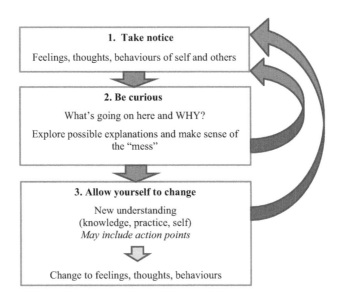

Figure 12.1 Humanistic Approach to Reflective Practice (in a parallel process, this illustration was crafted as I made sense of my reflective approach through writing this chapter)

This three-stage process can be applied both in-action (whilst I am still able to influence events around me) and on-action (once the event has passed), although the speed and depth of the process will invariably be different. Although the stages can function as a linear process, there is continual interaction between the stages, as I "take notice" of new discoveries that emerge and I reflect back on previous reflections to allow my thoughts to develop over time ("multiple staged reflection", Anderson et al., 2004). In order to reach stage three, critical reflection requires an open mind from the start. A mind that is too closed, is trying to cling to a fixed identity or is afraid to explore and understand what is *really* going on, will rarely get past stage one. Reflection at this level will likely be limited to surface-level description and is unlikely to reap the benefits that can be achieved when we take the risk of truly understanding (Rogers, 1961, 1990) and allow ourselves to change.

Critical Reflective Practice Examples

In this section, I will share three examples of the reflective process outlined in Figure 12.1 to illustrate the role different forms of reflective practice played in the development of my *knowledge*, *self*, and *practice* as I transitioned from full time academia to applied exercise psychology practice.

Example 1: Critical Reflection to Develop My Knowledge

TAKING NOTICE

I had been listening to a podcast with Sanjay Rawal talking to Dr Rangan Chatterjee about how running can be a spiritual experience (Chatterjee, 2019). Sanjay was talking about his experiences of running with the Navajo Indians and how they experienced running as a celebration of life, a teacher, and a means of connecting with the planet around us. Quite different from the Western approach to running characterised by timekeeping, headphones, and statistics.

BEING CURIOUS

This got me thinking, if we "ran naked" without the distractions of running watches, online comparisons, and self-imposed goals, might running in an urban UK environment be equally spiritual? If I wanted to help others with this, I first needed to explore this idea for myself. I decided every time I went for a run that month I would "run naked" (i.e., no distractions), reflect-in-action to explore my feelings and thoughts, then write my reflections in a journal to explore how the process was impacting me.

ALLOWING MYSELF TO CHANGE

Despite telling myself I was using my running watch "out of curiosity", when I "ran naked" I began to notice how much my emotions and behaviours were being controlled by the data on my watch (excerpt 6). The watch was no longer there, but the habitual thought patterns and behaviours remained. I noticed the habitual desire to put the watch on, to press "start" to tell me I could go, and "stop" to tell me I had finished. I experienced a sense of relief when I habitually went to check my pace and was unable to – there was no longer a risk of disappointment if I was not going as fast as I had hoped. And I noticed the internal "pull" that prevented me slowing down, talking to others, stopping at road crossings – because this would slow the pace on my watch. I discovered the watch was sucking so much pleasure from the joy of running!

Excerpt 6. Taken from Run Naked Journal Entry 1, 21 February 2021

> Immediately I felt a sense of freedom, it's a bit like when your phone runs out of battery and you don't have a charger – perhaps you're gutted at first, but then what comes with that is a sense of freedom that you can't be interrupted from life by technology.

The pros and cons of fitness technology are well-reported in the psychological literature (Nuss et al., 2021), but until I reflected on my own experiences, I was less aware of the mechanisms through which wearing a watch might impact on running behaviour itself. As the month went on, I noticed these habitual responses dissipate, in line with what I would have predicted through *Habit Theory* (Orbell & Verplanken, 2020) (since I was breaking the internal associations I had formed between specific events (arriving home) and my behaviour (pressing stop on my watch)). Reflecting on my own exercise experiences was helpful both in applying theory to "real life", but also in increasing self-awareness and alerting me to potential bias when working with clients (e.g., just because I perceived the desire to check my watch as a controlling pressure, does not mean everyone will perceive it this way). In case you are wondering, one year later and I rarely wear my running watch.

Example 2: Critical Reflection to Develop My Self

TAKING NOTICE

As I moved into the applied exercise psychology world, imposter syndrome became my "Jack-in-a-Box". I became overly risk averse and somewhat paranoid about slipping out of (what I perceived others perceived should be) my boundaries. I was also experiencing an exponential learning curve (through reading professional development literature, and working with non-academics, psychologists, and experts by experience) which was leading to a serious case of "the more I knew, the more I realised I didn't know".

BEING CURIOUS

In a process of staged reflection, I engaged in various forms of informal (e.g., conversations with peers, delivery of workshops) and formal (e.g., written reflections, supervision) reflective practice to explore the reasons behind my insecurities and to better understand my "true" competencies.

ALLOWING MYSELF TO CHANGE

I realised my insecurities were cultivated in a strange paradox of being an "academic expert" whilst at the same time feeling like a "neophyte practitioner". Through reflecting with my clinical supervisor, I became aware of the deficit-model through which I had been viewing myself (excerpt 7). Some of this was grounded in a hang-up I seemed to have about my title of "Sport and Exercise Psychologist". Through some illogical thought process, I was neglecting my many years' experience of working in weight management and providing health behaviour change interventions, and instead focused on the fact my title says "sport and exercise" so "that's all I can do". I also felt a "fraud" as I had been awarded Health and Care Professions Council (HCPC) Registration through the grand-parenting route (without engaging in the formalised period of supervised practice that trainees go through today). And whilst I had engaged in relevant professional development, including training in counselling skills, motivational interviewing, solution-focused therapy and mindfulness (the latter from a personal perspective) I had this overwhelming feeling that I was "self-taught". I realised then it was time to put a lid on my imposter syndrome and focus on my competencies rather than my title (as recently advocated by Dooley & Farndon, 2021).

Excerpt 7. Taken from reflective journal, 19 January 2022

> I'm always thinking what I'm missing rather than what I <u>can</u> do . . . in recognising I am not an "expert" in the world of practice, I've gone to the other extreme – and written myself off as a complete beginner . . . I'm actually presenting an untrue picture of myself as being less experienced/capable/qualified than I am . . . This isn't going to help me make a way in the applied world, it isn't going to help me "sell" my services to others, and it could possibly be off-putting for trainees coming looking for supervision.

Example 3: Critical Reflection to Develop My Practice

TAKING NOTICE

Exercise psychology as an applied profession (outside of academia) is in its infancy. There is a lack of awareness amongst the general public and potential employers about what exercise psychologists can offer, and training pathways are currently informed by a combination of sport psychology practice in high performance environments and academic physical activity behaviour change research. There is also a disconnect between the evidence base (dominated by non-psychologist-delivered behaviour change interventions), employment opportunities (I have never yet seen an advert for an exercise psychologist) and what many of us training and practicing as exercise psychologists aspire to do (psychological therapy with clients). Yet I have always felt exercise psychology has huge potential to make a difference in a world in which a lack of physical activity (Guthold et al., 2018) and unhealthy relationships with physical activity (MIND, 2022) are an increasing problem.

BEING CURIOUS

I wanted to better understand how I might be able to "find a place" for applied exercise psychology, and what implications this had for my approach to practice and how I supported trainees. How could I connect what I believed to be the *varna* (talent and passion of exercise psychologists) with the *seva* (universal need to develop healthy and sustainable relationships with physical activity)? One of the most pertinent reflections within this process was a 12-page reflective journal entry entitled "what am I learning about exercise psychology?" (Written three weeks after starting work with my first individual client).

ALLOWING MYSELF TO CHANGE

By the end of the 12 pages, I was able to draft a visual diagram of what I perceived to be two ends of an applied exercise psychology continuum (Figure 12.2). Mapping out my reflections in visual form helped me make sense of what I had written and provided me with a better understanding of how to move forward. I had a better idea how my skills could align with what clients need, and I could better support my trainees to target their development towards the type of work they want to do.

The left-hand side of the diagram (Figure 12.2) I labelled as "prevention", in which psychological principles are used in a covert/implicit manner to underpin physical activity behaviour change interventions (i.e., to promote adherence and a healthy relationship with physical activity). This is where the evidence base is most extensive and much of my applied research has focused (e.g., Buckley et al., 2020; Cowley et al., 2021; Watson et al., 2021). Prevention is about breadth rather than depth, and the involvement of psychologists is most likely to be in training and supervising others (e.g., exercise instructors) to integrate psychological principles into their practice, rather than psychologists delivering themselves. Individuals in this space may not perceive themselves to have a psychological "problem" with physical activity, therefore may be less likely to take up individual psychological support.

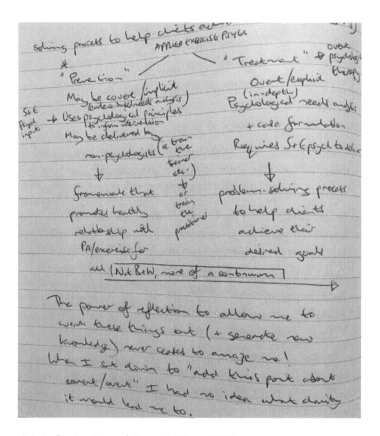

Figure 12.2 Reflective Journal Entry, 19 June 2020

The right-hand side I labelled as "treatment", in which clients explicitly seek psychological support for a physical activity-related problem (e.g., exercise dependence, complex weight management). This is the "depth", and requires psychological knowledge, counselling skills and the ability to formulate and tailor interventions to client needs (see Johnstone & Dallas, 2014, for a discussion of formulation in psychology). Individuals in this space may need more support than can be provided through standardised physical activity behaviour change interventions, and as such may benefit from therapeutic support from exercise psychologists.

Reflections on Reflection (Key Learnings)

Writing this chapter has brought home to me the deep and wide-ranging benefits of reflective practice. If I am ever in doubt of this, I just need to ask myself "how would things have been different if I had not engaged in reflective practice over the past 18 years?" Through the process of writing, I have been able to reflect on the aspects of reflective practice that have helped (and challenged) me most and would like to share key learnings in a quest to help others reap the benefits of critical reflection.

1. **Writing is important in developing my understanding.** Whilst I continuously derive learning from multiple sources of reflection, writing for me is the tool that brings sense and structure to these complex thought-processes. When writing reflectively, I rarely think about what I want to say before I write. The process of writing *is* my means of making sense of the situation.

2. **As a reflective practitioner, my thinking continually evolves over time.** This can be a scary prospect when writing reflections (particularly if they are to be shared in the public domain). It can be helpful to remember that the reflective process itself is a learning curve, and reflections are only ever a snapshot of our thinking at one moment in time. My thoughts may be different next week, and this chapter is just one in a stream of multiple reflections that will contribute to my continued growth.

3. **Being honest is the essence of critical reflection.** I sometimes hear trainees express a "fear" of critical reflection as writing something down makes it "true". This is a curious paradox, as the *avoidance* of reflection can actually lead us to carry around irrational thoughts that we perceive to be true (e.g., "I am less competent than peers who underwent more structured training pathways"). It is only through laying these thoughts on the table we see they are untrue and develop an alternative view (e.g., "I am a competent practitioner with many years of relevant education and experience"). If I am not honest, I cannot understand, and I cannot grow.

4. **Reflection is first and foremost a personal process.** I have been disturbed at times to find myself reflecting with an outward focus (e.g., writing creatively in my journal so I have good snippets to include in this chapter). I see the same external drivers in trainees, who endeavour to write "neat" reflections littered with academic references (in a quest to meet academic requirements). It is important to stay aware of these external drivers and put them aside to reflect freely and honestly. Unless I keep it personal, it will rarely be meaningful.

5. **To prompt a deeper level of critical reflection, the key question to ask is "why"?** If you notice something does not feel right, explore why. If you notice a session went well, ask yourself why. Whilst it would technically be possible to answer this question with a surface level "why" (e.g., "the coach didn't listen to my ideas because I'm only part-time"), the next crucial step is to dig deeper with a further "why" (e.g., "why does being part-time mean your ideas are less valuable?") and to consider alternative viewpoints (e.g., "could you think of any other possible explanations?").

6. **There may be value in introducing critical approaches to reflection from the outset.** Students are often eased into reflective practice with structured questions that do not naturally prompt deep-level thinking. Reflection then is seen as a tick-box activity, and it may be difficult to transition to the deeper

critical reflection that will impact professional development. If we were to teach reflection from a humanistic perspective from the outset (as I was taught), students may have a better understanding of how to reflect, why they are reflecting and how this will help them develop, which might better equip them to become lifelong reflective practitioners. Guided reflection focusing on the questions in point 5 might be helpful in this regard and might better prepare students for formal written reflection.

7. **It is important to recognise the strengths and challenges of my "reflective personality".** As a naturally reflective individual, reflective practice may come easier to me than some. My reflective tendencies can however turn into unhealthy rumination if left untapped. The process of writing, or sharing with another, allows me to "tame my can of worms" and arrange them neatly into containers that I no longer have to worry about. Alongside reflective practice, I've found mindfulness meditation (Nugent et al., 2011) to be helpful in a) developing the skills to "put my reflective brain aside" and stay present in the moment; and b) to increase my ability to "take notice" of my feelings, thoughts, and behaviours, which are important stimuli for critical reflection.

Conclusion

As I have been making the transition from academia to applied exercise psychology, I have come to understand reflective practice need not always be formal but might draw on multiple informal sources of information. As reflective practitioners, it is what we then do with this information that leads to deeper understanding and enables change to occur. This can be explained through a humanistic process of taking notice, being curious and allowing ourselves to change. Through sharing critical reflections from my own journey (which started as an M.Sc. student), I hope to have provided an insight into "how" critical reflection can be achieved, and the powerful impact it can have on our lives when we are truly honest with ourselves. "We cannot change, we cannot move away from what we are, until we thoroughly *accept* what we are. Then change seems to come about almost unnoticed" (Rogers, 1961, 1990, p. 19).

Acknowledgements

I would like to thank Mel Jones, Dr Lynne Johnston and Dr Laura Carey for providing critical reflective space and helping me recognise and align my strengths, values and priorities over this past 18 months. My thanks also go to Professor Zoe Knowles for encouraging me to write this chapter and believe in my ability as a reflective practitioner, Caz Earle for first introducing me to Carl Rogers, humanistic psychology and reflective practice and Dr David Gilbourne for facilitating the development of my critical reflection as an M.Sc. student. Finally, to the many colleagues, students and participants I've worked with over my 17 years in higher education – thank you for being a source of inspiration, support and making the journey fun.

13 My Reflective Journey

A Retrospective Request for Permission to Find My Own Way to Reflect

Laura Needham

Introduction

When I was asked to contribute a chapter to this book I felt like a bit of a fraud! After all, what does an exercise physiologist know about reflection? I began to reflect (the irony) on my personal reflective practice journey and also my own current reflective practices giving thought to when, how and what my approaches are. I was able to convince myself that, yes, I do reflect, and I do so continuously, although not in the traditional manner of how we novice reflective practitioners are led to believe it should be done. If I look back on my training and my early years, reflective practice was "sold" to me as having to sit in a room quietly, and work through a reflective proforma writing down your reflections as per Gibbs' (1988) or Johns' (1994) frameworks or similar. However, as this chapter will hopefully explain, I have moved away from this standardised and formulaic approach to a more open and flexible approach which has developed over time. I know now that this is best suited to me and my work and can allow me to draw on others (such as colleagues and other practitioners) as well as myself for comment. The "fraudster" in me still seems to be convinced that, in articulating my own reflective journey and the practices that have evolved for me, I need to seek, from those theorists who define, instruct, and guide on how to do reflective practice (e.g., Johns, 2017), permission to do it my own way. Don't get me wrong, there is most definitely a time and a place for the structured approach to reflective practice, and somewhat ironically, I still use Gibbs' (1988) framework regularly to structure my reflections especially when it is a very emotive situation, and there is a need to work through an experience to make proper sense of it – although this is now by *choice* and *design* as opposed to *by instruction*. I do, however, more so now having written this chapter, feel freed by the realisation that I can actually do reflection my own way and hopefully what follows will explain how I arrived at this point.

The Reflective Physiologist

Understanding how the body responds physiologically to the stress of exercise and knowing how to use physiological training stimuli to elicit adaptation is

DOI: 10.4324/9781003198758-17

probably one of the oldest examples of scientific support services being made available to coaches and athletes. Textbooks of "work" physiology (Åstrand et al., 2003) documented both the historical background and exercise physiology research that has been conducted to offer an up-to-date appreciation of the role of exercise physiology in both enhancing performance and in establishing and maintaining health and well-being. Throughout recent years, the discipline itself has evolved from routine laboratory testing to immersion in the daily training environment to support coaches and athletes in the training, design, and delivery more targeted athlete-specific work (Thompson, 2010). The aim of physiologists working in high performance sport today is to ultimately improve physical performance as part of an interdisciplinary support team. Generally, applied sport physiologists work in several broad areas, including: identifying and managing illness and injury; optimising physical condition; and maximising performance. These aims are achieved through having a clear understanding of the physiological demands of sporting performance, what characteristics are required to compete at the world class level and of how physiological parameters contribute to the holistic performance of the athlete. The physiologist is expected to measure and monitor key parameters, from which objective data can be used to advise the coach and athletes regarding training and competition. Throughout this process, physiology practitioners are required to translate scientific research into applied evidenced-based advice and interventions.

Given these role frames, the discipline of physiology is considered to be populated by the stereotypical *scientist* – those with the traditional positivist outlook and in constant pursuit of hypothesis-driven research inherent with rigorous research design, measured outcomes, and statistical procedures. The focus is perhaps more on the data and the outcomes it suggests rather than the athletes producing the data and the potential benefits that having that data affords the athlete. While a data-informed intervention can be shown to be effective, it is usually void of the human element and of how to apply the intervention in the complex environment the athlete operates in (Ross et al., 2018). Typically, published research articles may include a practical application section towards the end, but these are infrequent and refrain from offering comment on the humanistic nature of application (Morton, 2009). Whilst a robust evidence-base for applied scientific support is indeed imperative, it should come in conjunction with informed practice (Buchheit, 2017; Ross et al., 2018).

In the real world of applied physiology, the pace is fast and furious, and athletes do not inhabit the controlled environment of the lab quite as much as a positivist physiologist would like them to. Athletes are frequently travelling around the world either at holding camps, training camps, qualification or world ranking events, specific targeted training blocks (e.g., heat acclimation training) or recovery periods and the physiologist needs to be in close pursuit at all times testing, analysing, feeding back and supporting both coach and athlete in making training decisions and preparing for events. A four-year Olympiad can feel, and look, like a long time, but once you build in the varying demands identified above there is often little time left to plan and work with the athlete in a controlled environment. Therefore, being a physiologist is not just about being a physiologist.

The day to day technical and professional knowledge and skills associated with doing the job, whilst at the forefront of the applied practitioner's role, are only the foundations of being effective. To improve athlete performance is a necessity; practice though, is far too complex for a paint by numbers approach (Ingham, 2016; Ross et al., 2018). To build an effective practitioner's role on these foundations requires an appreciation of the human element of the role and the need to adopt and apply the craft knowledge and skills associated with applying science. Interpersonal and people skills are often underplayed as an essential part of a physiologist's tool kit. The applied elements of the discipline can be invasive, innovative, and even induce painful experiences for athletes, therefore, the ability to communicate and connect with both athletes and coaches is imperative. Whilst, as a physiologist, I might have a physiological concept I am trying to apply, I have to ensure the athlete feels informed about what I might be doing to them or feels a part of the decision-making about their performance and I feel that you cannot just tell an athlete what to do without picking up on the little cues in their reactions to influence your behaviour when working with them. Over the years, I have observed that applied physiology requires a unique blend of technical expertise and exceptional people skills. One such current example is my work in triathlon where I am working with a particular athlete towards the Paris Olympics. We have identified the optimal "numbers" the coach and I feel are required to be successful and can structure a training programme needed to achieve these, but the triathlete is the one that has to go out and do those training sessions and therefore has to buy in to the process. We cannot just say, "Here is the training programme, go and do it." We have to work *with them* to consider *how it works* with other commitments both in terms of their life and their racing schedule. The triathlete is ultimately the person who feels the training programme and we have to have the flexibility to adapt the training programme based on how the triathlete feels. This requires more than just physiology-based knowledge, it is about knowing and understanding the athlete, picking up on the human elements of their responses to training and taking into account all aspects of their life rather than just the pursuit of optimal training data.

I have found, from my experiences, that often I am the last person an athlete sees before they start their race to win or not win their Olympic medal or the first person they see after they have been successful or not. Indeed, it is at such a point when it is not about the numbers, it is about knowing what to do for that person and how to support them in that moment. That is about understanding the *athlete as a person* and how they want you to react and support them. Demonstration of such *craft knowledge* and skills allows athletes and coaches to trust their physiology support team – the holy grail of effective sport science as it is sometimes known! Those who I have seen to be the most successful physiology practitioners are those that can connect, engage, and translate science into practice. At the heart of the success is an incredible *openness to reflect*, which is a key step on the journey to increased self-awareness. The ability for physiology practitioners to be reactive and reflective in the moment to problem solve is imperative.

It is not in the traditional mindset of the physiologist to focus on the human element of either the athletes they are supporting or indeed of themself. From all the sport science disciplines it is of little surprise that it is those of us with the positivist mindset that have been the slowest and, arguably most reluctant, to embrace the concept of reflective practice as a means of professional development. Little evidence exists of a physiologist cataloguing their personal growth through reflective writing although there are notable exceptions (Doncaster, 2018; Morton, 2009, 2014).

Creating a Reflective Culture

I currently work at the English Institute of Sport (EIS), established in 2002 with an objective to support National Governing Bodies (NGB) by making "the best better" in Olympic and Paralympic sport within GB (Thompson, 2010). The EIS continues to expand and evolve over the Olympiads and now in July 2022 currently employs over 300 practitioners. The EIS supports elite athletes from a variety of medal potential and progressive sports to improve performance through the delivery of science, medicine, technology, and engineering. The practitioners responsible for this application of sport science and medicine support are often viewed as *the team behind the team* (Thompson, 2010).

A question often asked in high performance sport is who supports the support team? Within the EIS a series of technical leads for each discipline are responsible for the technical and non-technical development of practitioners with the responsibility to support, develop, and quality assure their practice. I currently have a unique joint role; as an embedded physiologist in a major British medal-winning sport and co-leading the physiology discipline. The two roles allow me to practice applied physiology whilst also lead the development and strategy for the discipline in the institute. In my dual roles, I aim to be a people-focused leader and practitioner, and have an appetite for enhancing human performance by using a blend of science and art. I believe the role as a practitioner is to be inquisitive into human performance by working in collaboration with the coach, athlete, and support team. I feel strongly towards an individual athlete-centred approach, whereby ethical decisions are made in the pursuit of excellence that are scientifically and/or experientially driven. I feel we at the EIS have a duty to work towards the pursuit of medals as a holistic process, but one that seeks excellence and paves the way for a world leading high performance system. I see this as being relevant in relation to my physiology practitioners as well as the athletes they work with. If we develop world-leading practitioners, then we are better placed to develop the world's best athletes. For me creating a culture that facilitates and nurtures the process of reflection is key to this. As both a practitioner and a Head of Service, I must try and create and retain such cultures in order that I, myself, can continue to reflect and also so that the practitioners in my team feel safe and able to reflect both individually and collectively as a group.

My philosophy as an applied physiologist is that nobody knows all the answers. Even if you have a PhD in an aspect of physiology you may still only know quite a lot about a little bit of physiology rather than everything about everything. Even then, in an applied setting, there are so many things that impact on the little bit of physiology that you know a lot about that you need to draw on knowledge of others to fully apply the knowledge. So, my philosophy is very much about collaboration and the need to draw the science knowledge from across the disciplines together with the application and implementation skills and the appreciation that all aspects of the person impact on the athlete. For me, reflections need therefore to be both personal – how did I do as a practitioner? And collective – how did we do as a support team? And in the latter instance there has to be an acceptance to "call each other out" with the focus being on why are we working with this athlete?

From a personal reflective perspective, I currently engage with several executive coaches, technical leads, and mentors to reflect on my own practice. This typically takes a variety of forms ranging from formal agenda-driven meetings to casual coffee chats. As such, I would argue that my reflective practices are not always, and do not need to be, formal in nature. I have probably had my most insightful reflective experiences chatting over coffee or one of the many walking meetings during the pandemic! I strongly believe that I now no longer need to ask permission to not use a reflective framework. I think we (sport science practitioners) should not be thinking that there is just one way to reflect – it takes place in all forms. You have to be able, as a practitioner, to pull on all experiences and just because it does not fit the box or look like what we are taught it should look like it doesn't mean that it is not meaningful and that your practice hasn't been informed. It may take some time, some reflection to uncover that.

I feel I have the need to try to establish a reflective culture amongst my team so that there are opportunities for them to reflect either individually and/or as a group. The following sections will explore, first my personal experience of reflective practices as a physiologist and then, second, as a technical lead for physiology, how I try to support those physiologists in my team to reflect and develop.

Me as a Reflective Physiologist

As I look back over the first period of my professional career, I note that my reflective journey has changed over the years and has become freer in style. In my early career, I very much engaged in traditional written reflective practice approaches, which would then be dissected with my supervisor (and I use this term deliberately). This was consistent with the demands of gaining professional body recognition (e.g., British Association of Sport and Exercise Sciences [BASES] Accreditation) where it was seen as a necessity to evidence that I was reflecting. Little focus was really put on the *value* or *impact* of the reflections themselves but so long as I could evidence that I was undertaking reflective practice that (for the purposes of the award criteria) was good enough. Now, as I write this chapter, there has been the realisation that, for me, it is the value and the impact of the reflections themselves rather than the physical evidence of them having taken place that is more important to my professional development. How and when the reflections occur is somewhat irrelevant to me (and I appreciate others in the book comment on exactly these things), that they have an *impact on my ability as a practitioner* is key.

If I were asked to identify a point in time or reason when or why I first felt constrained by the formalities of prescribed reflective approaches I am not sure I could actually pinpoint anything specific. However, as someone who likes to do things right, I think I started to feel as if I was failing by not completing my obligatory written reflective account after every experience. When working in a busy, dynamic, and constantly changing environment such as elite sport, where time and space to think is limited, written reflections are probably the first things to fall off the list of things to do. Therefore, when I realised that I was no longer completing my written reflections, something I had always done since my Supervised Experience days, I felt like I was failing as a practitioner by not allocating time into reflecting. I did then, however, realise that actually I was reflecting but I was just doing it in a different way and in fact that was OK. I remain unsure as to whether I am "allowed" to do it my way, which is why I guess I am asking permission from the theorists (and in some sense you as readers!) to move away from the structured approaches.

Fundamentally, I am a scientist at heart and, therefore, my default setting is that of a *positivist*. I absolutely believe in the scientific enquiry process and how understanding, critically reviewing, and challenging allows me to deliver a superior service to the athletes, coaches, and support teams I work with. In the early days, my reflections were, therefore, very much technical in nature, focused more on what I needed to learn from a physiology perspective to be a better physiologist. However, I soon learned that I could get away with not being the best physiologist – I can always read a book, a journal article or ask a more knowledgeable colleague if I want to learn about physiology and I can generally learn a new technical topic as it comes up within each Olympic cycle. Over the past decade, I have been captivated by how much of what every sport scientist does is so centred on what we deem as *non-technical* – those skills and qualities required to communicate and influence those who we work with. As such, now, very rarely will my technical knowledge be the topic of my reflections as it was in the early days. The challenge always comes with being able to influence and engage my athletes and coaches. I have learned that my "super-strengths" are my relationship building and influencing skills. A great reflective session for me will now result in me reflecting on my practice in relation to my values and behaviours. As a result, I have a heightened understanding of who I am, why I am the way I am and why I behave in the way I do. If we as practitioners all understand ourselves more, I believe we can be more effective in our practice. I want to be the best I can be for the incredible athletes I have the opportunity to work with, and reflective practice is an essential tool in my toolbox.

As a novice reflective practitioner, partly due to the technical nature of my reflections and also the "rabbit in the headlights" feeling often experienced by trainee practitioners, I seemed to focus my reflections on the here and now – what do I need to do now in order to get by? What do I need to know to survive tomorrow? Now, having learned how to get beyond tomorrow I use my reflections to look further into the future with the aim to advance and develop myself throughout my entire career; to pursue excellence in my role, in its broadest sense, just as my athletes do. I now believe by continuing to reflect in-action and on-action, I am able to take small steps towards being the more effective practitioner, scientist, and leader that I would like others to see me as being.

Whilst I argue throughout this chapter that I am constantly seeking permission to be free from the shackles of formal reflective practice models and to embark on my own "freestyle reflection" and I enjoy the interaction that group reflections can bring, I do still recognise the value of the more formal and solo approach. As mentioned previously, I do still utilise Gibbs' (1988) framework for what I would consider the more emotive situations. For me, I know that I can lead with my heart, emotion, rather than my head, so I use this approach as almost a safety mechanism and as an outlet for me to vent and capture any emotionally charged reflections on my own before having a considered discussion with others. I like to begin to make sense of the situation on my own and then when I am clear on what the issues are and am aware of where the emotion is coming from, I feel better prepared to share things with others. Over the years I have learned that my most emotional responses are due to the fact that what has happened has pulled on one of my values and I feel the need to personally make sense of the situation before I am prepared to share it. Gibbs' (1988) framework allows me to focus on the emotions and detach the situation from how I felt and be perhaps more holistic in terms of understanding myself and why I behave in the way that I do. I agree with the notion that the types of experiences we probably learn most from are those that we are most emotionally attached to, largely because it is usually our own personal values and beliefs that are challenged.

Reflections on My Effective Practice

Having reflected for many years now, initially formally to achieve BASES Accreditation and latterly more informally to improve my on-the-job applied practice, I have realised that reflection is not just about identifying weaknesses and beating yourself up about what you have not done particularly well. Reflective practice is importantly about celebrating what you have done well and your agency within it. My collective reflections have been a mix of both approaches and as a result of working with different sports, different coaches, and different EIS support colleagues, I can conclude that from those scenarios where things have gone well and also from those situations which have not gone to plan the following are key lessons that have emerged from my reflective practices. As a result of my reflections, I believe that as a physiologist I am more effective if I am able to:

1. Recognise that different sports, different coaches, and different athletes have different needs and cultures, and that physiology support is not a "one size fits all" approach and has to be adapted to fit the here and now of the sport at the time.

2. Understand the critical success factors and cultures that underpin performance in a particular sport and where physiology underpins or influences these factors.
3. Understand how I can monitor/track meaningful changes in both performance factors and cultural shifts.
4. Identify, explore, and advise on interventions that are believed to be beneficial to these critical success factors.
5. Understand and be respectful of the other aspects that influence these factors (e.g., technical, tactical, psychosocial).
6. Constantly reflect and evaluate the interventions and practices adopted.
7. Understand the need to do all of the above with integrity and respect by seeking understanding through effective communication and a person first approach.
8. Work with each athlete as an individual.
9. Always seek collaboration to enhance the insight, approach, technical, and non-technical elements that all contribute to the process of supporting athletes.

Me as a Reflective Facilitator

While reflecting on the strength of the technical lead model within the institute, I keep repeatedly coming back to the ability for a technical lead to pull the practitioners out of the day-to-day, lift their head up and engage in reflection with a critical friend, or group. In the role I have I can share my thoughts from both sides; I have been a practitioner working under a variety of technical leads for ten years, and I have provided technical leadership for five years. It is so easy for practitioners to get their head down and just crack on responding to the challenges they are immediately faced with, without taking the time, to stop and reflect on how it is all going.

At the EIS we have a number of what I would call "green" practitioners, by which I mean of limited experience, straight out of university and normally in their first job. They often lack credibility in the eyes of the coaches and athletes they are working with and being able to reflect on where you are in your career and thus what credibility you have is important. I know that through my reflections and even in the writing of this chapter I think my leadership role has been shaped by my own personal reflections of when I was in such a position. In my early years in the EIS environment, I felt like a bit of a fraud, and I didn't feel like I belonged, I didn't *feel* like a good scientist, and I wasn't doing anything that the senior scientists were doing. There wasn't this culture whereby it was OK to say you didn't know something. Now in my leadership role I try to do the opposite to this and create a safe space for practitioners to be vulnerable with each other and share stories and thus empower them to learn through reflection. For those working with us in the institute I sincerely hope this is felt.

I have been fortunate in my career to see first-hand the collaboration, excellence and care the performance support teams in the UK high performance system provide to the sports they work with. The most captivating mechanism for effective support is the network of fellow scientists and practitioners to engage with to problem solve and reflect with. While maybe not officially a reflective practice mechanism, the richness of the environment, questioning and outcomes are truly world class. This does not come naturally and requires time and effort from all those involved. One of the things we try to do within the physiology community at the EIS is move away from the idea of each of us having to know all the answers towards a climate where we are happy to accept that each of us does not know all the answers and by showing some vulnerability with each other we start to build really strong and trusting relationships. This practice allows strong bonds to develop and encourages us as a team to explore and collectively solve performance-based problems.

Group reflections as a team tend to take one of two forms. First, if a practitioner has a specific problem all those who are available may jump on a call and we "shoot the breeze." Whilst this is not necessarily a formal and structured process, I see my role with the team as a reflective facilitator in which I draw on my coaching and mentoring skills to guide the discussion with open questions to make the practitioners stop and think about the issue and consider solutions and alternative courses of action that they could have taken. Within the group setting we try to guide the practitioner who has the issue to finding their own solution or alternative approach with those amongst us who have had similar experiences offering insights as to what we may have done in previous situations. Second, we sometimes have sessions in which there is a common shared problem and because everyone's context may be different due to the different sports they work in, we each can offer a different lens on the problem. Some reflective practice purists might argue that such discussions are merely collective problem-solving rather than reflection. I would counterargue that, if a practitioner leaves such a forum having increased their understanding of a problem or added a new tool to their toolbox, then it has been an effective reflective process as it may bring about a change in their practice effectiveness for the future. The fact that this has been in an informal, group setting and not via a written structured reflective model does not mean that it is not reflective practice.

Such reflective pairing/circles can be very effective but a I have seen such events that have not been so successful! For me the less successful group reflections are characterised by people being guarded and not prepared to share vulnerability and perhaps simply just seeking the answers directly from other practitioners. A further reason behind some of our less successful group reflections is the lack of clarity around why people are involved and if people come to the event not knowing their role or the expectations on them then the session can be stilted and less effective. For me, the most successful group reflections are where either I, as the lead, or the group collectively, enable a practitioner to tease out the key issues and make sense of what is essentially their problem. I find practitioners do not want to be just told that "this is how I did it in swimming so go and do this." Rather, they want to be *guided* towards creating a solution which best fits the context of their problem. If practitioners turn up fully prepared to engage and provide challenge to those around them, they can be part of something special.

For us within the EIS context, characteristics of an effective group reflection would be one which is effectively set up so that the issue for discussion is well-framed and one whereby practitioners are prepared to be vulnerable yet feel safe to be so, are guided to find their own solutions to problems and are fully aware of the purpose and expectations of the event. The optimal group size also needs to be considered and the right people invited – "don't invite Bob" – where Bob is that person who you feel you should invite but who may not actually make any meaningful contribution – one of those people who do not fulfil a purpose but may end up detracting from it (Parker, 2018).

As technical leads, whether we are formally badged as mentors, executive coaches, supervisors, or reflective practice facilitators does not really matter, we are able to create a culture and environment where reflective practice can really be developed, embedded, and exploited. The key benefit, I believe, of reflecting with a critical friend is the ability for that person to question, dig deeper and pick up on those small cues that may have been missed if they reflected alone. A truly brilliant reflective session will allow a practitioner to explore what they did, what impacted their decision making, why they behaved/practiced in the way they did and what this means for their practice moving forward.

Summary

Gibbs' (1988) framework (which, as I have said before, I still love and use today) was actually written the year I was born. The world of sport has changed since then, and perhaps our perceptions of reflection need to modify slightly as we evolve. Fundamentally, the more formal reflective practice process Gibbs put forward is still, to me, a "no brainer." However, the dynamic nature of the professional support practitioner role perhaps requires practitioners to rethink the way in which we engage in our reflective questioning and methods to allow our reflective practices to be adaptable and conducted in a way which fits contemporary practice and its demands. Scientists are absolute sticklers for rules and processes, but we are still people who work with other people and whether we like it or not, our values impact on our behaviours and those we have the privilege to interact with daily. We owe it to our athletes who are striving to literally be the best in the world, to be the best practitioners in the world we can be. We can only do that by embracing both our personal and professional development in a way that allows us to truly understand what drives, motivates and makes us tick in our practice. We are literally exploring the complexity of the limits of human performance! Physiology is no doubt an amazing discipline (biased, I know!), but it impacts and is impacted by, emotion. Therefore, we should seek to understand ours so we can be better scientists, practitioners, and people.

My personal reflective journey started with me conducting formal, structured and solo reflections and time, maturity, experience, and effective reflections have led me to the realisation that even when the approach to reflection is random, informal, unplanned, and group-based it can still be effective so long as the right conditions are established and practitioners and myself are prepared to be vulnerable and to seek self-development. I am now content that I can choose to reflect in any way that suits me and the practitioners I work with and thus actually I do not need to ask for permission to find my own way. Here, through this chapter and articulating in such a way I believe I have already done that. I invite the reader to agree/disagree with me as to my conclusive position here as well as consider where they are placed on the "structured" to "freestyle" reflective practice continuum and the use of associated techniques. For me it's been quite a journey!

14 Winning on the Road

Critical Reflections from Life in the Fast Lane!

James Morton

Introduction

It has been ten years since I last wrote a "reflective" paper. I was 30 years old, and I was writing a reflective narrative of my experiences as a sport physiologist and nutritionist, largely an account of working in the applied worlds of professional football and boxing. Nonetheless, my reflections of life as an academic and applied practitioner were also intertwined with reflections from my personal life. My Dad had been killed in a car accident eight years earlier and during the process of writing my neophyte reflections, my Mum was also diagnosed with terminal cancer. Whilst my reflections were predominantly fuelled by critical thoughts on applied practice, they soon became a narrative of a young man struggling to come to terms with the death of his parents, of becoming a father, and of the desire to succeed, albeit from a professional perspective.

At the time of writing the present paper, I am actively planning my 40th birthday party. I am planning to return to my home. Although I have now lived in Liverpool longer than my hometown, Belfast will always be the most special place in the world to me. It has shaped my character, my values and defines who I really am, although I acknowledge there have been many times in the last decade that I have perhaps forgotten (and yet, rediscovered) myself. The transition from thirty to forty has been a particularly reflective journey. Professionally, my career has progressed exponentially, and I have continued to straddle both the academic environment and front line of elite sport. From an academic perspective, we are often considered as a successful applied research group, as evidenced by the volume and applied impact of our academic outputs but most importantly (in my view), the people we have helped to produce. As a practitioner, I also spent five years working with one of the world's most successful sports teams, a team who won five consecutive Tour de France races. On the outside, things could not have been better. I recall one conference where an academic colleague from another institution commented that he "thought he had a good year" until benchmarking himself against the "Liverpool group". Keynote conference invitations were coming thick and fast, taking me to corners of the world that I had only ever dreamed about as a young boy. On the outside, I was flourishing. I was living life in the fast lane.

DOI: 10.4324/9781003198758-18

On the inside, things were not always as they seemed. At home (and with family), I would often appear distant and preoccupied, my thoughts largely meandering between writing the next paper, securing the next grant, supporting students, line managing academic staff and of course, winning the next bike race. My thoughts were occupied with anything that would take me away from the realisation that I no longer had parents. I would spend one week on the road and one week at home, a vicious cycle of trains, planes, hotel rooms and mountains. Upon the return from each trip, I would often present in a daze-like state, taking days to adapt to the real world again, away from the bubble of professional sport. On the inside, I was slowly fading away, moving further and further from those closest to me.

When I accepted the invitation to write this chapter, I had initially hoped to provide a thought-provoking account of what it really means to be an effective applied practitioner. Indeed, my reflections from "Winning on the Road" have completely re-shaped my philosophy of how to support podium performances. Through close mentorship from others, I have learned the importance of leadership, the necessity of coaching and the art of translating science (knowledge) to practice (delivery). I believe I have learned how to impact performance. Without doubt, it has been the most rewarding phase of my career. However, as I began the writing process, I soon realised that I have a much more important story to tell. It, too, is also a hugely rewarding story. It is a story about an *older* man, a man who has *now* come to terms with the death of his parents, a man who has *now* embraced fatherhood and marriage, and a man who *will always* have that intense desire to succeed, albeit with different goalposts. My acknowledgements recognise those who helped with the writing process and yet at draft submission stage it felt it appropriate to invite someone else to comment. Following discussion with the editorial team, I agreed for Andy (Miles) to share "on paper" for the reader *their* reflections on *my* reflections and insights, and the impact of my reflective practice on them. Given that Andy works in a similar discipline to me (e.g., sport and exercise physiology) it seemed appropriate for him to comment and in doing so we hope that the commentary may prompt critical reflection for you, the reader.

Chapter Style

Readers who are unfamiliar with reflective writing are likely to already feel that this text is vastly different from traditional scientific writing. Indeed, it is unusual for an academic paper to open in the "first person". Nonetheless, Knowles et al. (2007) offer encouragement for such writing by suggesting that:

> If we are to encourage practitioners to reflect on their experiences, it is vital to stress that it is *their experiences* that matter more (in the first instance) than any associated theory that may or may not be illustrated through the narrative. (p. 111)

With this logic, I have chosen to tell my story by adopting an auto-ethnographic tone where "I" (the author) am talking directly to "you" (the reader). Interspersed throughout the narrative are a selection of events and critical moments that have eventually led to a new perspective on applied practice and moreover, a new way of being. Some of these moments have been formally captured in reflective diary extracts that were written over the last decade, whereas others, have simply been stored as memories in my mind that I can revisit as and when I need to. Such moments are recognised by indented text and are written in a confessional and creative non-fictional style where I am attempting to invite you to the same places in time that I have been. My inspiration for writing in this way has largely been drawn from the sport psychology, social sciences, and educational literature (Anderson et al., 2004; Gilbourne & Richardson, 2006; Gilbourne, 2012, 2013; Gilbourne et al., 2014; Knowles & Gilbourne, 2010), for there are few (if any) texts from *physiologists* for which to benchmark my writing against. Like my previous accounts (Morton, 2009, 2014), the writing process (i.e., the chapter that you are now reading) occurred over several weeks, an hour here, an hour there, often occurring whilst travelling (on trains) or in the quieter environment of home. There were no set times or location, I just wrote when I felt the urge to write.

Authors of reflective papers will likely have different motivations (and intended outcomes) that underpin their writing. Similarly, reviewers and readers of reflective narratives will critically appraise the quality of the writing and reflections through differing lenses, perhaps a hybrid appraisal that is based on relevant associated theory but also, how their *own* lived experiences interpret the narrative (Gilbourne et al., 2014). Notwithstanding such critical perspectives, I have reasoned, however, that perhaps the simplest criterion to judge, is to consider whether this paper *might* offer help to others. I hope that it does.

Leadership Begins With Excitement

In December 2014, I was effectively half-way through my fifth season working at a Premier League football club. I had loved every minute of it, though truth be told, I had gone stale as a practitioner. The excitement had slowly faded away and I knew that I was no longer challenging myself, nor was I being challenged by others. If I was to progress in my career, I knew that I needed a change. The opportunity for change presented itself over a coffee conversation with a colleague where he hinted if I would be interested in taking over his current position at what was regarded as the world's best cycling team. Although my knowledge of cycling (as a sport) was limited, the opportunity to study carbohydrate metabolism "in action" and with some of the world's best endurance athletes was hugely attractive. Furthermore, the team had a reputation as pioneers in human performance and a culture of excellence that was led by a Team Principal who was known for his approach of leaving no stone unturned (i.e., marginal gains) when it came to human improvement. In fact, it was the opportunity to study "leadership" that provided the biggest attraction.

Two weeks after *that* conversation, I found myself in Majorca at the team's pre-season training camp for what I had thought was a formal interview. However, "my interview" soon transitioned to my introduction to riders and staff as the team's new performance nutritionist. Dave (the Team Principal) had already made up his mind. I was to be one of his first hires for the 2015 season. The team had not won a Grand Tour in 2014 and it was time for a shake up and reset. Over the coming days, I was actively involved in a forensic review of 2014 and the beginning of the planning process for winning the 2015 Tour de France, frequently encouraged to give my opinion and views as a newcomer to the sport. It was a sport scientist's dream, working backwards from the demands of the event to create a nine-man team and lead rider capable of winning the world's biggest bike race. For three weeks in July, the riders would cycle 3,500 km over 21 days, riding in extreme heat and altitude pushing their bodies to the limit day after day. There was six months to get the team ready. Our discussions of "what it takes to win" were intertwined with the dangers of contentment and complacency, there was a buzz in the air and the evening "performance meetings" often ran into the early hours of the morning. There was an intensity and attention to detail that I had not witnessed in my previous experiences of professional sport. With every team meeting, the vision was continually communicated and discussed . . . "this isn't about being the world's best cycling team . . . it is about becoming the most admired sports team in the world". Both key staff and riders quickly took me under their wing, mentoring me on the culture of cycling, those critical performance priorities and continually reinforcing that I had a big role to play. Their thirst and desire to improve was relentless, a mindset that I loved being around. My moleskin journal was soon becoming busy with reflective scribbles, soundbites and key learnings from each meeting or person I was exposed to, often traced back to team's philosophy of "winning behaviours". In revisiting my notes on the return plane journey home, I quickly realised that I had already been introduced to the first rule of leadership . . . create excitement. I couldn't wait to go racing.

The Four Powerful Words

The initial few months of the season were spent engaging in a mix of technical, practical, and critical reflections. Cycling is a sport that is trenched in tradition and culture, and I was now working in a team that was actively trying to change the sport. My reflections were deliberate and structured, largely facilitated through personal journal writing (and drawing) but also shared reflection with the Team Principal, coaches, support staff and of course, key riders. Cycling races typically occur over days to weeks with a short stage race lasting four to seven days, whereas the cycling Grand Tours (i.e., the Giro d'Italia, Tour de

France and Vuelta Espana) are contested over 21 days. A typical day's racing begins at 10 am to 12 noon and usually ends between 3 and 5 pm, as dependent on the stage distance, racing tactics and racing conditions. In the interim period, I would reside in the team bus driving from the race start to the race finish. It was usually me, the Team Principal and the Head Coach, riding up front and positioned just behind the bus driver. Those two-to-four-hour drives provided a rich opportunity for daily shared reflection, essentially comparable to a never-ending action research project on "how to support performance". By day, we would discuss and debate all things "human performance" with the overarching aim of how we can be better tomorrow than we were today. The quest to improve was relentless. By night (in our evening "performance meetings"), we would discuss each rider's performance from the day's stage, with a view of any interventions that may need to be put in place before the next day's racing began. Nutrition was always high on the agenda and "under-fuelling", I would quickly learn, was often the cause of a below par performance. In fact, in many cases, it was the difference between winning and losing. There was an attention to detail and a focus on nutrition that I had not experienced in any sport before. Any key learnings would be noted and brought forward to our next race so that our on-race protocols were continually updated and improved. It was a process of continual improvement week-on-week. Dave likened it to "updating the operating system on your mobile phone", with each version slicker, smarter and faster than the previous. By the time we got to the Tour de France, our systems would be optimised to ensure we were ready to race and moreover, ready to win. Before sleeping each night, I would reflect "on-action" by journaling my field notes from the day's events. In drawing my "people map" (a map of people who circled and could influence each rider), I was becoming readily aware of the key relationships and behaviours that I needed to develop to support and impact each rider's performance. My reflections often focused on the requirement to "understand people" and I was embracing the process of reflection with greater focus, intensity, and consistency than ever before. However, despite the excitement and progression in my professional life, I was soon reminded that life should never be taken for granted.

> Natalie had just picked me up from the airport. It was good to see her, I had been away for eight days, and I had really missed both her and the kids, I didn't fully grasp it back then but looking back, it was a sign of things to come. I began to tell her everything I had experienced during the last week. I had found it tough being on the road, but it had been another successful trip . . . it was my third race and once again, we had won . . . our lead rider was now ranked number one in the world. He was a rider who I had worked with closely in the last six weeks and it felt like the nutritional plans we had put in place were now beginning to really manifest as performance gains. He was already down to a good racing weight and now regarded as one of the best climbers in the world. I knew I was making a difference . . . and he was on track to perform in July.

Despite my excitement, Natalie seemed a little distant and hesitant to engage in the conversation. I thought that she may have struggled with being on her own, perhaps having second thoughts amid the realisation that are lives were now vastly different with me now living on the road. When we got home, the mood really changed. "James, you'd better sit down . . . I've got some really bad news, it's Gracie (*my 10-year-old niece*). Your sister phoned a few days ago, Gracie's been diagnosed with leukaemia and will be starting treatment this week . . . I didn't want to tell you when you were away as I knew how you'd be". The tears instantly started rolling down my cheeks, "how can something like this happen to a 10-year-old little girl", I thought, and above all, "how will my sister cope with the prospect of losing her daughter as well her parents". Needless to say, I was straight on the phone to my sister and arranged to go to Edinburgh later that week to be with her.

The next day, I carefully crafted an email to Dave to explain what had happened. I mentioned that I would "likely need some time off and may not be able to travel for a few weeks, that if the team needed someone else who could fully commit to the riders and the race programme, then I would understand". I had learned from my previous experience from when my Mum was dying, that professional sport often doesn't wait for personal problems. Within 30 seconds of hitting "send", the phone rang. It was Dave. "Listen mate, take as much time as you need, get yourself up to see your family and do what you need to do. We'll support you with whatever you need. And listen, I know you've only been here a few months, but everyone can already see what an impact you're having, nutrition is front and centre and it's making a difference . . . and remember, *we believe in you*".

As I boarded the train to Edinburgh, I was dreading the thought of visiting yet another hospital. I have never liked hospitals, and I knew that the experience of visiting a ward full of sick children would be especially hard. As a coping mechanism, I soon took myself away from the images of sick children by doing what I had always done, quickly turning my thoughts back to work. Work had always been a safe space. Whilst it wasn't always easy, I loved my job, and I loved the challenge of competing with myself and others. Strange then, that at a time when my thoughts were largely occupied of potentially coping with more grief, I was also learning yet another fundamental rule of leadership. Indeed, in reflecting on his own philosophy of leadership, the late Bill Walsh, the former San Francisco 49ers coach, had previously written that the four most powerful words are "I believe in you" (Walsh et al., 2010). I had never fully appreciated these words, until they were spoken *to me*. The study of leadership is, of course, centuries old and the act of leadership can take many forms. In its purest sense, however, I reasoned that true leadership is about how you make people feel. Painting an ambitious and exciting vision of the future is just the beginning. The act of true leadership, however, is realised day-to-day by how you continually make people feel, instilling values, purpose, belonging and above all, making them feel that they can achieve greater things. As the train stopped at another platform to pick up more passengers, I reflected further. I felt more valued, committed, and with a greater sense of purpose than at any point in my career. Why? Because I knew that the team *believed in me*.

Performance Lessons From the Volcano

A rider's journey to the Tour de France is not an easy one. For a rider placed on the "long list" for potential team selection, they are typically provided with a six-month training and race programme that is intended to provide them with the necessary preparation to arrive on the start line in peak racing condition, at optimal racing weight and fully acclimatised to riding in extreme temperatures and altitudes. There will be setbacks along the way (e.g., injury, illness, crashes), and it may take longer than expected to for a rider to truly find their "racing legs". It is never a straightforward process. In a typical roster of 28–30 riders, only eight riders will be selected and moreover, only one or two will be designated as race leaders. The reality being, there is only ever a handful of riders in the world that are physically and mentally capable of winning the Tour de France. The rest are there to support and protect their leader, ensuring he remains as fresh as possible and ready to deliver in the high mountains after four to five hours of already being in the saddle. Aside from the requirement for an extreme physiological profile, my reflections have taught me that there is an essential ingredient that all Grand Tour riders must possess, that is, the ability to "suffer". Training can be brutal and yet, the best riders in the world have that ability to soak it up, to come back each day and suffer a little more. If today was planned for a six-hour ride, they would do seven. That is the mentality of a Grand Tour winner.

Suffering was most evident in the training camp environment. For three weeks in April and three weeks in May, we would live at the top of Mount Teide, a volcano in Tenerife that is 2000m above sea level. Those "altitude camps" would be minimalistic in nature, usually comprising a selection of those riders from the long list and a handful of support staff that would likely make up the staffing team at the Tour. Training would begin each day at 9.30 am, where we would ride down the mountain and return to sea-level. After several hours of "training efforts" up and down the mountain, we would eventually complete the final climb home, usually between 3 to 4 pm. Lunch would be followed by a rider massage, recovery time, an evening meal and sleep. Each day was simply a repeat of "eat, train, eat, sleep" and yet, each day was *so much* more. Whilst turning the pedals was the primary goal, the focused environment provided a rich opportunity to talk, an environment that facilitated shared reflection for both riders and staff to build those key professional (and often personal) relationships that would be necessary to perform in July. The Tour is one of the most intense sporting events in the world and we needed to know that we were all in it together, that we had each other's back for when it really got tough. Mount Teide provided the perfect environment to develop those high-performance relationships. Everyone knew that the Tour could be won or lost on *that* mountain.

> The phone rang, it was few minutes after 9 pm. It was Dave. "How's things at the top of that big volcano?!" he joked. "All good" I said, "you've actually just caught me in the final stages of writing my *Performance Strategy*". After a few minutes of wider reflections on strategic direction of the team, Dave soon taught me one of my most important lessons. "Listen" he said, "strategy is great, but when it gets to this stage of the season, the strategy is in the here and now, we've got eight weeks left to get ready to win the Tour again, at this stage, focus all your efforts on the rider who's going to make us win, give *him* the best support you can possibly give him, get detailed, get dialled, get coaching, and help get him to the start line in the best shape he can be for July". "Your strategy right now needs to be winning the Tour again!", he laughed. It was another life-long lesson and as always, delivered with humour, in a supportive style and with many years of reflections and anecdotes to support his reasoning. I turned to a new page and scribbled a new heading . . . "Sometimes the strategy is in the *here* and *now*".

The reflection that "I should focus on the winners" was a little uncomfortable at first. I had just spent five seasons at a Premier League football club where I had been used to supporting a first team squad of more than 25 players. Nonetheless, as I reflected on that experience in the coming days, weeks, and years, I reasoned that I had never *truly* supported performance. Rather, I had merely provided a service to a squad of "football players". Without doubt, the quality of nutrition provision certainly improved during my time at the club and for sure, there were individual players who measurably improved their knowledge and behaviours surrounding key principles of performance nutrition. However, players often *got the same*, provided with the same protocols, teaching methods and resources to improve their training adaptations, match day performance and recovery. There was no real individualisation or personalisation of the support. Although I am often considered a brutally harsh self-critic, in benchmarking against my current self, I can honestly say that I wasn't an effective practitioner in my neophyte years. Whilst my academic background ensured I had sufficient technical knowledge and my down-to-earth approach allowed me to build relationships, I did not possess the leadership or coaching skills to improve "individuals". I needed to improve my ability to see the *person first* and the *athlete second*. I needed to improve my ability to *coach*.

In the coming years, I would learn that a bike rider can typically be characterised into one of four categories. There are those that are *racing to win*, usually the more experienced and senior athletes. This cohort are at the top of their game. There is still room for improvement, but you must work harder and smarter to achieve the smaller gains. There are those that are *racing to support winning*, these are the riders who will never win a major stage race or Grand Tour. Rather, winning for them must be framed around the concept of supporting a winning performance. They can still stand on the podium, albeit they will never wear the Yellow Jersey. Finally, there are the development riders and neo-professionals. In this group, there are those that are *learning to (one day) win* for themselves or alternatively, those that are *learning to support winning*. The development group also need high quality support, but they can usually achieve much bigger performance gains for less overall time investment. This is a group who may not require marginal gains. With an intense focus on "coaching", I would soon learn to tailor their performance strategy for what they needed, according to the stage of their career. Above all, I would soon learn and apply the basic principles of coaching and behaviour change that is required to improve the individual. Indeed, my reflections have taught me that performance support can never be a one size fits all approach. Although the basic essence of performance support begins with understanding the demands of the event and identifying the critical performance priorities, the actual delivery of the support process entails improving those performance priorities that are specific to the level of each individual athlete. What limits performance in one athlete (or rather, the opportunity for improvement) may not necessarily be relevant for another athlete. Through valid, reliable, and consistent assessments (both objective and subjective), a multidisciplinary individual athlete performance plan should subsequently be developed. There must be alignment, belief, and commitment to the plan whilst also recognising that all good plans should be flexible and adaptable to change. Most importantly, the delivery of the performance plan should be brought to life by *coaching the behaviours* that are required to achieve the desired performance outcome. After all, it is what we *do* that counts, not just what we think.

The Tour de France: A Race of Self-Sacrifice and Goal Harmony

The Tour de France is like no other sporting event in the world. For the fans and spectators, the Tour represents a carnival like atmosphere, a three-week holiday in July where, day after day, they get to watch their heroes (from within touching distance) push their bodies to their limits. For the riders and support staff, the intensity of the Tour can be likened to competing in an Olympic or Champions League Final for 21 consecutive days. Every day is a high-pressure situation where a mistake on just *one* day is likely to affect performance in the coming days or week. Indeed, although the Tour is unlikely to be *won* on any given day, it is accepted that the Tour can be *lost* at any moment in time. A day of getting caught in the crosswinds, under-fuelling, poor recovery, or illness can result in minutes being lost on a single stage. Such time-losses are hugely important considering that despite three weeks of racing, the margin separating the Yellow Jersey and second place may only be a handful of seconds. It is this urgency, attention to detail and consistent pressure to perform "day-in, day-out" that positions the Tour as the most demanding sporting arena of all. The Tour has taught me many things, not least, some of the essential ingredients that make a winning team, the willingness to self-sacrifice for others and the ability to align to a goal and deliver your part of the plan. In a sport where only one athlete wins, it is perhaps ironic that I now consider cycling to be the world's greatest *team* sport.

It was Stage 20, the final day of racing that would culminate on one of the sport's most iconic climbs, Alpe d'Huez. Although the Tour lasts 21 days, the final stage is considered a processional stage of the race winner, through the streets of Paris and arriving at the famous Champs Elysees. Today was the last day of racing, we would win or lose today. We start the stage at two minutes and 38 seconds in the lead of the overall standings. The general classification doesn't tell the whole story though. Our lead rider had developed a chest infection, he lost 30 seconds yesterday and cracks were beginning to show. It is hard or virtually impossible to sustain your peak racing condition for three weeks. We had come into the race at the top of the curve, but now we were on the downward slope. Anything could happen today, we knew the attacks would come early, they would come thick and fast.

At the foot of Alpe d'Huez, the race really kicks off. Our lead rider only has two support riders left with him, the rest have been burned up earlier in the stage, they did their job to deliver him to the bottom of the climb. Now it was the other riders' job to take him up as far as they could. Our rival attacks, we seem to be suffering and lose his wheel. A gap opens . . . eventually our support riders (riding in front of our lead rider) reel him back in. He attacks again, another gap and another feat of support riding to bring him back. He attacks again . . . but this time our lead rider can't follow. Our support riders stay with him, they need to keep him in the race. We're losing time and there is still a long way to go. I'm watching it play out at our hotel near the finish line. Our worst fear begins to play out. A few minutes ago, we were getting ready to celebrate winning the Tour, and now we could be losing it, on the final few kilometres of the final mountain of the final day's racing.

The support riders keep riding, grimacing with every pedal stroke, self-sacrificing themselves and suffering to prevent us from losing this race, but riding in the knowledge they will not win themselves, riding in the knowledge that they are giving everything for someone else. They know their jobs, they are committed to the plan, their whole season has been preparing them for moments like this, moments when they would need to step up, when they too could also prove they are a winner. With several kilometres to go, one of them "pops", he has given his all and nothing left to give. We are still losing time. Just one more support rider left. In another minute, he also empties himself, the pedals stop turning at the same speed they were in the last kilometre. It is just our lead rider left, holding on for dear life . . . eventually, he crosses the finish line, winning the Tour by just over a minute, but having lost one minute and 20 seconds on the stage. He is the champion, but he will soon thank his teammates. He knows, more than anyone, that the Tour de France is never won on your own.

The time between the end of Stage 20 and Stage 21 always presented as an opportunity for emotive reflection. Although the riders would later travel by plane on the morning of Stage 21, the staff would (almost immediately) begin their journey to Paris by road, stopping at a "half-way hotel" overnight. In those initial few hours after Stage 20, the feeling of euphoria would also be mixed with a sense of relief, relief that we had won but also a relief that we had not lost. It is a feeling that is hard to describe but it is an *addictive* feeling, a feeling that you have been part of something special, a feeling that you will always remember and want to experience again and again. I would always complete the "final leg" of the journey to Paris on the team bus on the Sunday morning of Stage 21. There would usually be a handful of staff, it was another opportunity to reflect on the previous six months. Although there were plenty of more racing days to come (not least the final Grand Tour of the season, the Vuelta Espana), we would allow ourselves a few hours to not think of future races, but to simply enjoy the moment. I often felt a sense of calmness and contentment on that drive to Paris. It was also where I took stock of what I had learned. On one particular year, I was preparing for a conference presentation that I was soon due to present (centred on the theme of Winning Cultures) to another sporting governing body. I wanted to leave them with a take home message that could summarise my reflections from "Winning on the Road". With several drives to Paris now under my belt, I was able to settle on the below:

> Winning consistently is not a fluke. It is characterised by super talented athletes who are continually hungry for success. They are supported by hardworking multidisciplinary support staff who, like the athletes, are willing to self-sacrifice in order to achieve goal harmony. A winning culture is underpinned by leadership that promotes a team of teams, winning behaviour, continual improvement, and a performance first approach. Ultimately, it is the progressive and shared understanding of ourselves and the people that we work with that really underpins winning performances. The priority for performance support staff is to proactively ask, answer and deliver practical solutions (i.e., translate the complex to simple) to the key performance (priority) questions. The mission is to improve performance. The goal is to win.

The Personal Cost of Winning

Winning *consistently* is the hardest thing in sport. With each successive victory, there is a danger of complacency and contentment creeping in, a danger that the hunger begins to fade. The act of winning therefore presents a distinct set of leadership challenges. Where once it was failure that prompted critical reflection and performance reviews, it is success that can often lead to a more rigorous, thought provoking and forward-thinking debrief. The search for meaningful performance gains becomes harder each year but if you look hard enough, they can *always* be found. The competition will eventually close the gap, your challenge is to not get caught.

The challenge to *win again* was often brought to life by the requirement (or perception) of doing something different each year. There had to be a new performance theme, a new process, or a piece of innovation to keep riders and staff engaged. It had to convey that we were smarter than the opposition. It had to improve on what we currently did and above all, it had to make us go faster. The desire (or perhaps pressure) to win again became an obsession, occupying more of my thoughts with each passing month and unknowingly, impacting my mood, self-esteem, and presence at home. I don't recall a specific moment in time, but eventually I realised that I was spending more time thinking about my relationships with bike riders than I was with the people who really matter.

It's the eve of another Tour de France. The key support staff (sports directors, coaches, medical staff) are all sitting on the team bus, parked in the car park of the hotel where several other teams are also staying. The bus was *our office*, the place where we would continually debate, discuss, and align our views of how to win. At a few minutes past mid-night, it was time to wrap things up. "Listen lads" said Dave, "we've been sitting here for the past two hours thinking of everything that could happen in the next few weeks. Look out the window now and you can see (a rival team) in the hotel bar, all having a jolly and getting on the beers. That's why we're going to win this race. We're the team who works harder and smarter than everyone else, we're the team who can be bothered do all the little details that no one else can be bothered to do, we're the team who will sit in a bus until midnight and keep working. That's why we're going to win this bike race". I knew he was right.

The intensity of preparing for the Tour ramps up as the months get closer. The final 8–12 weeks is all about suffering in training, sharpening up in those last few races and for a potential Grand Tour winner, shifting those last couple of kilos to get down to racing weight. It was tough for the riders, but the staff also felt a progressive increase in work intensity in those final months. With every race, my reflections began to increasingly consider that of "staff self-sacrifice". I had felt it more this year. There were more days away from home, more days of watching my children grow older in photographs and FaceTime. More days of missing Charlie score goals and more days of missing bed-time stories with Georgia.

I stayed on the bus a little longer, writing a few notes of things I needed to get right the next day. I looked out the window again and saw our lead mechanic preparing the bikes for tomorrow. I knew he spent more time on the road than he did at home. "That won't be me" I told myself, "Just a few more races to win".

As my children got older, I would find the drive to Paris get harder each year. One particular journey springs to mind. We had won another Tour de France with another British rider, a rider who I had worked with closely in the preceding four years and a rider who had really embraced the support process. Our relationship was professional but also personal, a climate in which I tend to work best. The team had now won four consecutive Grand Tours and riders and staff had pub-licly acknowledged the role of nutrition in supporting their performances. It had been the most uncomfortable, challenging and yet, rewarding phase of my career. I had learned that true growth often comes when we are at our most uncomfort-able. Several months earlier, I had also been promoted to Professor, a milestone that I had always thought would bring a sense of achievement and contentment but rather, a short-term high was soon greeted with a sense of emptiness and searching for what was next. Although I was seemingly winning on the road, my reflections on driving to Paris that year hinted of something missing from my life.

> I changed my playlist to one of my favourite bands, Snow Patrol. As a band from Northern Ireland, it made me think of home. For one reason or another, I began to scroll through Facebook, the lives of my "old mates" from Belfast soon appeared. I realised that I had not seen or spoke to some of them in years. In fact, I had not been home for over a year. I thought of Dad, my Mum, the streets where I grew up, the fields where I played foot-ball. I thought of the "troubles", I thought of Belfast, what it stands for and the lessons it had taught me. I thought of who I once was but also who I'd become. A tear fell from my eye. I'd lost the connection with my home. I'd lost the connection with my family. I'd lost the connection with myself.

The months that followed represented a period of intense reflection where I questioned what I really wanted from life. I was soon due to get married but a lot of shared reflection at home prompted me to seek counselling. I was about to embark on the next chapter of my life but to do so, I realised that I needed to close a few chapters from the previous decade. Although I did not consider myself depressed, I was consciously aware that I was not *happy*. A breakthrough moment came in one of those early sessions.

> "I know you like the process of reflection", she said, "so I'd like you to con-sider your life as a tree and draw the branches of your life as you currently see it". After a few minutes, I realised that my tree was flourishing on one side, but the other had not grown in years. Those branches that were rich in life were those related to my career, those that were not, were those related to my family, my friends, to me and to my home. Those were the branches that *really mattered* and yet, I had not watered them in years. When I cycled home from that session, another tear fell from my eye. Strangely, it didn't feel like a tear of sadness. Rather, it felt like a tear of contentment, representing an important step towards rediscovering myself and becoming the man that I always wanted to be, a man, like my Dad, who looks after his family.

There were many themes that were explored in those sessions, too many to cover in this chapter. However, the process of shared reflection (albeit with a stranger) as well as finally "opening up" to Natalie, my sisters and close friends allowed me to eventually work through the process of grief and to identify where

I had made a wrong turn many years before. I realised that things started to unravel when my son (Charlie|) was born. I had struggled to come to terms with being a parent whilst simultaneously dealing with the fact that he would never meet his Grandad. I needed my dad to teach me how to become a father and I missed him immeasurably. Where once I spoke to him every day, there was now a huge void in my life, at a time when I needed him more than ever. When my daughter (Georgia) was born six weeks after my Mum died, I sank a little deeper. A feeling of loneliness is perhaps how to describe it best. I *stopped* talking, but I *kept* working. In fact, it was a time that represented the most successful years of my career. Counselling helped me to realise the importance of opening-up again, it helped me to connect with my former self and most importantly, it helped me to recognise the role of balance in my life. I realised that the past doesn't have to define your future, I realised that the relationships that really matter are the ones that are closest to you. Those people will always be there, regardless of whether you win or lose. I realised that it was Natalie and my children who really needed me to "be at my best each day". It was time to finally close those chapters and start writing a new one.

> I'm sitting at the "top table", my parents aren't here but my sisters sit in their place. I'm holding my wife's hand. My Dad's cousin (also my Uncle) gives a speech on behalf of my Dad, he talks about how proud Jim and Elizabeth would be of the man that I had become. It was soon my turn. I look out at the room. It was full of people who really mattered. Friends that I first met as a toddler in nursey, friends from Belfast, from playing football, from university, my family, all people who had been with me at key times of my life. I look out again, I see Gracie (and her Dad), now 15 years old and a beautiful young woman, I see and hear Georgia heckling me at the back, people laugh. I look at Charlie, my sisters, and my wife. It is a day that I will never forget. I was ready to move on, I was ready to "come home". I was ready to be happy again.

In the weeks after I got married, I decided to resign from the cycling team. There were many reasons that underpinned my decision. Professionally, I reasoned that I had probably seen all that I needed to see. Indeed, my reflections from "Winning on the Road" had completely changed my philosophy as a practitioner, and I now had a much clearer methodology imprinted in my mind of how to support performance. It was now time to share that with others and to try and create my own path. From a personal perspective, "Winning in Life" became my new pursuit, as supported with a style of play where *balance* became the tactic. I spent less time on my laptop. I went back to the gym. I played competitive football again, even though my last game had been ten years earlier. I began coaching my son's football team. I joined a golf club, a sport that I played consistently in the summer holidays of my childhood but had not played in almost 20 years. I made more effort to connect with family and old friends. I made new friends. I spent more time with my wife. We went on holidays. Most importantly, I was now "present" when I was at home. I was talking more.

Final Thoughts

The present paper is the culmination of ten years of critical reflections on both professional practice and personal being. It represents an intense period of professional and personal growth, with a continual framing and re-framing on the essence of winning. Whilst some of this story has been told in lectures and conference presentations, this account represents the first time that my reflections have been documented in a format that will always be available for others to see. The reflective journey has entailed a variety of reflective methods encompassing both personal (journal writing and drawing) and shared reflection (critical conversations, mentorship, and counselling), as occurring over a timeframe incorporating immediate (daily) and staged reflection (weeks, months, and years). Although I have long favoured reflective writing as a preferred method of reflection, readers of this story might also suggest that it was the process of "talking" that underpinned the times of greatest growth and change of being. I, too, have also arrived at this conclusion.

As with my previous reflective accounts, it is at this stage of the writing process (i.e., reflecting on reflecting) that I begin to wonder (and worry) about how my reflections may be received. Readers of this story are all likely to *see*, *hear* and *feel* very different things, likely determined by a perspective that has arisen from your own lived experiences. Some of it may resonate, some of it may not. Rightly or wrongly, I have chosen to reflect on my reflections through the lens of a *man* contemplating the life of *another man*. In looking back, I see a man whose dad was his hero, but unfortunately his dad was taken away at a time when he still had many more lessons to teach his son. The death of his dad seemed to strip away some of the essence of his own being, perhaps also a contributing factor to gradually losing his connection with his home. I see a man, who like many others, chose to deal with his grief by bottling it up, probably perceiving that it was *weak to talk*. There is also a man, like many others, who did not readily adapt to the transition of becoming a parent, perhaps the process of grieving hindered his early progression as a father. There is also a man, like many others, with an ambition and desire to succeed professionally but who lost sight of *who* and *what* really matters in life. In looking forward, I now see a man who appears content with his life. He knows he is blessed, and he never takes anything for granted. He is a man who wants to be the best husband and father he can be. He is a happy man. He is a man who will *always* have that intense desire to win, but he has now recognised what *winning really means*.

Andy's Reflections on James' Reflections

Typically, when introducing neophyte practitioners to the concept of reflective practice there is a tendency to oversimplify the concept and also an urge to "processify" it into a set of guidance as to how to reflect and instructions as to what they should reflect on. In so doing its complexity and its untidiness may be missed and the seemingly mature concept is not done full justice. In his chapter James illustrates just how complex reflective practice can be and how impactful on the whole self it can be if given the right conditions to flourish. He offers a 'free-flow' reflection that is not constrained by a model or hampered by a specific focus, just a willingness to question his own role in both his profession and also his personal life and (without being flippant) simply . . . just reflect . . . ! Such an autoethnographical approach can allow the reflector to be more critical in their insightfulness.

When we, as trainers of new practitioners, offer our "introduction to reflective practice" we tend to adopt Anderson et al.'s (2004) observation that reflective practice may serve different interests or purposes, namely technical, practical and critical. In such a notion, technical reflective practice examines the "mechanical aspects of practice" (Anderson et al., 2004, p. 192), practical reflective practice explores "personal meaning in a situation" (ibid) and critical reflective practice "questions values and actions that may hither to have been taken for granted" (ibid). It is clear to me that in this chapter James has embarked on critical reflective practice in which he questions the relationship between his "practitioner self" and his "personal self" and, dare I say it, reaches the conclusion that he has sacrificed the latter for the former and feels that now, as a result of his reflective practices, is the time to restore a balance and bring his "personal self" back to the fore in his and his family's life. Whilst reading this chapter in its initial stages I felt somewhat moved on two counts.

Firstly, I felt a sense that James felt the need to "apologise" and worry how his reflections would be received with the inference that his reflections documented here were "wrong" and that such a professional reflective piece (perhaps orientated by the brief the authors set) should not necessarily be influenced by personal life reflections. For me, the two should be intertwined linked to notions of the whole self and there was, and remains, no need to make an apology for the fact that here they are presented as such. I would argue that James' reflections show that, whilst he remains relatively young from a practitioner perspective, he has accumulated a wealth of experience which belies this age. In this chapter James shows a level of mature critical reflection – to be able to acknowledge that the person you are impacts on the professional that you are and possibly vice versa is an amazing acceptance. Nelson-Jones (1997) has previously advocated, in respect of counsellors, that a practitioner is a person first and practitioner second and that the individual's personal characteristics not only influence how they practice but rather than hinder should be a resource on which they should positively draw.

Secondly, when reading James' story, it resonated somewhat with my own. This is not about me so I won't dwell on my backstory but suffice it to say that the death of my own father and the subsequent loss (emotional rather than physical) to dementia of my mother and perhaps, some would say, an accompanying unhealthy relationship with work evoked many of the same emotions in me that James reveals here. I found myself nodding in agreement with the sentiments that James proffers and actively reflecting on his examples to find parallel examples of my own. The phrase *"lost sight of who and what really matters in life"* really stirred an inner emotion and has triggered a recognition that James might not be the only one!

It was never intended by way of initial invitation that this would be a multiple author contribution. Yet perhaps provoked by James' work with critical friends and recognition of the author's final thoughts, in particular that of worry and resonance, in consultation with James I "joined" the chapter at its latter stages. In this chapter James, for me, clearly shows a shift in his life, from a state where he felt that his applied practice and professional growth was being influenced by his personal life, to a time and place where there is now a recognition that his personal life is being negatively impacted by his professional one. In finalising the chapter, therefore, I wonder what James makes of my reflections on his reflections . . . a conversation for another day (soon) perhaps.

Acknowledgements

This chapter is dedicated to my parents. I would also like to thank all of those "critical friends" who read and commented on earlier drafts of this chapter, including Dr Andy Miles for his reflective commentary. It was the notion that these writings prompted reflection *within yourselves* that encouraged me to publish in its current format.

15 Critical Reflective Practices of a Strength and Conditioning Coach

A Case Study of What Turned into Post-Structural Refracting

Brian Gearity and Clayton Kuklick

Introduction

In alignment with my (Brian, first author) philosophy as a post-structural scholar-coach and postmodern sensibilities, I do not believe in a single, unified understanding of reflective practice. Rather, I believe there are many discourses of reflective practice. This translates for me to consider relations of power-knowledge, their meaning, utility, and effects, and an alertness of Foucault's advice on the possibility of any discourse or practice being dangerous (see Mills et al., 2022). Theoretically speaking, I can engage in problematising (i.e., awareness and critique) traditions and dominant reflective practice discourses, while practically speaking, I still must make choices effected by these discourses and remain vigilant to my unfolding everyday realities. A useful alliteration capturing this discursive philosophy is the 3Cs of *constructive*, *critical*, and *creative*. Knowledge is socially constructed, fallible, and potentially useful but also limiting and potentially damaging. I can be critical of knowledge and practice without being dismissive. As individual coaches, we can push our personal thoughts, emotions, and behaviours towards new ways of living and coaching. As scholar-coaches, we can implement these changes and push towards social change by writing and disseminating new and creative knowledge and practices. Throughout this chapter, I will tell and show the reader how this post-structural approach to reflective practice affected me and my practice as a strength and conditioning (S&C) coach.

Limited and Delimited to the Physical: Reflecting With Natural Science Evidence-Based Practice

I cannot recall exactly when I became familiar with the term reflective practice, but I suspect it was somewhere in the early 2000s while I was in graduate school and a practicing S&C coach at the University of Tennessee (UT) from 2001–2009. In my undergraduate degree programme (completed in 2001) in Physical Education and Exercise Science with Athletic Training and Fitness Specialist concentrations, students were not formally exposed to reflective practice. However, back then, I am pretty sure I was taught evidenced-based practice (EBP). My

DOI: 10.4324/9781003198758-19

initial understanding of science was from a positivist paradigm, and I was explicitly taught about experiments, hypothesis testing, and statistics. As an athletic trainer and S&C coach, positivist science was, and still is, the dominant paradigm from which I learned to solve my coaching problems.

At UT, I worked primarily as the head baseball S&C coach and an assistant with (American) football. One day, the head football S&C coach returned from a meeting with the head football coach and assistant football coaches to inform us that we, the dozen or so S&C coaches in the men's S&C department, needed to determine how to prevent so many shoulder injuries from occurring to our offensive linemen. "G" as they called me, "Look up some research and see what we can find out about offensive linemen shoulder injuries. The coaches are mad as hell, and we need to figure out why it looks like we're having a rash of shoulder injuries with our offensive linemen."

I knew something about being an offensive lineman as I played that position throughout high school and my first year of college. Offensive linemen are usually the biggest players on the football field and common shoulder injuries include rotator cuff strains, shoulder joint (i.e., acromioclavicular) sprains, and labrum (i.e., cartilage) tears. As a student in my undergraduate degree, we studied care and prevention of athletic injuries and rather ironically, the same week we covered shoulder injuries, I dislocated my shoulder as a defensive lineman tackling the quarterback. I stuck my arm out (i.e., horizontally abducted with external rotation) and the quarterback "ran through" my arm, forcing the top part of my arm (i.e., humerus) to pop out of the socket (i.e., scapula). Talk about experiential learning!

At UT, I had developed a bit of a reputation for being a bookworm and unofficial sport scientist, before those roles were as common as they are today. Like any good scientist, I engaged in what I would consider to be EBP. The problem, patient, and population were our offensive linemen as a group and their shoulder injuries, which for us ranged from rotator cuff to labrum tears. I recall sitting down at my work computer and searching the academic databases for research on offensive linemen and shoulder injuries. Having been the baseball S&C coach for several years, I kept a folder of research on pitching shoulder and elbow injuries that I could glean from as well.

There was no doubt that shoulder injuries, particularly injuries that resulted in weeks of being unable to perform or that required surgery, were serious problems. Moreover, if we were or were not doing something that contributed to these injuries, that was a serious problem as it could be seen by ourselves and our co-workers as a S&C departmental failure. Furthermore, if it was the football coaches doing something that contributed to these injuries, that too was a serious problem and perhaps the most troubling given the organisational micropolitics that would have to be navigated. I was a relatively novice coach in my 20s and new to UT, without relational and organisational capital (i.e., credibility currency to buy me personal favour). I could see two major challenges. First, telling the head S&C coach what was likely contributing to the shoulder injuries and then effectively revising the S&C programme. Second, the S&C coaches would need to interact, with any luck collaboratively, with the football coaches to mitigate shoulder injuries. The former was more of a biological problem, the latter more psychosocial, but in everyday life they came together biopsychosocially. For now, however, this case of reflective practice focused on the physical problems of the shoulder injuries, not on the organisational management and interpersonal relations in the workplace. My job at the time was not to fix all the problems, but to focus on the shoulder injuries, which is what I did.

Problem-Solving Using the Natural Sciences

After spending several hours across several days searching the academic databases, I came across a terrifically fitting article – a single-subject case study diagnosing and treating a shoulder injury in an American offensive lineman. While I currently cannot find a copy of the study, I remember three key aspects: mechanism of injury, offensive lineman blocking techniques, and strengthening key shoulder muscles. The offensive lineman's job is to protect the quarterback during a passing play or block the defensive lineman or linebacker in front of them for a running play. Offensive linemen are routinely taught on passing plays to punch the defender in front of them to stop their movement and to lockout their arms to keep back the defender. Defensive linemen that UT competed against routinely had a height between 6'0''- 6'5'' (183–213 cm) and weight between 275–330 lbs (125–150 kg). Clearly, these are massive athletes generating extremely high forces and understanding if we can even prevent injuries is worthy of science and practice. The mechanism of shoulder injury, or cause, is believed to be the defender forcing the offensive lineman's arm (i.e., locked-out forearm through humerus) posteriorly. This can occur either acutely with great traumatic force or chronically with repetitive traumas.

If offensive linemen block with their elbows slightly bent, this is thought to reduce the posterior forces to the lineman's shoulder coming from the defender, and thus reduce shoulder injury. However, this bent elbow position is considered weaker and less desirable by offensive line coaches because it is presumably harder for the offensive lineman to block without the benefit of bone-on-bone (i.e., elbow joint locked-out straight). Additionally, the bent elbow position means the defender is closer to the offensive lineman, which provides the defender with a tactical advantage compared to being farther away in a locked-out blocking position. The researchers in the article identified these risks and benefits, while arguing that the bent-arm position could be supported with additional strengthening of the triceps and rotator cuff muscles. The triceps muscles are on the back of the upper arm (i.e., humerus) and their function is to extend the elbow. The rotator cuff muscles stabilise the shoulder joint. In summary, a bent-arm position with strengthening the triceps and rotator cuff muscles should result in fewer shoulder injuries, while preparing the offensive lineman to block.

I provided the research article and a version of this summary to the head S&C coach, who then presented it to the football coaches. For all intents and purposes, we made the changes suggested in the article. Our offensive line coaches started instructing a slight bent-arm technique. We incorporated additional triceps strengthening in the S&C programme for our offensive linemen, along with additional triceps strengthening immediately prior to football practices. The S&C coaches or equipment managers would move dip machines to the entrance of the practice fields where the offensive linemen would do a couple dozen dips before practice. While I also had concerns about the potential for injury with athlete performing dips, the range of motion was limited, and it appeared that no unintended negative consequences occurred.

At the time, as we were coaches, we did not conduct a research study while implementing our intervention. There was no comparison or control group. Rather, our EBP considered the most pertinent research evidence mixed with our clinical or coaching expertise. We assumed the athletes' (i.e., patient or client) values and needs. While we may not be certain that our changes caused a decrease in shoulder injuries, we did find a reduction in their occurrence.

This sort of physical body injury, sport and S&C techniques, and performance problem is widespread within S&C contexts. Positivist science and its tools, adapted to everyday practice, are useful to evaluate, treat, and improve athletic injury and performance outcomes. The humerus is the humerus (i.e., biological composition of bone is complex but also rather straightforward), forces are developed that cause strains and sprains, and all sorts of technology (e.g., MRI, X-ray) and methods are available to understand athletes' bodies. Like my positivist science colleagues, the post-structural scholar in me might be cautious of and reconsider the mechanism of injury and ponder if we got the diagnosis right. While post-structural theory does not dive deep into experimental studies, I can still appreciate its goals to determine causality in injury and injury prevention. Diverse scholars and practitioners alike would reconsider how football practices and S&C programming may contribute to injury. Maybe we need less full contact hitting? The risk and bodily damage outweigh the benefits. Or maybe S&C sessions should have less high velocity lifts that place the shoulder in near-end range of motion positions? Perhaps there is a place for more exercises involving slower, sustained contractions of the rotator cuff and back muscles to strengthen muscles, tendons, ligaments, and bones without similar wear and tear on these tissues. A post-structuralist, not the positivist sport scientist, is likely to question how American football became such a popular spectacle, if we might alter or abandon it completely, and show other negative social and individual effects of encouraging adolescents (and adults) to bang up, or destroy, their brains, hearts, and the rest of their bodies. Also, a post-structuralist is likely to consider relations of power more and wonder in the previous case where the athletes were in this context, what their relationship is to their bodies and the S&C coaches, and how the sport coaches' disciplinary practices contribute to injury, injury prevention, and rehabilitation? Post-structuralist reflective practice would zoom out from the microscopic details of what was portrayed as a specific physical problem to the interactions of biology, psychology, and sociology. How are all these moving parts connected?

Expanding Problem-Setting and Problem-Solving: Reflecting With the Social Sciences

As an athlete, S&C coach, and student, I was interested in exercise physiology, biomechanics, and nutrition. From the time I was a teenage football player and powerlifter, through my college football playing days and as an undergraduate student, the knowledge bases associated with these disciplines helped me understand why, what, when, where, and how to train. However, the pull of the social sciences, and their strength to reflect on all the sciences, drew me in as a scholar. Throughout graduate school I studied sport psychology, sociology of sport coaching, coaching science, and cultural studies of education. With this new knowledge came new ways of seeing the world and asking new questions. Reflecting socially, the "why" I lifted was not only to become a better football player or powerlifter, but to cope with the death of my mother from cancer when I was 13, to avoid teenage apathy and drug use, and to improve my self-esteem, body image, and sense of self. Post-structuralism and other critical social sciences gave me new tools, such as power, discipline, identities, becoming, archaeology, genealogy, hidden and reverse discourses, micropolitics, and ethics, to make sense of scientific and practical issues in S&C. The sort of issues that coaches would talk about, as would positivist scientists, but I found our theorising in this area lacking and where I could add benefit and insight. Shoulder injuries still occurred, and I used positive science throughout my coaching, but new questions (e.g., what was the role of creativity or leadership as a coach?) and problems (e.g., amotivation, injury, and even death during training, under performance, poor communication) came up too. Since then, I have zoomed out and written about these issues (see Gearity & Mills, 2012; Gearity & Henderson Metzger, 2017; Gearity & Szedlak, 2022).

Earlier in this chapter, I alluded to some questions that a post-structuralist might reflect on with regards to sport and S&C. Although I had been exposed to post-structuralism and postmodernism in my graduate-level cultural studies courses, attending the North American Society for the Sociology of Sport (NASSS) annual conference in 2008 accelerated the paradigm shift in my reflective practices. With my understanding of S&C deepening by drawing upon social science and its theoretical tools, I was able to start crafting insightful arguments and make sense of my own observations and debates and discourses within S&C. Reflective practice was no longer limited to the physical, transactional, and narrow problem-solving. Social theory and the branches of philosophy swung swiftly as I took on taken for granted assumptions and made the familiar strange. S&C was also a social practice, and I was learning to say something about that.

For my doctoral dissertation that I completed in 2009, I did what I would consider to be a typical sport psychology study. I completed an interview-based study with athletes asking them to reflect on their experiences of poor coaching. In reviewing the literature, I read how the field of sport psychology and the burgeoning research on coaching science had conceptualised and studied quality in coaching. I also reviewed related literature on how coaches learned to coach, where reflection was becoming a hallmark of quality coaching. I continued attending the NASSS annual conference in subsequent years, and with the support and mentoring of Dr Jim Denison and reading his work, I became more interested in thinking, researching, and practicing with post-structural theory. Reflective practice existed in Denison (2007), but it was not explicitly called that; it was informed by Foucault's theorising, and not Schön's (1987), who most coaching science researchers at the time used to guide their reflections in learning to coach.

Many overlapping experiences happened in the next five years that affected my reflective journey. I was moving more into post-structural theory and published a critical autoethnographic reflection on my experiences as a S&C coach at UT (see Gearity & Mills, 2012). Also, I was chairing the dissertation committee of (the now Dr) Clayton Kuklick, who was studying coach learning (Kuklick, Gearity, Thompson, & Neelis, 2015) and whose dissertation ultimately used Schön's (1987) theory of reflective practice to examine the efficacy of undergraduate coaching-students' reflective practice (Kuklick et al., 2015a, 2015b). And, to top it off, I volunteer coached high school football for two seasons as a full-participant ethnographer, a team for whom I was also the S&C coach. In the following section, I expand on my growing understanding of reflective practices that resulted from these experiences, particularly from my emerging post-structural perspective, which I propose is different than the technical-physical EBP case offered earlier.

Multiplicities of Reflecting: From Schön to Foucault, to Deleuze too?

Reflective practice is often thought of as a way of transforming experience into knowledge, by thinking back on something that happened to make better sense of it, not making the same mistake again, and, therefore, enhancing an outcome in the future. As a S&C coach, in addition to the physical injury problem addressed earlier, highly essential and frequent tasks include motivating athletes and designing programmes to enhance performance. These interactive and dynamic tasks occur through the coach-athlete relationship. Schön (1987) theorised the reflective practice cycle consists of a reflective conversation that is initiated by one's role frame. A *role frame* is generated from one's previous experiences, which acts as a lens for viewing, interpreting, and perceiving a problem that starts *the reflective conversation*. In this *reflective conversation*, one *appreciates* a problem based on their *role frame*, then *generates strategies* to overcome the issue, and then actively *experiments* with a strategy. One may experience a satisfactory outcome or need to re-appreciate or re-frame the problem until a satisfactory outcome is experienced. As a S&C coach informed by positive science research, my role frame led me to view athletes as problems, the physical body as a problem that should be understood with positivist science, and with my expertise and education in S&C and athletic injuries my implemented evidence-based programme would lead to the best outcomes (i.e., aforementioned EBP story).

After reading Denison's (2007) article critiquing normal, disciplinary coaching practices, I could see more clearly how my own coaching practices might be producing unintended consequences or the very problems that I was trying to avoid, which impeded athletic performance. I could start to trace the discourses or ways of knowing that I was taught or socialised into. I was able to more fully appreciate that they were not the *truth*, but discursive constructions that could be problematised to become freer to coach in other ways. The dominant way of doing sport and S&C coaching aligns well with Foucault's work on contemporary relations of power-knowledge and why Shogan (1999) said reading Foucault's *Discipline and Punish* was like reading a how-to coaching manual. S&C coaches, like sport coaches, plan and create minutely detailed training sessions to build a factory-like model with nearly absolute control of time, space, and the flow of athletic bodies.

If an athlete was out of line, literally or metaphorically, *discipline* them. If an athlete needed to gain muscular strength, *prescribe* more weight training. If you had to train a group of athletes, *plan* every minute element performed in sequence to maximise productivity. The strategy generated to solve problems, or to just do our job, was more control. We never called it control. There was no need. We all knew it was simply good coaching. And by not calling it control, power could remain out of sight, more effective, and us coaches could feel good about what we were doing in the best interests of athletes. Guided by select discourses and practices that never challenged concealed power relations (i.e., physiology, biomechanics, nutrition, testimony of expert/winning coaches, authoritative leadership), we found it nearly impossible to re-frame problems. This is how contemporary power is insidious, subtle, and remarkably effectively. Our role frames never critiqued the so-called big picture or the technologies of discipline, power, and dominant discourses that were constraining and impeding our interpretations. On this near invisibility of powers in disciplinary societies, Foucault (1978) wrote "power is tolerable only on condition that it masks a substantial part of itself" (p. 86).

Despite all the evidence showing negative effects from too much discipline and disciplinary practices (Denison, 2007), we were not aware that we and the dominant way of doing S&C and sport coaching were so disciplinary. We were so busy generating and implementing strategies to reinforce this disciplinary system, we never stopped to challenge our taken for granted assumptions. My co-authored paper reveals the numerous negative effects from ordinarily unseen disciplinary practices (see Gearity & Mills, 2012), and it was at this time that serendipitously I got back into coaching. I had received an email from a local high school football coach who was looking to hire a new head middle school football coach. I recommended one of our new graduates for the position, and I asked the head coach if he would consider me to volunteer coach with his football team. I suggested I could be a great help with S&C while I learned to coach high school football, which I had never done. We set up a meeting to discuss the possibility, but before we met, I sent him my resume, as he requested.

Continuing the theme in this chapter on reflection, when I prepared to meet with the head football coach, I kept in mind the research in the sociology of sport coaching (Potrac & Jones, 2009) using Goffman's (1959) presentation of self and organisational micropolitics. I was careful not to come across as a know-it-all, big-time college coach or as an eggheaded, ivory tower professor. Arrogance or abstraction did not seem like an effective first impression. In earnest, I wanted to coach and while I thought myself to be a pretty good coach, I knew I did not have all the answers. Not even close. I could have, probably should have, done a bit more research on the head coach before we met, but I just thought to play it humble and get my foot in the door. He graciously invited me to come meet with him in his office in the football locker room, so that was a good sign that a door was opening.

> "Well Coach Gair-Uh-tee," he said in a deep slow Southern drawl, "Is that how you say it?" I nodded affirmatively, although his hitting of the syllables sounded off. I got used to it as this is how he pronounced my last name for the next two years.
> "I see here," he looked down at my resume and pointed to the paper with his thick, wrinkled fingers, "You were a strength and conditioning coach at Tennessee."
> "Yes, Coach. That's correct. I worked with football and baseball the most for my eight years there. I finished my PhD, decided to become a professor, and got the job at Southern Miss."
> "Uh hmm. Well, do you think you could help us with coaching the kids to run 40s (yard sprints)? I got this video here by a speed coach and we're okay with it, but is that something you can do?"

At this point I thought a few things. I was well aware that coaches present themselves in a manner to gauge your response, feel you out a bit. I had seen this before and the coaching science research leaned into my consciousness. This was an informal test. Another part of me wanted to laugh at the absurdity of the question. After all, I had been a Division I S&C coach for eight years, I had three certifications with USA Track & Field, and I had programme designed speed training and instructed athletes' sprint technique with well over a thousand football and baseball players. Yes, I could coach some high schoolers to run 40s. I was also familiar with the coach in the instructional video he held up, a good coach from what I heard, and I thought it a bit curious that he had bothered to purchase the video and have it nearby while we met.

The 60+ year old head coach had a certain cleverness to him. He was calm, not outwardly enthusiastic, and certainly not gushing at the chances that a qualified S&C coach-professor-coach educator dropped into his lap by good fortune. We had a good chat and he told me to come back the next week when they started summer evening conditioning. When the season started that August, the head coach was surprised when I showed up for Sunday film review; this bought me additional credibility that I was a real coach, there to learn, and be there for the team.

This background is important as it sets up my post-structural informed reflection as a football and S&C coach. The coaching staff was comprised of five coaches who had all coached together for a handful of years. This was a relatively tight knit group. My fieldnotes from August 2012 identified that their experience working together resulted in them knowing often what the other would say or do. Their practice plans were structured, and they would talk in shorthand because they intuitively understood each other. I did not. It took me months to acquire their vocabulary.

My observations of their summer conditioning and eventually pre-, in-, and post-season football practices mostly align with the technologies of discipline identified earlier. For weight training, the athletes were grouped into three stations – squat, bench press, and power clean. There were subgroups within each station. The weight training was led by one of the coordinators and he used a whistle and group numbers to start each set.

> "Alright, group 1 ready," and the whistle blasted. Group 1 performed their set of back squats.
> "Alright, group 2 ready," and the whistle blasted.

This was the routine. There was discipline. There was hardly any time for anything but discipline. There was so much discipline that there was marginal instruction for exercise technique. Coaches were not buzzing about giving a lot of demonstrations, instruction, or feedback. The athletes' power clean techniques varied from poor to mediocre; feet spread too wide, not dropping deep under the bar, and catching the bar that looked like a reverse curl or very awkward and painful front squat. Bench press looked pretty good. Squats were okay. Forty-yard sprints varied like power cleans. I knew I could instruct all this better, but I was worried if I came on too strong that I might disrupt the coaching staff's relationships and find myself excluded or, worse, asked to leave. That is what Foucault noted happens in disciplinary systems – subtle corrections to bring people in line. I wanted less discipline and more "coaching", by which I meant a better pedagogical environment for engaging, learning, and performing, not docile bodies (i.e., useful and easily controlled). But I was careful never to overstep. As the weeks went on, I offered more instruction and problem solving related to S&C programme design and implementation. By September, after volunteering for about three months, I ended up taking over most of the S&C programming. It worked out well as the football coaches were more interested in football, and as a S&C coach learning to coach football, I was happy to improve the S&C component.

One unintended consequence of my enthusiasm for S&C resulted in me leading the weight room with some athletes while the coaches would review film, install strategy and tactics with other players, or even run practices, particularly on Thursdays before Friday's night game. I would often take a few promising first or second year players to lift, stretch, or condition instead of doing Thursday's walk throughs. I was often assigned to do what I did best (i.e., S&C) because I provided that extra coach for the head coach, which meant for me personally I missed out on coaching a bit more football. Knowing now that Foucault (1977) referred to the disciplinary instrument, hierarchical observation, or head coaches' numerous assistants as the "perfect eye that nothing would escape" (p. 173), I could help them do S&C during football practice and other things that previously they could not do due to lack of qualified eyes. Similarly, at football practice I could pull some guys aside to do some reps instead of silently watching; if they were "good" football players they watched practice carefully, "bad" ones zoned out.

In the Summer and early Fall, I worked most with the power clean group as I did state that this was where I thought I could be most effective. It was the most task-complex lift and it was rare to see any of the other coaches instruct it, although the other coordinator would offer cues and feedback, and eventually he would come to ask me a lot of questions about S&C. The following year I asked the defensive coordinator what my greatest contribution to the team was and he replied – proper instruction on Olympic lifting. Athlete autonomy was rare. Athletes doing what they were told and commanded by a whistle and a booming voice was omnipresent.

One of the coordinators and another assistant coach both worked the offense. The coordinator had coached the assistant when he was a high school athlete and they had worked together with the offensive line and tight ends for several years. In my fieldnotes, I described how I could "feel" like I was being watched by the one assistant. I was an odd newcomer – a former Division 1 S&C coach turned professor who asked to volunteer at this rather run-of-the-mill, but well-respected high school football programme. Everything about this situation was abnormal. I wanted to take the reins and run with the S&C programme, to continue some disciplinary practices but disrupt others. Would most S&C coaches not lack awareness of power-knowledge and instead desire near total discipline? Later during my first season, I told the head coach that I had written a paper on discipline and as a result, I was trying to coach in less disciplinary ways. He agreed that the best players developed themselves and did not merely follow orders, like sheep follow the herd. But to what extent were we allowing players to lead? Disrupting disciplinary practices was not the equivalent of facilitating self-directed learning, but it was a start. Can critical self-direction or anti-docile bodies be created within a mostly disciplinary system of S&C and football? How could we know if, or when, too much discipline was a problem?

I wanted to get rid of the whistles, offer more instruction to achieve greater athlete technical proficiency, and assign training loads with greater precision. Some things I wanted to control, other things I wanted to control less. A bit schizophrenic. By August, I had written that we needed to spend more time on nutrition as body composition changes were not going to occur with just whistles and work. I started taping up nutrition and workout advice on the white cinder blocks in the weight room and the cork bulletin board in the locker room. By year 2, I completely changed our pre-practice warm-up and had taught the athletes numerous new stretches. When I saw a handful of them doing these stretches before one of the games, I thought that they had really learned something and that by doing these stretches on their own, they were engaged in self-development and autonomy. I was providing them with tools for becoming athletes, without controlling everything. Then again, maybe I was just fooling myself and they were just doing what they were told and trying to please me.

In the off-season, as I took on the S&C lead, I kept some of their novel and effective practices, but changed a lot from the warm-up to speed training, lifting, plyometrics, and conditioning. I used to run and lift with some of them, especially guys that were not playing much in-season. I changed the exercise selection and progression to develop greater lifting competence, as well as strengthen key stabilising muscles, and teach from a deeper and wider S&C toolbox. At times, we would still have stations and groups, but with better technique and an understanding of what the technique was supposed to be. During the team lifts, for all intents and purposes, time on task was required, but the whistles were down, and instruction was up. Also up were the loads of weight lifted and unquestionably, we were faster, stronger, and in better overall football physical preparation in year two.

Throughout my time coaching the football team, I reflected on so many things, continuously thinking of ways to disrupt power, knowledge, and the dozens of subjectivities bounding about. Was I disrupting my coaching docility or athlete docility? A bit of both most likely. Table 15.1 illustrates some of the ways I disrupted disciplinary practices.

Refracting on Reflecting

But did these kids need more, or less, discipline? Something else entirely? A benefit of reflecting post-structurally is the recognition that so many things can be changed. As Foucault argued, we are freer than we think (Martin, 1988). Also (not but), in this context, there were so many overlapping systems, norms, and needs that possibilities were constrained. We needed to get 11 football players lined up correctly and then execute their responsibilities simultaneously. We needed them to eat well daily, but when I would talk to them about calories and the nutritional value of varying foods, they often had no idea how this worked. Nobody is supposed to miss practice, but two of the players, brothers, missed a couple of practices in-season after they were evicted from their apartment. A 17-year-old transfer student from a nearby school who joined our team in the summer during conditioning was killed in car accident a month into the season. The head coach pointed out to me early on that not a single starting athlete on the defence had a two-parent household. Many of the players lived with a single parent or close relative (e.g., grandmother). One of the kids I coached daily in the weight room and in my position group on the football field decided to swallow a handful of his dad's Adderall at school because he thought he was going to get caught with them when he was surprised by a knock on the bathroom door. He practiced that day, pale as a ghost, unusually struggling with a few sprints that he normally dominated. I knew he was off, but only understood why after the fact. Following another overdose later that year, he would transfer to an alternative school. I never saw him again. Maybe my own focus on disciplinary practices,

Table 15.1 Outcomes of Disrupting Disciplinary Practices

Space & Flow	Time	Panopticon & Means of Correct Training
Varied where lifts and activities were performed; moved inside to outside; built new pullup bars outside near field; did not get locked into stations or self-contained training racks.	Used intuition or emotion (e.g., felt need to have greater variety, team building, challenge, or fun) to guide S&C programme design and made changes in relation to football practice and season performance and energy.	Based on head coach's desire, we performed max repetition testing in-season mid-week, which is definitely not in any periodisation model and turned out to be a great lift, with great energy, and no negative consequences.
Removed old weight machines that were unused in locker room, greater variety in stations and exercise selection.	Accepted that 10–20 minutes before or after practice was possible and beneficial, not just a longer chunk of designated time.	Recognised the interconnectedness of so many things and that reductionism is severely limited if not fatally flawed.
Used different parts of the football and practice field in multiple ways (e.g., several shapes).	Quality of work guided lifting or conditioning, not pre-determined programme.	Embracing non-linear athlete and coach development and unforeseen challenges.
Incorporated games and friendly competition into lifting sessions.	Greater athlete control of time, not waiting on the coach's whistle and command.	Relationships, diversity, questioning, and planning sessions amongst coaches resulted in different and new practices.
Grouped athletes differently, not just based on seniority or age.	Provided a specified period (i.e., "You got 5 minutes") for athletes to do as they choose.	Recognised the need to be nearby for supervision, safety, and reduce legal liability without surveilling every single repetition, exercise, or sprint.
Used lined football field temporally and based on athlete effort, not lines or pre-determined distances (i.e., touching the line or finishing through the line was disciplinary, arbitrary, and at times ineffective).	Extended coaching time with handouts, social media, email, 1–1 discussions; think about how to coach when not in-person or adapt based on what else is going on (i.e., off-season other sports) or head coach's planning/preferences.	Coaches and athletes experimenting; head coach stating in practice we were going to experiment with different players in a new formation and that we did not know exactly how it was going to work.
Changed exercise order and did not follow "best practices" according to limited physical science research.	Allocated more time to nutrition, mental skills, injury prevention, stretching, technique, film, anything.	
Athletes chose lifts to perform after prescribed portion of S&C programme.	Coach lifts with athletes; model what being a lifter looks like to complement head coach's meaning of being a football player, not just somebody who plays football.	
Asked questions and offered choices during lifting stretching.		

disrupting them to advance coaching science research, resulted in missed opportunities to address these kids' needs and realer problems.

Systematic (perhaps formulaic) approaches to reflective practice (e.g., Schön) and EBP are often portrayed as rather neat and tidy sequential processes involving a couple of factors; problem (shoulder), identify solution (mechanism of injury & efficacious adaptations), achieve satisfactory outcome (fewer injuries). They can reduce the values, complexities, and dynamism of coaching to facilitate problem solving. Engaging in the messiness of post-structural reflecting *jars* my sense of paradigms and reality, *criticises* neutrality, reductionism, and lifelessness, and *induces* me to wonder if I have missed the forest for the trees. Generally, in practice, in the everyday life of a S&C coach, there is always so much going on concurrently and numerous biological, psychological, sociological, and interdisciplinary interpretations are possible to make sense of what is going on. When I sat down to write this chapter, I did not know where I was going. I likely would not have had the courage to write it as such if I knew what I would say at the end (Martin, 1988). When done well, it is quite conceivable that post-structural reflection (maybe I should have written *refraction*) can be a technology (i.e., tool) of the self (development) via active self-examination (Foucault, 1988). Writing this chapter has helped me consider the contact between technologies of domination and technologies of the self (Foucault, 1988). I think I wrote this chapter to become something I was not yet. What good is refraction (there, I've done it) if it acts like a mirror? I can hear the post-structural possibility of danger alarm ringing! I do not want to obsess too much as then I may lapse into self-surveillance (Markula, 2003).

Perhaps, for clarity I should offer comment on my use of the term refraction in preference to reflection. Put plainly, reflection tends to be incremental, linear, reductionistic, and reenforcing of dominant identities, systems, and relations of power. Much like an operational definition of reflection from physics, it is a subtle change that returns into the original medium; reflection is a mirror image. Refraction, developing it and drawing from post-structural theory, constructs, critiques, and creates simultaneously, recursively, and continually. A coach engages in refraction, it is not a thing unto itself. Refracting engages relations of doing, knowing, power, and becoming. Like an operational definition of refraction from physics, refracting passes through, picks up, leaves behind, and bends to something else. We know what the reflective practitioner is, but what can a refractive practitioner do?

If you got this far in the chapter – in earnest, thank you. If this assemblage was not for you (or even if it was), then try another. Better, create another (Deleuze & Guattari, 1987). As for me, I must admit, without confessing (Foucault, 1988), I am no longer a post-structural scholar-coach. Well, I am, but I am multiple, becoming more. What is true for love relationships, for writing, for refracting, is true for S&C, football, and life: The game is worthwhile insofar as we do not know where it will end (Martin, 1988). This is not the end.

In sum, we offer the following considerations:

- S&C coaching is much more than sport science, EBP, and interacting with an athlete's biological tissue, which are dominant discourses in S&C.
- Frameworks or models of reflection exist that can be useful for problem-setting and problem-solving, but some are rather formulaic and constraining as they tend to reinforce ways of knowing and practicing rather than challenging them, whilst washing over the messy realities of reflection in everyday life.
- Some scholars, such as post-structural and postmodern theorists, encourage artistic, creative, experimental, and refracting thinking, or what Foucault called "thinking differently," which was modelled at the end of this chapter.

16 Reflective Practice During the HERizon Physical Activity Intervention Project

The Utility of Group Reflection and Lessons Learnt from Exercise Psychology Students

Hannah C. Wood, Amelia K. Simpson, Amelia K. McIntosh, and Emma S. Cowley

Introduction

This chapter aims to critically reflect on how engaging with reflective practice formed an integral part of our work with adolescent girls who were participating in the *HERizon* physical activity (PA) intervention (Cowley et al., 2021). We offer this reflection from our perspective as students and neophyte practitioners. We (Hannah, Amelia S and Amelia M) worked on HERizon as "Activity Mentors" during our M.Sc. Sport Psychology degree at Liverpool John Moores University (LJMU) to fulfil our applied placement module requirement. The HERizon Project was Emma's multidisciplinary PhD project at LJMU; she offers her researcher perspective to the chapter (by initially outlining the context of HERizon and then contributing to our group reflection evaluation towards the end of the chapter). The PhD initially set out to design and evaluate the effectiveness of a remote PA intervention for adolescent girls. Through this the HERizon Project was developed, which aimed to support inactive girls in improving their relationship with PA to create sustained participation in an activity they enjoy.

To locate the context of the case study, we first offer a brief overview of HERizon and what our role as Activity Mentors entailed, before discussing what reflective practice means to us and how we used it during HERizon. Following this, we explore key "reflections on reflection" and consider how reflective practice aided our development as neophyte practitioners. We then evaluate our approach to reflection, particularly focusing on group reflection as this was the most unique aspect of our approach, before offering recommendations for others conducting group reflection based upon our experiences. We conclude by reflecting on how much we have learnt (both about reflective practice itself and what we have learnt through engaging with it) and finish by summarising what we wish we had known at the start of our ongoing journey with reflection, in the hope such tips may be useful to other neophyte reflective practitioners (and supervisors of these individuals).

DOI: 10.4324/9781003198758-20

Providing the Context: The HERizon Project

The HERizon Project (Cowley et al., 2021) was a 12-week randomised controlled trial (informed by Self-Determination Theory; Ryan & Deci, 2017) that aimed to increase the PA of adolescent girls in the UK and Ireland. Participants were asked to complete three PA sessions each week but were free to choose any activity (e.g., swimming, team sports). All girls received a PA logbook that included: a calendar to record their PA sessions; a "PA menu"; and weekly worksheets designed to support participants in creating new PA behaviours (see Figure 16.1). The PA menu provided links to various PA types that did not need specialised equipment or large space and could be completed at home (e.g., follow-along boxing, yoga classes). Participants were invited to try these suggested activities and complete the weekly worksheets, but neither were compulsory.

Participants were assigned to one of four intervention arms, with some groups receiving additional intervention components to the PA logbook. The four arms were: (a) a PA programme group, involving group workout classes and access to an online social community; (b) a behaviour change support group; (c) a combined PA programme and behaviour change support group; and (d) a comparison group (i.e., no additional components). Participants in groups (b) and (c) both received individual behaviour change support through weekly 15-minute videocalls with an allocated Activity Mentor (our role in HERizon). Of the 12 mentors, seven were LJMU M.Sc. Sport Psychology students and five were

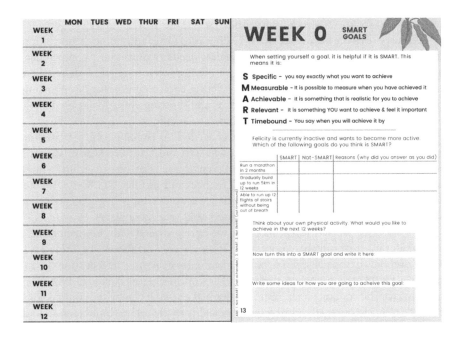

Figure 16.1 Example Pages from the PA Logbook

Table 16.1 Overview of the Behaviour Change Support Calls

Week	Description of session	Duration
Week 0	Introduction – rapport building and goal setting	30 mins
Week 1	Setting action plans	15 mins
Week 2	Barrier identification	
Week 3	Action plan review (no specific topic)	
Week 4	Action plan review (no specific topic)	
Week 5	Coping planning	
Week 6	Reflect on achievements	
Week 7		
Week 8		
Week 9	Coping planning	15 mins
Week 10		
Week 11		
Week 12	Reflect on achievements Coping planning	30 mins

Stage 2 trainee Sport and Exercise Psychologists (either completing a Professional Doctorate or the British Association of Sport and Exercise Sciences' [BASES] Sport and Exercise Psychology Accreditation Route [SEPAR]). Each mentor was assigned several mentees (approximately eight across two staggered intake waves) to work with for the 12-week intervention (see Table 16.1 for an overview).

The purpose of the behaviour change calls was to foster autonomous motivation in mentees by supporting their psychological needs of autonomy, competence, and relatedness (Ryan & Deci, 2000). All mentors were trained to deliver in a needs-supportive style (the "how"; e.g., offering choice [autonomy], supporting opportunities for progression [competence] and showing empathy [relatedness]; Teixeira et al., 2020) and to use six behaviour change techniques (the "what"; e.g., goal setting, action planning; Michie et al., 2011). Training took place online over two and a half days and was led by a Health and Care Professions Council (HCPC) Registered Sport and Exercise Psychologist (also one of Emma's PhD supervisors), with assistance from Stage 2 trainees and another HCPC-Registered Psychologist. Training involved both guidance on procedures (e.g., safeguarding and child protection) and competency-based tasks (e.g., role plays).

To standardise support across mentees, we were provided with pre-planned session guides for each call (based upon the PA logbook worksheets; see Table 16.1 for an overview of topics). Each session had a similar structure: (a) reflection on the prior week's PA; (b) discussion of the weekly worksheet/topic; and (c) PA action planning for the coming week. Although we had a session plan with required content, we were encouraged to bring our personality to the calls to build rapport and had the scope to tailor the sessions to each individual mentees' needs.

Reflective Practice During HERizon: Activity Mentors' Perspective

Prior to HERizon, our experiences of reflective practice varied. Hannah had no previous experience whereas Amelia S and Amelia M had engaged with reflection during their B.Sc. Sport Psychology degree. As a result, our perceptions of reflection before HERizon also varied (e.g., Amelia S and Amelia M had already experienced the value of reflection whereas Hannah was perhaps more sceptical). Regardless, HERizon was our first experience of one-to-one applied client work and we all quickly came to view reflection as integral to our development as neophyte practitioners.

We subscribe to Knowles et al.'s (2014b) definition of reflective practice, viewing it as an ongoing, purposeful process that bridges the gap between experience and learning and results in change. In this way, reflection helped us to make sense of our experiences and identify learning that we could apply to future work. Through continued engagement with reflection (and learning from our peers during group reflection) we came to understand how reflection was allowing us to make informed decisions during and after client work (Knowles et al., 2014b). As our understanding developed, we began to realise that our undergraduate reflections had remained largely at the descriptive level (e.g., identifying what went well and what we could improve; Knowles et al., 2001), whereas our HERizon experience was challenging us to move towards more critical levels of reflection (e.g., considering why we responded in a certain way). For example, we experienced how reflection could lead to the fruition of unconscious (and occasionally uncomfortable) internalised narratives (Anderson et al., 2004). This sometimes led us to question our own beliefs and values. Whilst this could be challenging, it increased our self-awareness and helped us to recognise how we could further develop (as both people and practitioners). In this way, we feel we are starting to "get" reflective practice, rather than simply learning "how to do it" (Trelfa & Telfer, 2014). If we had not engaged with reflection, we would not have learnt nor developed as much from our placement experience. We used both reflection-in-action (i.e., during our calls to help guide our decisions) and reflection-on-action (i.e., after our experiences to identify learning) during HERizon (Knowles et al., 2014b; Schön, 1983, 1987). However, we mainly discuss on-action reflection throughout this chapter. We used three different forms of on-action reflection: individual reflection, group reflection and individual supervision.

Individual Reflection

We all used a journal to reflect individually. Like many who are new to reflection, we began by using Gibbs' (1988) framework (e.g., Collins et al., 2013) due to its simple, cyclical structure (Willis, 2010). Then as we started to gain confidence we moved away from this simple structure, either using it more flexibly or exploring other reflective models. Below, Amelia M gives an example of how she engaged in individual reflection:

> Throughout HERizon, the logbook was used by both mentees and mentors to guide us through each call with tasks and worksheets to complete. Approximately halfway through our calls, one of my mentees mentioned that they had never received the PA logbook that I had been referring to each week! When the mentee disclosed this information, I immediately began reflecting-in-action: my mind raced as I felt a sense of guilt and confusion (because I had regularly asked "can you see on page . . ."); however, I tried to maintain the flow of the call so that she would not feel awkward or uncomfortable. Afterwards, I used Gibbs' (1988) framework to guide my written reflection. Initially, I remained extremely self-critical and questioned "what else could I have done to be aware of the situation?". I felt disappointed in myself for not creating an environment in which she felt she could be honest. However, through this reflective process (particularly focusing on making sense of the situation), I began to rationalise and accept the situation. I acknowledged that I had no reason to doubt her when she told me she was using the logbook and with the calls taking place online there was little more I could have done (as I could only see what she showed me on camera). Furthermore, I considered the mentee's perspective, perhaps she had felt the logbook was not necessary as we had talked through each task together. In this way, individual reflection was particularly important in helping me to move forward without fixating on my mistakes (without reflection I may have continued feeling this sense of guilt which likely would have impacted on my future work with the mentee).

Group Reflection

All mentors, supervising psychologists, and Emma (the researcher) engaged in weekly online group reflection meetings using Zoom video-conferencing software (reducing in frequency as the mentee calls became less frequent). The purpose of these one-hour sessions was broad, giving us the opportunity to share and discuss our individual reflections as well as reflect together on our similar experiences. Typically, we started with an informal catch-up, during which Emma would provide new updates or discuss any issues with the research aspect of HERizon. Then we would split into three smaller breakout rooms with our assigned reflection group, providing "the opportunity and time for quality relationships to develop and a depth to group-based reflections to emerge" (Huntley & Kentzer, 2013, p. 60). These groups were designed to have individuals with a range of experience and were facilitated by Stage 2 trainee psychologists. In our groups, we would spend 25–30 minutes reflecting together on our previous week of calls, sharing challenges, learnings, feedback, and support. Each mentor could bring any of their individual reflections to the meeting to share and discuss; equally, the facilitator would pose questions based on our similar experiences (e.g., we reflected together on how we ended our relationship with the first wave of mentees and what we could learn from this experience to implement in concluding the second wave of calls). Whilst we mainly reflected together on our work with the mentees, we also discussed wider topics, such as what we were learning about applied exercise psychology that we could apply in future work. For the last 10–15 minutes we would come back together as one group to share learnings and discuss issues that had arisen from our small group reflection.

Supervision

We also met individually with our supervisor (the same psychologist that conducted the training and group reflection sessions) to participate in conversational reflection when we felt it was required. The purpose was either to seek advice on a specific issue that had arisen with a mentee (following safeguarding procedures) or to reflect on our experiences, helping to deepen (and add a level of expertise to) our individual reflections (Knowles et al., 2007). Below, Amelia S gives an example of how she used individual supervision:

> Early on in HERizon I started to become concerned about one of my mentees who was over-exercising and had mentioned feeling unhappy with her eating habits on a couple of occasions. Consequently, following agreed child protection guidance, I met with my supervisor to discuss the situation, which also gave me the opportunity to reflect on how I had handled the situation. Using Gibbs' (1988) framework, I looked at my assumptions and beliefs underlying why I had become concerned about my mentee. Furthermore, my supervisor reassured me that I had made the right decision to approach her with my concern and we discussed next steps. We decided that in future calls I would: discuss the importance of rest days, explore her feelings if she mentioned food again to better understand her perspective, have weekly supervision meetings to discuss further steps and continue to reflect on how well I was supporting my mentee.

The above situation also led to the development of a "talking about weight and related problems" help-sheet to provide guidance to all mentors about having conversations around weight (if mentioned by mentees), which was discussed during a group reflection session. This gave all mentors the opportunity to reflect on how we would manage a similar situation, illustrating how each form of reflection we used complemented one another to aid our development.

Reflections on Reflection

To illustrate how engaging with reflective practice positively impacted our placement experience (not only by developing our skills as reflective practitioners, but also by improving our work with our mentees) we offer the following three examples of our reflections during HERizon and discuss what we learnt from each experience.

"Did I Really Just Say That?" – Identifying and Challenging Our Beliefs and Assumptions

Some of the most valuable lessons we learnt from reflection were about ourselves and our underlying beliefs, and how such beliefs and assumptions might have been impacting our applied work. Previous literature has demonstrated how engaging with reflection can result in new insights to the self and environment (Cropley et al., 2007; Huntley & Kentzer, 2013; Neil et al., 2013). Moreover, by reflecting on such insights you can consider whether your beliefs are serving you (and align with your values) or whether they need challenging. Whilst this can be an uncomfortable process, it leads to greater self-awareness and, therefore, increased competence as a practitioner. In the following example, Amelia S discusses how an in-action reflection led her to identify and challenge an underlying belief:

> During one call I acted in a way that conflicted with my values. I was working with my mentee to complete an activity in the PA logbook around confidence strategies. The first strategy was "be kind to yourself", which encouraged mentees to write down something they liked about themselves. I provided examples as I was explaining this but realised, as I was talking, that I had only given appearance-related examples (e.g., "I have a nice smile"). Yep, I really had just indirectly told an impressionable teenager that a woman's self-worth and confidence is determined by appearance – how awful! This message strongly conflicts with my values; one of the main reasons I applied for HERizon was the opportunity it offered to empower young females through PA and mentoring. Therefore, I reflected on why I had acted in this way. Coincidentally, I had recently begun reading de Beauvoir's "The Second Sex" (1949) which turned my analysis to societal norms. I reflected on how the male gaze is indirectly internalised from a young age; for example, in films when the male character chooses the woman who performs the Western ideal of femininity and "prettiness" (Given, 2020). I realised I had passed on to a young female what had been passed on to me: personal experiences of being reduced down to appearance (which was so ingrained into my subconscious that it became my default way of thinking). Although this realisation was extremely uncomfortable, this critical reflection was one of my most important learning curves during HERizon. It demonstrated how internalised societal narratives may affect the practice you deliver to clients. Due to this reflection, in the following call I explicitly discussed with my mentee how I had unintentionally given all appearance-related examples and replaced them with phrases such as "I am empowering" and "I am a talented dancer". Furthermore, going forward I will be more consciously aware of the language I use with clients and what effect this could have. Without reflecting on this moment, I would not have recognised this embedded narrative and therefore I believe I am now in a better position to deliver good practice.

While helping us to uncover underlying beliefs, reflection also encouraged us to consider our assumptions about the mentees themselves, particularly when responding to the "feelings" stage of Gibbs' (1988) Reflective Cycle. The service a client receives should not be contingent on a practitioner's personal feelings or assumptions about them; such behaviour would compromise the practitioner's integrity (British Psychological Society [BPS], 2018). Therefore, it is important to recognise how any prior assumptions may influence our subsequent behaviour towards clients. In the following example, Hannah discusses how she reflected on her assumptions about quieter mentees (compared to more outgoing mentees) to bring these implicitly held assumptions to consciousness:

> When reflecting-in-action during a call with one mentee I realised that I was feeling frustrated with her one-word responses to my questions and experienced similar frustrations with other quieter mentees. Analysing these feelings in subsequent individual reflection led me to recognise that I felt frustrated because I was assuming that quieter mentees were disengaged from the process. However, a group reflection discussion about working with shy mentees highlighted to me how we can never truly know what a client is getting out of our work with them. In other words, we may have been having a significant impact on a mentee, but they might not show it in a way we would recognise (based on our own beliefs and assumptions). Therefore, I tried to follow La Guardia's (2017) advice and, instead of getting frustrated, use my reactions as information to help me consider how to better support the needs of quieter mentees. My supervisor helped me to achieve this as we discussed how the goal is not to treat all mentees equally (as each is an individual). Instead, a skilled practitioner works with all mentees differently to enhance the chances of an equal outcome (i.e., providing an equitable service). As a result, I implemented deliberate actions when working with quieter mentees (e.g., leaving more pauses in the conversation to encourage further expansion) and continued to reflect individually on how my assumptions might be affecting my behaviour, an issue I likely would not have explicitly considered without regular reflection.

"Am I Stepping Outside of my Role?" – Navigating Professional Boundaries

HERizon was our first experience of navigating professional boundaries, an ethical issue because it is imperative to operate within your professional competencies (BPS, 2018). We were conscious of not stepping outside of our role, particularly when mentees raised topics not directly related to exercise psychology (e.g., asking for specific PA advice). Such experiences led us to reflect on what the role of an applied exercise psychologist should entail; for example, how much scientific knowledge do we need around PA frequency, intensity, and type? Essentially, where does the role of an exercise psychologist end and that of a fitness coach begin?

Navigating this boundary was particularly challenging because applied exercise psychology literature is currently limited to a few discussion papers (e.g., Castillo, 2020; Hutchison & Johnston, 2013; Swann et al., 2018). As the literature offered limited guidance, reflection was crucial in exploring this boundary. Supervision and group reflection were particularly useful because we gained the input of more experienced individuals (i.e., our supervisor and Stage 2 trainees). This discussion of our boundaries was prompted during group reflection by a mentor sharing that in one of her final calls the mentee said that she planned to continue improving her strength by "doing more cardio". As a group we discussed whether the mentor had an obligation to correct the misunderstanding or whether advising on type of exercise was outside of our competencies. At the end of HERizon we felt that there was currently no clear boundary to the limits of our role. However, we have continued to reflect on this issue together while writing this chapter (and sought our supervisor's experienced opinion) and have therefore clarified our thoughts. Our answer that follows is the outcome of this staged reflection (Knowles et al., 2001), an example that has highlighted to us the importance of revisiting earlier reflections.

As exercise psychologists, we have a responsibility to keep our clients safe (BPS, 2018) and, consequently, we need enough PA knowledge to avoid potential harm and identify errors in understanding, such as the example above. In this case, the mentee may have continually increased her cardio exercise and felt frustrated when she did not achieve her expected results, potentially harming her well-being. Instead, the mentor was able to correct the misunderstanding and educate the mentee on strength-based PA. Having a good understanding of the current UK government PA guidelines (Department of Health and Social Care, 2019) was crucial for the mentor to competently help the mentee; such guidelines are arguably the minimum knowledge we need as neophyte exercise psychologists. Upon revisiting the available exercise psychology literature, we found it also supports this conclusion as, generally, it suggests a base knowledge of PA for health is required (Pauline et al., 2006) but, equally, we are not qualified to prescribe exercise for example and, indeed, this is not our purpose (Shannon & Zizzi, 2018). In this way, staged reflection has developed our thoughts on this issue and identified an area of knowledge we need to further develop to be competent exercise psychologists.

"It Just Went Well" – Drawing Learning from Positive Experiences

A somewhat paradoxical challenge arose from the success the mentees experienced; many of our calls were very positive. Often mentees increased their PA with relative ease, resulting in a dearth of "critical incidents" for some mentors (defined as significant moments impacting on practitioner development; Furr & Carroll, 2003; Woodcock et al., 2008). Previous practitioners have identified the danger of reflective practice becoming a "tick-box" exercise or just something that "has to be done" (Cropley et al., 2010b, p. 524). We believe this is particularly the case in the absence of negative or challenging events as reflections may become repetitive or remain at surface-level observations if all experiences are similarly positive. Below, Hannah reflects on how she tried to ensure her reflections remained meaningful:

> To extract as much learning from the experience as possible, I reflected on why things were going well and how to replicate similar success in future (e.g., had I not fully engaged in training and preparation, I may have encountered more situations requiring me to think on my feet). I also followed Lindsay et al.'s (2007) suggestion of ensuring I was reflecting on emotions (alongside behaviours and thoughts); for example, allowing me to identify the feelings of frustration with quieter mentees discussed earlier. I made use of Gibbs' (1988) Reflective Cycle but, in retrospect, I perhaps should have explored other reflective models, which may have diversified my insights.

Our HERizon experience challenged our previously implicitly held view that reflection was mainly about improving on negatives. Indeed, Trelfa and Telfer (2014) discussed how students often feel like they need "big, worthy events leading to fundamental change" to reflect (p. 50). Perhaps this perception comes from how we are introduced to reflection: typically, we look to published reflective writing to find out how to "do" reflection. However, such writing is likely the "highlights reel" of the author's reflection and maybe does not accurately represent their everyday reflection; hence, our perception of what reflective practice "looks like" becomes warped. Alternatively, our supervisor suggested to us that students new to reflection often evaluate (e.g., what worked well and what could be improved?) rather than critically reflect (e.g., what could I learn from this experience about myself or my role?), echoing the different levels of reflection (see Knowles et al., 2014b). Moreover, descriptive or evaluative reflection usually requires an "event" to reflect upon whereas critical reflection can be applied to a broader range of scenarios and experience. Thus, when we lacked challenging moments to reflect on during HERizon, we perhaps naturally began to move beyond descriptive reflection to more critical reflection (thereby changing our view that we needed negative or challenging events to meaningfully reflect). For example, discussing how to reflect on positive experiences during group reflection led to the wider topic of how we viewed the purpose of the calls. Below, Hannah reflects on her experience of this discussion and what personal realisations this led to:

> We discussed letting go of the perception that we as practitioners have to "fix" something (or offer tangible suggestions to the client) to be helpful, a notion previously described as our "inner solutioneer" (Lindsay et al., 2007, p. 345). I undoubtedly held this belief prior to HERizon; however, through exposure to alternative viewpoints during group reflection, I realised a client intervention does not mean "fixing" something (indeed, this would be ill-aligned with the needs-supportive delivery we were aiming to achieve). Instead, an intervention can constitute any kind of interaction that instigates some form of change (which could be to

behaviour or to other aspects such as thoughts, emotions, perceptions etc.). This shift in my understanding allowed me to view the calls as a conversation first and foremost, through which I realised that I had previously been listening to respond (while worrying about what solution I could offer) rather than listening to understand, and therefore I was not fully focused on the mentee (Katz & Keyes, 2020). Changing my perspective made active listening more natural and thereby increased my competence as a practitioner.

In this way, we think reflecting on positive experiences helped us to develop our ability to critically reflect. Descriptive level reflection quickly became repetitive as our positive experiences were often similar, which created a challenge to make sure our reflection remained meaningful. To combat this, we somewhat naturally moved towards more critical reflection (a development likely also influenced by our improving ability as reflective practitioners).

Evaluation of Our Approach to Reflective Practice

Overall, engaging with three different forms of reflection was extremely beneficial to our development. As neophyte practitioners, we found written reflection using Gibbs' (1988) cycle was often encouraged; however, through HERizon we also experienced verbal and group reflection, which allowed us to identify the form we personally found most useful. The three forms of reflection we engaged in (e.g., written, group, verbal) also complemented one another; for example, during group reflection we not only shared our individual reflections, but we were also encouraged to reflect on those initial reflections through probing questions from our peers. Equally, issues raised during group reflection discussions could prompt further individual reflection. Thus, using multiple reflective practices enhanced the effectiveness of our reflection as it ensured we thoroughly explored our experiences and feelings (with external input from our supervisor and peers). This will have also increased the likelihood that we experienced the benefits of reflection, including gaining applied practice-based knowledge (Cropley et al., 2007), improving our understanding of self within the applied context (Fletcher & Maher, 2013) and assessing our own effectiveness (Knowles et al., 2007).

Benefits of Group Reflection

As group reflection is a more novel approach, and we feel that we perhaps gained the most out of it (compared to individual reflection and supervision), it warrants further evaluation. One main benefit we experienced was that it normalised our anxiety (a somewhat inevitable part of starting applied work; Tod, 2007) by giving us the opportunity to reflect together on the challenges or concerns we were experiencing (and to learn that these were extremely common;

Hings et al., 2020; Owton et al., 2014). Discussions about imposter syndrome ("persistent thoughts of intellectual phoniness"; Hutchins & Rainbolt, 2017, p. 1) were particularly useful, not only to normalise the experience but also to generate action plans to reduce such feelings. We addressed other challenges of being a neophyte practitioner in a similar way. For example, many of us felt exhausted once we started to work with clients but were somewhat unprepared for this as it is perhaps not explicitly discussed within literature. Together, we reflected on why we were experiencing such feelings (likely partly due to the pressure we were putting on ourselves to always "get it right") and what self-care strategies we could use.

Second, as the group comprised individuals with varied previous experience (and at different academic levels) we were exposed to alternative ideas and perspectives that we may not have considered had we only been reflecting individually (Rhodius & Huntley, 2014). We were also able to learn vicariously through listening to others' developmental moments and discussing how we would deal with a similar scenario, exposing us to a wider range of situations, challenges, and successes. The person sharing may have also learnt new ways to engage with the mentee under discussion.

In addition to our personal learning, a wider benefit was the impact group reflection had on the research project itself. Below, Emma reflects on the utility of the group reflection sessions to her research:

> Group reflection was important from the research perspective as it provided information on intervention delivery (i.e., was the intervention being delivered as it was intended?). Capturing mentors' reflections was important in evaluating the intervention implementation (Anderson et al., 2002), data that were later used to inform a detailed process evaluation of HERizon (Cowley et al., 2022). By meeting weekly with mentors, I could make note of any deviations from the intervention protocol that may have impacted objective outcome measures. I could also collect information on the perceived acceptability of the intervention components based on mentors' videocalls with their mentees (e.g., were the topics discussed on calls interesting and relevant? Were the participants using their PA logbook as planned?).
>
> Further, I was able to gain a better understanding of the reach of the intervention and the participants enrolled in it. While the focus of group reflection was on the psychological needs-supportive delivery, information on the participants' PA interests and the context in which the intervention took place were useful in understanding the study population (e.g., participants who were part of local sports teams or mentors' awareness of the decline in participants' engagement during school exams).
>
> Lastly, group reflection gave insight into the mentors' varying delivery styles and their acceptability of the intervention, as well as providing an understanding of the challenges mentors faced during delivery and how

these might be overcome. This information can be used by the research team to refine future intervention delivery training. This insight was important to create an intervention that is scalable and sustainable, with a standardised intervention delivery.

Challenges of Group Reflection

Although group reflection was highly beneficial to our development, there were challenges to conducting it in an effective way. The main challenge we experienced was (not) feeling able to fully engage. Reflection can be deeply personal and, at times, an uncomfortable experience; thus, it can be difficult to discuss this openly in a group. Sometimes we felt hesitant to discuss an issue for fear of being judged or coming across as incompetent, particularly as neophyte practitioners. This was exacerbated by power dynamics in the group between different academic and experience levels, as some mentors did not want to look "wrong" in front of others who were perceived to be more qualified, something that needs to be carefully managed when a diverse group of people reflect together. It is important to make sure everyone understands that challenging or contrasting views are normal and constructive for professional development and enhancing self-awareness, they are not personal or character attacks. Equally, everyone can learn from anyone else, regardless of prior experience. If these ideas had been emphasised more, we feel it would have increased the psychological safety of the group reflection sessions for all involved. However, we recognise that individuals need sufficient self-confidence to share within a group, irrespective of the environment created for them to do so, an inherent challenge with group reflection (Huntley & Kentzer, 2013). Social desirability will also likely have impacted what was discussed, a further limitation with group-based reflection (Cropley et al., 2010b; Huntley & Kentzer, 2013).

We should also highlight that our sessions were conducted entirely online (out of necessity due to the COVID-19 pandemic) as this will have undoubtedly affected our experience. Many of us had never met in person so we had to build trust and rapport with each other online. As no doubt everyone has experienced, it is harder to sustain conversation online and interpret individuals' tone in the way they had perhaps intended. Communicating over videocall removes many of the body language cues you would normally have access to in person, so you do not have the "full picture" from which to interpret. This is arguably particularly significant when challenging other people on their views or reflections.

A further online challenge was that individuals could disengage by muting themselves or turning their cameras off in a way that would not be possible in-person. Although this occurred infrequently, when it did happen it made the group feel less psychologically safe as you could not see the person's reaction or be sure they were in a private space. We think in-person reflection would have increased the psychological safety of the group by removing some of these challenges (if it had been possible at the time).

Recommendations for Facilitating Multi-Career Stage Group Reflection

Based upon our experience we recommend facilitating group reflection (alongside traditional supervision and individual reflection). However, to be effective, it must be a psychologically safe space and the group dynamics need to be carefully managed. Our suggestions include:

1. Use small groups comprising the same individuals for each meeting to help them develop rapport. If possible, a social occasion before commencing the meetings would help everyone get to know each other.
2. Encourage everyone to think beforehand about what they can bring to the meeting to reflect on (whether that is individual reflections to share or common issues they wish to reflect on with the group). You could also have some discussion topics prepared for each meeting if any group does not have individual scenarios to discuss.
3. Remind everyone of the "ground rules" (Huntley & Kentzer, 2013) at the start of every session (at least for the first few sessions). Emphasise that it is okay to disagree and challenging each other is encouraged: such challenges are not personal attacks! Also stress that everyone can learn something from everyone; possibly share the facilitator role within the small groups so that a different individual does it every week to help reinforce this.
4. If possible, conduct meetings in-person to help build rapport within the group (which we believe is vital to feel able to be honest with your reflections), although we recognise the benefit of online meetings in that location of participants does not matter.

Conclusion

Our understanding of reflection has developed considerably since beginning our journey as reflective practitioners. At the start of this journey, reflective practice seemed a somewhat vague concept that we had read about in the literature, but now it is something much more tangible that has helped us develop as both people and practitioners. As such, we feel the only real way to learn about reflective practice (and the value of engaging with it) is by doing it. Moreover, this does not have to mean reflecting individually in a journal and writing only about how to improve; instead, focusing on what went well is equally important and finding alternative ways to reflect (e.g., group reflection) can also be highly beneficial. In this regard we agree with Knowles et al. (2014b): reflection should be a creative, individual experience and if you view it as such you can avoid "becoming sanitised by the norm" (p. 11). Ultimately, reflective practice has helped us learn from our experience, increased our self-awareness and confidence as neophyte practitioners and therefore, arguably, increased our competence as well. With this in mind, we wish to conclude by summarising what we wish we had known about reflection at the start of this journey in the hope that this may prove useful to other neophyte reflective practitioners (as well as those tasked with supervising them).

Our Tips for Other Neophyte Practitioners

1. Try out multiple methods to find what works for you. Written reflection is often promoted but other methods could be more effective for you. In our experience, some mentors found they engaged in deeper, more meaningful reflection when done individually, whereas others found group reflection to be most impactful on their learning.

2. Reflective practice will likely be a requirement of your qualification so you may as well take the time to make it meaningful! Try to put it into practice as part of your life and be as honest in your reflections as possible. Remember that no one is going to read your individual reflection unless you choose to share it so try to discount what others may think and focus on being honest with yourself (we have found this has led to the most authentic and useful reflections). Sometimes reflections are uncomfortable but that is okay! We are not expected to get it "right" first time and, arguably, we will never be the finished article: there is always something to learn. Use reflection to help you identify that learning.

3. Equally, you do not need to have "deep" reflections all the time; we have found that in reality sometimes there is not much to reflect on about an experience. However, reflections can build up over time. For example, a collection of seemingly surface-level observations may accumulate in your journal that, when revisited several months later, reveal a pattern of deeper reflection that you can explore. Indeed, we feel we have perhaps engaged in the deepest reflection (and learnt the most about reflective practice) through writing this chapter together and reflecting on our reflections.

Our Tips for Supervisors to Help Neophyte Practitioners See the Value of Reflection from the Outset

1. Recognise that students new to reflection will likely be sceptical to begin with because it is something we feel you can only really understand the value of by experiencing it.

2. Introduce reflective practice as an integral part of an applied experience (rather than an addition).

3. Encourage creativity in reflection. Structured written reflection is often highly useful (particularly for learning how to reflect); however, students may see this as the only option if other approaches are not discussed.

4. Share some example reflection of your own to make it tangible for your students (we found group reflection to be so valuable for seeing first-hand what reflection actually looks like in practice).

Acknowledgements

We wish to thank: our supervisor (Dr Paula Watson), other supervising psychologist during group reflection (Dr Laura Carey), and the rest of the mentor team (Chiara Mansfield, Ella Whitcomb-Khan, Izzie Cacciatore, Nicole Wells, Abbie Bowman, Ellie Glover, Jennifer Ballinger, Payal Gore, and Suzy Aram).

Section 5

Reflecting Forwards

17 Reflecting Backwards and Forwards

Summary, Recommendations, and Future Directions

Andy Miles, Emma Huntley, Zoe Knowles, and Brendan Cropley

"Follow effective action with quiet reflection. From the quiet reflection will come even more effective action."

– Peter Druker (A. A. Milne)

Introduction: Emma Huntley

It is a huge honour to be asked to write the opening section to our final chapter as an editorial team, which aims to consolidate such a wide range of high-quality chapters into a few pages. In the spirit of this book, and indeed that of the former (Knowles et al., 2014a), reflecting back on the last two years or so, the period has not been without challenge, not least in navigating the "swampy lowlands" of a global pandemic. However, the chapter contributors to this edition have made the journey more than worthwhile. I, on behalf of the editorial team, would like to thank each and every one of you for sharing your experiences, thoughts, insights, and ideas about a topic for which we share a common interest, and I hope these have favourably translated to you, the reader, as you arrive at this final section of the text. The remainder of the chapter provides an editor's summary of each of the book's subsections and concludes with some recommendations for practice and future research. The final line of the first edition of this text, concluded in saying (about reflective practice), "We are valued for being different, thinking differently and bringing innovation into what we do" (Knowles et al., 2014c, p. 191). I truly believe that the chapters in this updated version represent this sentiment entirely; every chapter is different and is valued for being so, each contributor has their own perspective on reflective practice, which is clearly evident in Chapter 3, and through this book as a resource, we hope from here you are able to bring innovation to your reflective practice, whether you have lots of experience, or you are just starting out.

DOI: 10.4324/9781003198758-22

The Conceptual Landscape and Critical Perspectives of Reflective Practice in Sport & Exercise Science and Allied Disciplines: Brendan Cropley

The collection of chapters in sections one and two of this text offer critical perspectives on conceptual and practical issues regarding reflective practice. In doing so, the authors present a series of debates that should stimulate ongoing discussion and critique with the purpose of improving understanding and application of, and engagement in, reflective practice in a way that results in profound personal and professional growth. As someone whose reflective practice journey began approximately 20 years ago, having the opportunity to work with the authors of these chapters, has personally been a timely endeavour. Certainly, the chapters have encouraged and stimulated thoughtful analysis of how I understand and continue to develop as a reflective practitioner (Chapter 3), and in accord how I elicit meaningful reflective practices (Andy and Emily, Chapter 5), how such reflective practices link to mindful self-regulation (Gareth and colleagues, Chapter 4), and my willingness to embrace the "risk" of engaging in reflection-in-action (Jo and Hamish, Chapter 6).

Underpinning debates in these sections of this text with different theoretical perspectives (e.g., Heidegger and Wittgenstein, Chapter 5; neoliberalism, Chapter 6) has added to the presentation of distinct and novel insights. Such diversity in thinking is perhaps typified in Chapter 3, where all authors provided their own views on "what it means to be a reflective practitioner" – and while the editorial team were able to draw on some commonalities, the nuanced vignettes offer us all opportunities to critically explore what this term (or position) means to us. One point that stood out within the authors' vignettes in this chapter was the understanding that the reflective practitioner should adopt a philosophical position that "promotes the use of evidence to reason between alternative solutions to practice-based problems, making such individuals open to a range of perspectives". This argument may, in part, account for the previous (and perhaps ongoing) reluctance of practitioners working in certain disciplines (e.g., biomechanics) to embrace the concept of reflective practice as a fundamental aspect of applied service delivery due to the traditionally positivistic philosophical assumptions underpinning these disciplines, which are in conflict with the position of relativism. It is not suggested that disciplines alter their philosophical stance *per se*, but with some reflexivity, it would seem worthwhile that those involved in the professional service delivery of all sport and exercise science (SES) and allied disciplines reflect on their own position to understand whether this may be facilitating or inhibiting their reflective practices.

To support this disciplinary and individual reflexion, Gareth and colleagues (Chapter 4) provide an in-depth analysis of the extant literature in which researchers have attempted to empirically understand the impact of reflective practice on service delivery effectiveness. As part of their purpose, Gareth and his team synthesised a conceptual model of "how reflective practice works", considering the interplay between reflective learning, mindfulness, self-regulation, and improved practice-based behaviours. The presentation of this model has the potential to offer the level of empirical evidence that attests to the importance of reflective practice often sought by the more positivist practitioners and researchers in the SES.

My final thoughts based on the chapters presented in the first two sections of this text relate to what appears to be a collectively agreed need to move beyond what we currently know about reflective practice and how we go about it. As a caveat to this, it also appears important to challenge perhaps not *what is known* but *what is accepted* – for example, we understand the importance of critical, meaningful reflective practice, yet in many sectors we accept descriptive, bland accounts of practice and pass these off as *reflective practice*. Indeed, Andy and Emily (Chapter 5) argue that many (e.g., practitioners, education and training providers) accept approaches to reflective practice that are "overly systematised" and instead contend that reflective practice should be engaged with in a more meaningful way by critiquing the constraints that are placed upon reflective practices by the overt use of rationalistic frameworks. Similarly, Jo and Hamish (Chapter 6) critique current approaches to reflective practice that simply deliver the "status quo" and challenge everyone to embrace the risk of exploring experience and practice in critical ways – examining and questioning boundaries and the "normal" values held in sport and exercise settings. We (the field) are, therefore, presented with a decision – to carry on engaging in reflective practice in a way that is merely compliant with the professional training and accreditation needs of the field, or, to move beyond such comfort, accept the "risk", explore ways that our reflective practices might become more meaningful, and prioritise our development as reflective practitioners for the betterment of ourselves, those we work with, and those we work for.

Pedagogical and Applied Issues: Zoe Knowles

The collection of chapters here, for me, clearly depicted a sense of quiet evolution not revolution between that of the first book and this one. The movement is one of recognition, debate, and applied focus beyond that of the individual reflective practitioner (not withstanding their importance and agency) and prescription of reflective practice (still recognised as being helpful to initially embark on reflective practice), to that of community, philosophy, culture, safety, and preparedness. For the reflective practitioners themselves there is a need to take responsibility as learners, develop reflective skills and associated attitudes, focus on who they are (and purposefully explore that of others who they are not), and to undertake reflective practice for authentic interest, not just for meeting criteria or an award. We learned through the contributors how reflective practice needs to be *meaningful* otherwise it becomes a redundant ritual, it can be *adapted* such as that of "freestyle reflection" and has been *aligned* with that of philosophical origins and cultural implications. There still, however, remains contention with that of establishing *quality* of reflection (for outcomes and criteria/judgement purposes) and concerns within Think Aloud as to it being a mechanism that can create questions of, "Am I thinking correctly?".

All chapters have raised the role of others and, in particular, that of supervisors. Indeed, interesting questions are raised here in that are supervisors reflecting on their role of supervision and facilitating reflection? Do *they themselves* need specific training/support for this role and what may it contain? In facilitation of reflective practice, how do they establish supportive conditions such as space, time, and a psychologically safe environment as well as commit to exploration of culture, racism, oppression, blind spots, and bias? It is accepted that reflection is a cognitive exploration process and as such risks are inherent. Should supervisors check in on their own and supervisees' well-being and mental health through supervision within the dyadic relationship and that of support elsewhere such as counselling/mentoring? There is much inspiration and good practice from other professions allied to our own and perhaps it is there we start to create this and support those supporting others on their reflective practice journeys.

We have learned from the chapter authors that reflective practice is driven by a purpose, which should drive the approaches taken to facilitate the process. Perhaps for those who establish curricula and make judgement on reflection by way of competency assessment this "purpose to approach" explanation should be part of the required process. Specifically:

- **To the practitioner/candidate:** What are you reflecting on/for? How best is this served? Is the purpose to approach congruent?
- **To the assessor:** Are/were there different approaches in the portfolio of evidence employed based on purpose, situation, experience with reflective processes? Is there evidence of maturity in reflective skill development.

Finally, from editing this section, and as a reflective practitioner researcher for over 20 years, I find myself excitingly contemplating movement towards that of a temporal reflective practice model. I wrote it several times in a notebook, in different guises, and it looks like this: (1) reflection-in-action (TA to capture thinking); (2) reflection-on-action (immediate and captures outcome, emotion laden, links to memory gap); and (3) reflection-on-action (delayed purposely to allow processing time). I purposely leave it here for readers, educators, and researchers to contemplate its purpose, utility, and acceptability moving (or should that be *reflecting*) forwards. I shall be doing that too with enthusiasm and vigour and thank the section authors for their inspiration!

Applied Case Studies: Andy Miles

The authors in this section all shared a sense of excitement and commitment for reflective practice and grasped with enthusiasm and genuine acceptance that it is an effective means of personal and professional development. However, in advocating reflective practice and its value to them, it was apparent that none saw reflective practice as fitting in with the traditional, theoretical model that is often presented. It is clear that the authors all "get" reflective practice – Hannah and her team (Chapter 16), our youngest contributors, report simply that "we feel we are starting to 'get' reflective practice, rather than simply learning 'how to do it' " – but all chapter authors appear to "get" it in different ways.

Several issues emerged which reflect a shift away from the traditional perception of reflective practice by practitioners. In evidencing these shifts some authors tread cautiously and offer considered evidence-based argument and reasoning for their alternative views (Amanda, Chapter 11; Paula, Chapter 12) or seek permission to reflect outside the norms (Laura, Chapter 13), whilst others are more buccaneering and adopt a contrasting philosophical lens through which to view reflection (Brian and Clayton, Chapter 15) or just go for it freestyle (James, Chapter 14).

The primary observation is that practitioners do not see reflection as being as simplistic as described in the literature. Indeed, I recall a debate with Paula about the use of the word "purposeful" and whether reflection had to be "intentional" or whether it could just happen without having been planned. Also, we debated what "critical reflection" meant to her and it seemed that it meant something different to her than it did me and she articulates her thoughts on these points in Chapter 12. Brian and Clayton similarly challenged the norm with their preference for the term "refraction" as opposed to "reflection" (Chapter 15). Such contrasting views are indicative of the discussion we provide in the introduction to this text (see *Reflecting on Reflective Practice*). Second, the authors make only passing comments about traditional frameworks (e.g., Gibbs, 1988), preferring instead to evidence their use of alternative approaches. It feels as if the level of reflective maturity of the authors has allowed them to partly (Hannah, Emma, and the two Amelia's in Chapter 16 evidence their continued use of such frameworks and Laura retains her appreciation of Gibbs' framework in Chapter 13), if not wholly (James writes autoethnographically in Chapter 14), abandon the theoretical frameworks to develop their own hybrid or self-designed frameworks (Amanda's Four A's Framework in Chapter 11). Third, the loneliness of solo written responses to structured questions is seen as a less favourable approach. Shared experiences amongst peers, especially amongst early career practitioners, seems to be of increasing value. Hannah's team advocate the value of group-based approaches (Chapter 16), as does Laura (Chapter 13). Both chapters offer comment about the need for someone to facilitate shared reflections to establish a safe environment for practitioners. Perhaps a *reflection facilitator* is replacing the *framework* as the question poser and reflection prompter? A place still exists though for solitary reflections and both Paula and James (Chapters 12 and 14 respectively) find solace in crafting their own thoughts and then sharing the finished product rather than the process itself.

We sought input from within and across the SES and related disciplines in the hope that we could spotlight reflective practitioners from outside of the sport psychology domain and stimulate other disciplines having seen the utility and benefit for others. From physiology, James (Chapter 14) offers a different perspective from working in nutrition in one of the most physically demanding events where nutrition is key to performance, and Laura (Chapter 13) offers advocacy for the effectiveness of reflective practice amongst her team of physiologists also working in elite sport. Brian and Clayton (Chapter 15) offered in conversation that their group of psychosocial colleagues, whilst having written about reflection in strength and conditioning previously, are fairly atypical. Hannah and her team (Chapter 16) report on how they have utilised reflective practice in a health and physical activity context, whilst Paula (Chapter 12) reflects on her own personal journey in a sport psychology context, and Amanda (Chapter 11) reinforces the use of reflection in sport psychology within an elite team sport context. Noticeable by its absence is any contribution from biomechanics. Indeed, it was only in the final days of editing this book that Emma (co-editor) revealed she had discovered a piece of reflective writing by a biomechanist (see Lees, 2019) although joy turned to disappointment once she realised that the article appears to only provide the article appears to provide "a somewhat 'person-absent' view, more akin to an opinion piece of the external context, rather than an introspective, self-reflective view on oneself". The key point drawn from across the disciplines is that reflective writing in the SES is no longer solely the domain of the sport psychologist. Those practitioners typically aligned to the positivist paradigm are beginning to look beyond their clients' data and are turning their lens on themselves and how they can improve their effectiveness. As Laura says, "We owe it to our athletes who are striving to literally be the best in the world, to be the best practitioners in the world we can be."

In an applied setting, reflective practice is now being undertaken across a range of disciplines and it means different things to different people. How it is done varies and it would seem that there is an increasing digression away from the more prescribed approaches to more personalised, self-designed and bespoke approaches. Given the strongest references to using established frameworks come here from the younger practitioners in our author pool I would argue that trying the standard framework-based approaches and developing appreciation, understanding and experience of reflective practice is part of the necessary evolution of an applied practitioner. There is a need to learn the skills using the established techniques and then when ready, go freestyle. Once liberated by the recognition that you "get" reflective practice you can "do" reflective practice however you want. Hopefully these chapters will help many practitioners "get" reflective practice and be given the required permission to be free to reflect, or "refract", and find their own Dharma.

Reflecting Forward: Future Directions

In concluding this text, we leave you with a set of emerging, future challenges and/or recommendations for the field. Within this text, we (editorial team), and the contributing authors, have situated reflective practice as being core to helping practitioners at all levels of development, across all disciplines, understand themselves, their practice, and the context in which it occurs. Reflective practice is, therefore, presented as a fundamental mechanism and way of being that affords individuals the opportunity to develop the knowledge and skills they need to manage and navigate the complexity that is inherent within applied service delivery in the SES and allied disciplines. Moving forward, we contend that the following points should be at the forefront of ongoing debate and action. We invite you to contemplate individually and within groups, and for you to hopefully take some action through public comment, debate, and research to advance the field.

- Although the reflective practice literature in the SES has undoubtedly grown over the past decade, a wider evidence-base is needed that explores the development of context-specific knowledge, understanding and practice across all disciplines in SES and allied sectors. This potentially requires a paradigmatic shift in certain disciplines and a commitment to value different forms of knowing that will help to support the growth of a body of literature that focuses on professional applied practice. This commitment also requires disciplines to create the necessary open and supportive environments required to encourage individuals to feel free (and safe) to share honest and truthful reflections on practical experiences. So, **how can commitment to and facilitation of reflective practice be achieved in those disciplines that are, to date, under-represented with reflective practice literature?**
- Engaging in debate about approaches to, and frameworks for, reflective practice is an important necessity as we start to shape individuals' understanding that the purpose of the reflection should drive the approach to reflective practice – meaning that individuals should become skilled at engaging in a range of approaches and reflective modalities. However, this debate should not come at the expense of wider discussions concerning what it actually means to be a reflective practitioner and how we might support individuals to accept this position and develop the necessary philosophical position, skills, and attributes. So, **what does it mean to be a reflective practitioner, what is needed by way of understanding, skills, and experience?**
- In accord with the previous point, new and innovative approaches to reflective practice that help to nurture learning and facilitate more lasting and consistent engagement should be considered. No single approach to reflective practice is more suitable than another. Consideration should be given to the use of technology in supporting novel approaches to reflective practice, and discussions concerning the development of a culture of reflective practice should be continued. So, **how could technology help reflective practice – are we moving towards that of the e-reflective practitioner?**
- The preceding points attest in some way to the ongoing need to discuss what meaningful reflective practice "looks like" and how education and training providers (including mentors and supervisors) might facilitate critical reflective practice in students, trainees, and neophyte practitioners. There is a continued need to support individuals in their movement away from the perspective of engaging in reflective practice as a form of compliance, to one that embraces the potential of critical reflective practice to result in transformative and emancipatory outcomes. So, finally, **what commitment do we make to meaningful reflective practice, how do we achieve this, what impact does it have, and how might we represent it?**

References

Abbott, A., Button, C., Pepping, G.-J., & Collins, D. (2005). Unnatural selection: Talent identification and development in sport. *Nonlinear Dynamics, Psychology, and Life Sciences, 9*, 61–88.

Abuhamdeh, S. (2020). Investigating the 'flow' experience: Key conceptual and operational issues. *Frontiers in Psychology, 11*, 158. https://doi.org/10.3389/fpsyg.2020.00158

Ahadi, H. S., & Guerrero, L. A. (2020). *Decolonizing your syllabus, an anti-racist guide for your college*. Academic Senate for California Community Colleges. Retrieved February 16, 2022, from www.asccc.org/content/decolonizing-your-syllabus-anti-racist-guide-your-college

Alfano, H., & Collins, D. (2020). Good practice delivery in sport science and medicine support: Perceptions of experienced sport leaders and practitioners. *Managing Sport and Leisure, 26*, 145–160. https://doi.org/10.1080/23750472.2020.1727768

Andersen, M. B. (Ed.). (2000). *Doing sport psychology*. Human Kinetics.

Andersen, M. B. (Ed.). (2005). *Sport psychology in practice*. Human Kinetics.

Anderson, A. G. (2014). The (sport) psychologist in spite of himself. In P. McCarthy & M. Jones (Eds.), *Becoming a sport psychologist* (pp. 87–96). Routledge.

Anderson, A. G., Knowles, Z., & Gilbourne, D. (2004). Reflective practice for sport psychologists: Concepts, models, practical implications, and thoughts on dissemination. *The Sport Psychologist, 18*, 188–203. https://doi.org/10.1123/tsp.18.2.188

Anderson, A. G., Mahoney, C., Miles, A., & Robinson, P. (2002). Evaluating the effectiveness of applied sport psychology practice: Making the case for a case study approach. *The Sport Psychologist, 16*, 432–453. https://doi.org/10.1123/tsp.16.4.432

Araujo, D., & Davids, K. (2009). Ecological approaches to cognition and action in sport and exercise: Ask not only what you do, but where you do it. *International Journal of Sport Psychology, 40*, 5–37. https://psycnet.apa.org/record/2009-04771-002.

Argyris, C., & Schön, D. A. (1974). *Theory in practice: Increasing professional effectiveness*. Jossey-Bass.

Arnold, R., Collington, S., Manley, H., Rees, S., Soanes, J., & Williams, M. (2019). The "team behind the team": Exploring the organisational stressor experiences of sport science and management staff in elite sport. *Journal of Applied Sport Psychology, 31*, 7–26. https://doi.org/10.1080/10413200.2017.1407836

Åstrand, P. O., Rodahl, K., Dahl, H., & StrÃ, S. B. (2003). *Textbook of work physiology: Physiological bases of exercise*. Human Kinetics.

Atkinson, H., & Nixon-Cave, K. (2011). A tool for clinical reasoning and reflection using the international classification of functioning, disability and health (ICF) framework and patient management model. *Physical Therapy, 91*, 416–430. https://doi.org/10.2522/ptj.20090226

Bachelard, G. (1960/1969). *The poetics of reverie: Childhood, language and the cosmos.* Beacon Press.

Bain, A., Lancaster, J., & Zundans, L. (2009). Pattern language development in the preparation of inclusive educators. *International Journal of Teaching and Learning in Higher Education, 20*, 336–349.

Baird, B., Smallwood, J., Mrazek, M. D., Kam, J. W. Y., Franklin, M. S., & Schooler, J. W. (2012). Inspired by distraction: Mind wandering facilitates creative incubation. *Psychological Science, 21*, 1117–1122. https://doi.org/10.1177%2F0956797612446024

Banks, S., & Nøhr, K. (2003). *Teaching practical ethics for the social professionals.* European Social Education Training.

Banning, M. (2008). A review of clinical decision making: Models and current research. *Journal of Clinical Nursing, 17*, 187–195. https://doi.org/0.111/j.1365-2702.2006.01791.x

Barney, S. T., & Andersen, M. B. (2014). Meta-supervision: Training practitioners to help other on their paths. In G. Cremades & L. Tashman (Eds.), *Becoming a performance psychologist: International perspectives on service delivery and supervision* (pp. 339–346). Routledge.

Bartlett, J., & Drust, B. (2021). A framework for effective knowledge translation and performance delivery of sport scientists in professional sport. *European Journal of Sport Science, 21*, 1579–1587. https://doi.org/10.1080/17461391.2020.1842511

Bartone, P., & Homish, G. G. (2020). Influence of hardiness, avoidance coping, and combat exposure on depression in returning war veterans: A moderated-mediation study. *Journal of Affective Disorders, 265*, 511–518. https://doi.org/10.1016/j.jad.2020.01.127

Béres, L. (2017). Maintaining the ability to be unsettled and learn afresh: What philosophy contributes to our understanding of 'reflection' and 'experience'. *Reflective Practice, 18*, 280–290. https://doi.org/10.1080/14623943.2016.1269003

Berman, S. L., Down, J., & Hill, C. W. L. (2002). Tacit knowledge as a source of competitive advantage in the national basketball association. *Academy of Management Journal, 45*, 13–31. https://doi.org/10.2307/3069282

Binks, C., Jones, F. W., & Knight, K. (2013). Facilitating reflective practice groups in clinical psychology training: A phenomenological study. *Reflective Practice, 14*, 305–318 https://doi.org/10.1080/14623943.2013.767228

Blackmore, C. (2010). *Social learning systems and communities of practice.* Springer Science & Business Media.

Blaikie, N. (2007). *Approaches to social enquiry: Advancing knowledge.* Polity.

Borleffs, J., Custers, E., van Gijn, J., & ten Cate, O. (2003). Clinical reasoning theatre: A new approach to clinical reasoning education. *Academic Medicine, 78*, 322–325. https://doi.org/10.1097/00001888-200303000-00017

Borton, T. (1970). *Reach, touch and teach.* McGraw-Hill Paperbacks.

Botelho, N. (2020). Reflection in motion: An embodied approach to reflection on practice. *Reflective Practice, 22*, 147–158. https://doi.org/10.1080/14623943.2020.1860926

Boutcher, S. H., & Rotella, R. J. (1987). A psychological skills education program for closed-skill performance enhancement. *The Sport Psychologist, 1*, 127–137. https://doi:10.1123/tsp.1.2.127

Boyd, E. M., & Fales, A. W. (1983). Reflective learning: Key to learning from experience. *Journal of Humanistic Psychology, 23*, 99–117. https://doi.org/10.1177/0022167883232011

British Association of Sport and Exercise Sciences, BASES. (2019). *Sport & exercise psychology accreditation route competency profile.* www.bases.org.uk/imgs/separ_candidate_handbook526.pdf

British Association of Sport & Exercise Sciences, BASES. (2021). *BASES supervised experience guidelines.* www.bases.org.uk/spage-professional_development-supervised_experience.html

British Association of Sport & Exercise Sciences, BASES. (2022). *About sport and exercise science.* www.bases.org.uk/spage-about_us-about_sport___execise_science.html

British Psychological Society. (2018). *Code of ethics and conduct.* www.bps.org.uk/news-and-policy/bps-code-ethics-and-conduct

Broderick, J. E., Stone, A. A., Calvanese, P., Schwartz, J. E., & Turk, D. C. (2006). Recalled pain ratings: A complex and poorly defined task. *The Journal of Pain, 7*, 142–149. https://doi.org/10.1016/j.jpain.2005.09.012

Brookfield, S. (1998). Critically reflective practice. *The Journal of Continuing Education in the Health Professions, 18*, 197–205. https://doi.org/10.1002/chp.1340180402

Brooks, J. (2007). Reflections on the Athens Olympics and the Paralympics: My work as a sport psychologist working with equestrian. *Sport and Exercise Psychology Review, 2*, 5–40.

Buchheit, M. (2017). Houston, we still have a problem. *International Journal of Sports Physiology & Performance, 12*, 1111–1114. https://doi.org/10.1123/ijspp.2017-0422

Buckley, B., Thijssen, D. H. J., Murphy, R. C., Graves, L. E. F., Cochrane, M., Gillison, F. B., . . . Watson, P. M. (2020). Pragmatic evaluation of a coproduced physical activity referral scheme: A UK quasi-experimental study. *British Medical Journal Open, 10*, e034580. https://doi.org/10.1136/bmjopen-2019-034580

Bull, S. J. (1991). *Sport psychology: A self-help guide.* The Crowood Press Ltd.

Butterworth, A., & Turner, D. (2014). Becoming a performance analyst: Autoethnographic reflections on agency, and facilitated transformational growth. *Reflective Practice, 15*, 552–562. https://doi.org/10.1080/14623943.2014.900014

Carson, F., Leishman, B., Hinck, K., & Hoffmann, S. M. (2021, ahead of print). Identifying the habitual needs of novice strength and conditioning coaches. *Journal of Hospitality, Leisure, Sport & Tourism Education, 28*. https://doi.org/10.1016/j.jhlste.2021.100313

Cassidy, T., Handcock, P., Gearity, B. T., & Burrows, L. (2020). *Understanding strength and conditioning as sport coaching: Bridging the biophysical, pedagogical and sociocultural foundations of practice.* Routledge.

Cassidy, T., Jones, R. L., & Potrac, P. (2015). *Understanding sports coaching: The pedagogical, social and cultural foundations of coaching* (3rd ed.). Routledge.

Castillo, E. A. (2020). Developing a professional philosophy for applied exercise psychology: Integrating theory and practice. *Journal of Sport Psychology in Action, 11*, 183–195. https://doi.org/10.1080/21520704.2020.1755401

CEP-UK. (2022). *What is a CEP?* www.clinicalexercisephysiology.org.uk/

Chatterjee, R. (Host) (2019, October 16). *How running can transform your life with Sanjay Rawal* [audio and video podcast]. Feel Better Live More (episode #79). https://drchatterjee.com/how-running-can-transform-your-life-with-sanjay-rawal/

Cheetham, G., & Chivers, G. (1998). The reflective (and competent) practitioner: A model of professional competence which seeks to harmonise the reflective practitioner and competence-based approaches. *Journal of European Industrial Training*, *22*, 267–276. https://doi.org/10.1108/03090599810230678

Chow, G. M., & Luzzeri, M. (2019). Post-event reflection: A tool to facilitate self-awareness, self-monitoring, and self-regulation in athletes. *Journal of Sport Psychology in Action*, *10*, 106–118. https://doi.org/10.1080/21520704.2018.1555565

Christensen, D. A., & Aoyagi, M. W. (2014). Lessons learned consulting at Olympic trials: Swimming through growing pains. *The Sport Psychologist*, *28*, 281–289. https://doi.org/10.1123/tsp.2013-0092

Colistra, A. L., & Brown-Rice, K. A. (2011). *When the rubber hits the road: Applying multicultural competencies in cross-cultural supervision.* American Counseling Association. Retrieved February 17, 2022, from www.semanticscholar.org/paper/When-the-Rubber-Hits-the-Road%3A-Applying-in-Colistra-Brown-Rice/562fea4b8d83ac04b3c9c952bc28a01c3a731d55

Collins, D., Evans-Jones, K., & O'Connor, H. L. (2013). Reflections on three neophyte sport and exercise psychologists' developing philosophies for practice. *The Sport Psychologist*, *27*, 399–409. https://doi.org/10.1123/tsp.27.4.399

Conway, J. (1994). Reflection, the art and science of nursing and the theory practice gaps. *British Journal of Nursing*, *3*, 14–18. https://doi.org/10.12968/bjon.1994.3.3.114

Cook, J. L. (2006). College students and algebra story problems: Strategies for identifying relevant information. *Reading Psychology*, *27*, 95–125. https://doi.org/10.1080/02702710600640198

Cowden, R. G., & Meyer-Weitz, A. (2016). Self-reflection and self-insight predict resilience and stress in competitive tennis. *Social Behavior and Personality: An International Journal*, *44*, 1133–1149. https://doi.org/10.2224/sbp.2016.44.7.1133

Cowley, E., Foweather, L., Watson, P. M., Belton, S., Thompson, A., Thijssen, D., & Wagenmakers, A. (2022). What happened in 'The HERizon Project'? – Process evaluation of a multi-arm remote physical activity intervention for adolescent girls. *International Journal of Environmental Research and Public Health*, *19*, 966. https://doi.org/10.3390/ijerph19020966

Cowley, E., Watson, P. M., Foweather, L., Belton, S., Mansfield, C., Whitcomb-Khan, G., . . . Wagenmakers, A. (2021). Formative evaluation of a home-based physical activity intervention for adolescent girls – The HERizon project: A randomised controlled trial. *Children*, *8*, 76. https://doi.org/10.3390/children8020076

Cronin, C., Knowles, Z. R., & Enright, K. (2020). The challenge to care in a Premier League Football Club. *Sports Coaching Review*, *9*, 123–146. https://doi.org/10.1080/21640629.2019.1578593

Cropley, B., Baldock, L., Hanton, S., Gucciardi, D. F., McKay, A., Neil, R., . . . Williams, T. (2020). A multi-study exploration of factors that optimise hardiness in sport coaches and the role of reflective practice in facilitating hardy attitudes. *Frontiers in Psychology*, *11*, *1823*. https://doi.org/10.3389/fpsyg.2020.01823

Cropley, B., Baldock, L., Mellalieu, S. D., Neil, R., Wagstaff, C. R. D., & Wadey, R. (2016). Coping with the demands of professional practice: Sport psychology consultants' perspectives. *The Sport Psychologist, 30,* 290–302. https://doi.org/10.1123/tsp.2015-0125

Cropley, B., & Hanton, S. (2011). The role of reflective practice in applied sport psychology: Contemporary issues for professional practice. In S. Hanton & S. D. Mellalieu (Eds.), *Professional practice in sport psychology: A review* (pp. 307–336). Routledge.

Cropley, B., Hanton, S., Miles, A., & Niven, A. (2010a). The value of reflective practice in professional development: An applied sport psychology review. *Sports Science Review, 19,* 179–209. https://doi.org/10.2478/v10237-011-0025-8

Cropley, B., Hanton, S., Miles, A., & Niven, A. (2010b). Exploring the relationship between effective and reflective practice in applied sport psychology. *The Sport Psychologist, 24,* 521–541. https://doi.org/10.1123/tsp.24.4.521

Cropley, B., Hanton, S., Miles, A., & Niven, A. (2020). Dohme Developing the effectiveness of applied sport psychology service delivery: A reflective practice intervention. *Sport & Exercise Psychology Review, 16,* 38–60.

Cropley, B., Miles, A., Hanton, S., & Niven, A. (2007). Improving the delivery of applied sport psychology support through reflective practice. *The Sport Psychologist, 21,* 475–494. https://doi.org/10.1123/tsp.21.4.475

Cropley, B., Miles, A., & Knowles, Z. (2018). Making reflective practice beneficial. In R. Thelwell & M. Dicks (Eds.), *Professional advances in sports coaching: Research and practice* (pp. 377–396). Routledge.

Cropley, B., Miles, A., & Nichols, N. (2015). Learning to learn: The coach as a reflective practitioner. In J. Wallace & J. Lambert (Eds.), *Becoming a sports coach* (pp. 11–26). Routledge.

Cropley, B., Miles, A., & Peel, J. (2012). *Reflective practice: Value, issues, and developments within sports coaching.* Sports Coach UK.

Crum, M., & Hendrick, K. (2014). Multicultural critical reflective practice and contemporary art. In L. Evans & J. B. Acuff (Eds.), *Multiculturalism in art museums today* (pp. 271–297). Altamira Press.

Csikszentmihalyi, M. (1975). *Beyond boredom and anxiety.* Jossey-Bass.

Csikszentmihalyi, M. (1996). *Creativity: The psychology of discovery and invention.* Harper Collins Publishers.

Culver, D., & Trudel, P. (2006). Cultivating coaches' communities of practice: Developing the potential for learning through interactions. In R. L. Jones (Ed.), *The sports coach as an educator: Re-conceptualising sports coaching* (pp. 115–130). Routledge.

Culver, D., & Trudel, P. (2008). Clarifying the concept of communities of practice in sport. *International Journal of Sport Science & Coaching, 3,* 1–10. https://doi.org/10.1260/174795408784089441

Cushion, C. (2018). Reflection and reflective practice discourses in coaching: A critical analysis. *Sport, Education & Society, 23,* 82–94. https://doi.org/10.1080/13573322.2016.1142961

Cushion, C., & Partington, M. (2016). A critical analysis of the conceptualisation of coaching philosophy. *Sport Education and Society, 21,* 851–867. https://doi.org/10.1080/13573322.2014.958817

Daniel, G. R., Auhl, G., & Hastings, W. (2013). Collaborative feedback and reflection for professional growth: Preparing first-year pre-service teachers for participation in the community of practice. *Asia-Pacific Journal of Teacher Education, 41,* 159–172. https://doi.org/10.1080/1359866X.2013.777025

Dao, P., Nguyen, M. X. N., & Chi, D. (2020). Reflective learning practice for promoting adolescent EFL learners' attention to form. *Innovation in Language Learning & Teaching*, *15*, 247–262. https://doi.org/10.1080/17501229.2020.1766467

de Beauvoir, S. (1949). *The second sex*. Vintage Classics.

Deleuze, G., & Guattari, F. (1987). *A thousand plateaus: Capitalism and schizophrenia*. University of Minnesota Press.

Denison, J. (2007). Social theory for coaches: A Foucauldian reading of one athlete's poor performance. *International Journal of Sports Science and Coaching*, *2*, 369–383. https://doi.org/10.1260/174795407783359777

Department of Health and Social Care. (2019). *Physical activity guidelines: UK chief medical officers' report*. https://assets.publishing.service.gov.uk/government/uploads/system/uploads/attachment_data/file/832868/uk-chief-medical-officers-physical-activity-guidelines.pdf

Dewey, J. (1933). *How we think*. DC Heath & Co.

Dixon, M., Lee, S., & Ghaye, T. (2013). Reflective practices for better sports coaches and coach education: Shifting from a pedagogy of scarcity to abundance in the run-up to Rio 2016. *Reflective Practice*, *14*, 585–599. https://doi.org/10.1080/14623943.2013.840573

Dixon, M., Lee, S., & Ghaye, T. (2016). Strengths-based reflective practices for the management of change: Applications from sport and positive psychology. *Journal of Change Management*, *16*, 142–157. https://doi.org/10.1080/14697017.2015.1125384

Dohn, N. B. (2011). On the epistemological presuppositions of reflective activities. *Educational Theory*, *61*, 671–708. https://doi.org/10.1111/j.1741-5446.2011.00428.x

Doncaster, G. (2018). From intern to practitioner to academic: The role of reflection in the development of a sports scientist. *Reflective Practice*, *19*, 543–556. https://doi.org/10.1080/14623943.2018.1538951

Donovan, S. J. (2021). Harm, healing, and joy: Syllabus shifts in English education with an anti-bias anti-racist (ABAR) lens. *Oklahoma English Journal*, *34*, 5–11.

Dooley, C., & Farndon, H. (2021). *Best practice in psychologist recruitment*. www.bps.org.uk/news-and-policy/best-practice-psychology-recruitment

Double, K. S., & Birney, D. P. (2019). Reactivity to measures of metacognition. *Frontiers in Psychology*, *10*:2755. https://doi.org/10.3389/fpsyg.2019.02755

Drigas, A. S., & Papoutsi, C. (2018). A new layered model on emotional intelligence. *Behavioral Sciences*, *8*, 45. http://dx.doi.org/10.3390/bs8050045

Driscoll, J., & Teh, B. (2001). The potential of reflective practice to develop individual orthopaedic nurse practitioners and their practice. *Journal of Orthopaedic Nursing*, *5*, 95–103. https://doi.org/10.1054/joon.2001.0150

Dube, V., & Ducharme, F. (2015). Nursing reflective practice: An empirical literature review. *Journal of Nursing Education & Practice*, *5*, 91–99. https://doi.org/10.5430/jnep.v5n7p91

Duke, S., & Appleton, J. (2000). The use of reflection in a palliative care programme: A qualitative study of the development of reflective skills over an academic year. *Journal of Advanced Nursing*, *32*, 1557–1568. https://doi.org/10.1046/j.1365-2648.2000.01604.x

Eberhardt, J. L. (2019). *Biased: Uncovering the hidden prejudices that shape our lives*. Windmill Books.

Edwards, J. C. (1982). *Ethics without philosophy: Wittgenstein and the moral life*. University Press of Florida.

Einar Thorsen, D. (2010). The neoliberal challenge: What is neoliberalism? *Contemporary Readings in Law and Social Justice, 2*, 188–214. https://doi.org/10.1525/ctx.2007.6.3.13

Englander, R., Cameron, T., Ballard, A. J., Dodge, J., Bull, J., & Aschenbrener, C. A. (2013). Toward a common taxonomy of competency domains for the health professions and competencies for physicians. *Academic Medicine, 88*, 1088–1094. https://doi.org/10.1097/ACM.0b013e31829a3b2b

Eraut, M. (1994). *Developing professional knowledge and competence*. Routledge.

Ericsson, K. A. (2007). An expert-performance perspective of research on medical expertise: The study of clinical performance. *Medical Education, 41*, 1124–1130. https://doi.org/10.1111/j.1365-2923.2007.02946.x

Ericsson, K. A., & Simon, H. A. (1993). *Verbal reports as data*. MIT Press.

Evans, M. B., Shanahan, E., Leith, S., Litvak, N., & Wilson, A. E. (2019). Living for today or tomorrow? Self-regulation amidst proximal or distal exercise outcomes. *Applied Psychology: Health & Wellness, 11*, 304–327. https://doi.org/10.1111/aphw.12160

Faubert, J. (2013). Professional athletes have extraordinary skills for rapidly learning complex and neutral dynamic visual scenes. *Scientific Reports, 3*, 1154–1157. https://doi.org/10.1038/srep01154

Fifer, A., Henschen, K., Gould, D., & Ravizza, K. (2008). What works when working with athletes. *The Sport Psychologist, 22*, 356–377. https://doi.org/10.1123/tsp.22.3.356

Finlay, L. (2008). *Reflecting on 'reflective practice'*. Practice-Based Professional Learning Paper 52. The Open University.

Fish, D. (1998). *Appreciating practice in the caring professions: Refocusing professional development and practitioner research*. Butterworth Heinemann.

Fitts, P. M., & Posner, M. I. (1967). *Human performance*. Brooks/Cole.

Fletcher, D., & Maher, J. (2013). Toward a competency-based understanding of the training and development of applied sport psychologists. *Sport, Exercise, and Performance Psychology, 2*, 265–280. https://doi.org/10.1037/a0031976

Fletcher, D., & Wagstaff, C. R. D. (2009). Organisational psychology in elite sport: Its emergence, application and future. *Psychology of Sport and Exercise, 10*, 427–434. https://doi.org/10.1016/j.psychsport.2009.03.009

Fletcher, T., & Wilson, A. (2013). The transformative potential of reflective diaries for elite English cricketers. *Leisure/Loisir, 37*, 267–286. https://doi.org/10.1080/14927713.2013.865982

Flett, M. (2015). Creating probabilistic idiographic performance profiles from discrete feelings: Combining the IZOF and IAPZ models. *Sport Science Review, 6*, 241–266. https://doi:10.1515/ssr-2015-0018.

Foltz, B. D., Fisher, A. R., Denton, L. K., Campbell, W. L., Speight, Q. L., Steinfeldt, J., . . . Latorre, C. (2015). Applied sport psychology supervision experience: A qualitative analysis. *Journal of Applied Sport Psychology, 27*, 449–463. https://doi.org/10.1080/10413200.2015.1043162

Fonteyn, M., & Ritter, B. (2008). Clinical reasoning in nursing. In J. Higgs & M. Jones (Eds.), *Clinical reasoning in the health professions* (pp. 236–244). Butterworth-Heinemann.

Forsberg, E., Ziegert, K., Hult, H., & Fors, U. (2014). Clinical reasoning in nursing, a think-aloud study using virtual patients – a base for an innovative assessment. *Nurse Education Today, 34*, 538–542. https://doi.org/10.1016/j.nedt.2013.07.010

Foucault, M. (1977). *Discipline and punish: The birth of the prison* (A. Sheridan, Trans.). Random House.

Foucault, M. (1978). *The history of sexuality volume 1: An introduction* (R. Hurley, Trans.). Random House.

Foucault, M. (1988). Technologies of the self. In L. H. Martin, H. Gutman, & P. H. Hutton (Eds.), *Technologies of the self: A seminar with Michel Foucault* (pp. 16–49). University of Massachusetts Press.

Fox, M. C., Ericsson, K. A., & Best, R. (2011). Do procedures for verbal reporting of thinking have to be reactive? A meta-analysis and recommendations for best reporting methods. *Psychological Bulletin, 137*, 316–344. https://doi.org/10.1037/a0021663

Fullagar, H., McCall, A., Impellizzeri, F., Favero, T., & Coutts, A. (2019). The translation of sport science research to the field: A current opinion and overview on the perceptions of practitioners, researchers and coaches. *Sports Medicine, 49*, 1817–1824. https://doi.org/10.1007/s40279-019-01139-0

Furr, S. R., & Carroll, J. J. (2003). Critical incidents in student counselor development. *Journal of Counseling & Development, 81*, 483–489. https://doi.org/10.1002/j.1556-6678.2003.tb00275.x

Galipeu, J., & Trudel, P. (2005). The role of the athletic, academic, and social development of student-athletes in two varsity sport teams. *The Applied Research in Coaching and Athletics Annual, 20*, 27–49.

Gardner, F. L., & Moore, Z. E. (2019). Mindfulness in sport: Neuroscience and practical applications. In M. H. Anshel, T. A. Petrie, & J. A. Steinfeld (Eds.), *APA handbooks in psychology series: APA handbook of sport and exercise psychology* (pp. 325–342). American Psychological Association.

Gathu, C. (2022). Facilitators and barriers of reflective learning in postgraduate medical education: A narrative review. *Journal of Medical Education and Curricular Development, 9*, 1–8. https://doi.org/10.1177/23821205221096106

Gearity, B. T., & Henderson Metzger, L. (2017). Intersectionality, microaggressions, and microaffirmations: Towards a cultural praxis of sport coaching. *Sociology of Sport Journal, 34*, 160–175. https://doi.org/10.1123/ssj.2016-0113

Gearity, B. T., & Mills, J. (2012). Discipline and punish in the weight room. *Sport Coaching Review, 1*, 124–134. https://doi.org/10.1080/21640629.2012.746049

Gearity, B. T., & Szedlak, C. (2022). Developing as a coach: Leadership, culture, and purpose. In A. Turner & P. Comfort (Eds.), *Advanced strength and conditioning: An evidenced based approach* (2nd ed., pp. 396–408). Routledge.

Ghaye, T. (2010). *Teaching and learning through reflective practice: A practical guide for positive action*. David Fulton Publishers.

Gibbs, G. (1988). *Learning by doing: A guide to teaching and learning methods*. FEU.

Gigerenzer, G. (2014). *Risk savvy: How to make good decisions*. Penguin.

Gilbourne, D. (2012). Contemplations on sport, complexity, ages of being and practice. *Sports Coaching Review, 1*, 4–16. https://doi.org/10.1080/21640629.2012.689491

Gilbourne, D. (2013). Heroes, toxic ferrets and a large man from Leeds. *Sports Coaching Review, 2*, 86–97. https://doi.org/10.1080/21640629.2014.888298

Gilbourne, D., Jones, R. L., & Jordan, S. (2014). Applied utility and the autoethnographic short story: Persuasions for and illustrations of writing critical social science. *Sport, Education and Society, 19*, 80–92. https://doi.org/10.1080/13573322.2011.632405

Gilbourne, D., & Richardson, D. (2006). Tales from the field: Personal reflections on the provision of psychological support in professional soccer. *Psychology of Sport and Exercise*, *7*, 325–337. https://doi.org/10.1016/j.psychsport.2005.04.004

Gillmer, B., & Markus, R. (2003). Personal professional development in clinical psychology training: Surveying reflective practice. *Clinical Psychology*, *27*, 20–23.

Gilmore, S., Wagstaff, C. R. D., & Smith, J. (2018). Sports psychology in the English premier league: 'It feels precarious and is precarious'. *Work, Employment and Society*, *32*, 426–435. https://doi.org/10.1177/0950017017713933

Gilroy, P. (1993). Reflections on Schön: An epistemological critique and a practical alternative. In P. Gilroy & M. Smith (Eds.), *International analyses of teacher education* (pp. 125–142). Carfax Publishing Company.

Giroux, H. (2019). Neoliberalism and the weaponizing of language and education. *Race & Class*, *61*, 26–45. https://doi.org/10.1177%2F0306396819847945

Given, F. (2020). *Women don't owe you pretty*. Octopus Publishing Group.

Gobet, F., & Charness, N. (2006). Expertise in chess. In K. A. Ericsson, N. Charness, P. J. Feltovich, & R. R. Hoffman (Eds.), *The Cambridge handbook of expertise and expert performance* (pp. 523–538). Cambridge University Press.

Goffman, E. (1959). *The presentation of self in everyday life*. Doubleday.

Goodman, J. (1984). Reflection and teacher education: A case study and theoretical analysis. *Interchange*, *15*, 9–27. https://doi.org/10.1007/BF01807939

Guthold, R., Stevens, G. A., Riley, L. M., & Bull, F. C. (2018). Worldwide trends in insufficient physical activity from 2001 to 2016: A pooled analysis of 358 population-based surveys with 1.9 million participants. *The Lancet*, *6*, E1077–E1086. https://doi.org/10.1016/S2214-109X(18)30357-7

Hägglund, K., Kenttä, G., Thelwell, R., & Wagstaff, C. R. D. (2021, ahead of print). Mindful self-reflection to support sustainable high-performance coaching: A process evaluation of a novel method development in elite sport. *Journal of Applied Sport Psychology*. https://doi.org/10.1080/10413200.2021.1925782

Handcock, P., & Cassidy, T. (2014). Reflective practice for rugby union strength and conditioning coaches. *Strength & Conditioning Journal*, *36*, 41–45. https://doi.org/10.1519/SSC.0000000000000020

Hanrahan, S. J., Pedro, R., & Cerin, E. (2009). Structured self-reflection in adult recreational salsa dancers. *The Sport Psychologist*, *23*, 151–169. https://doi.org/10.1123/tsp.23.2.151

Hanton, S., Cropley, B., & Lee, S. (2009). Reflective practice, experience, and the interpretation of anxiety symptoms. *Journal of Sports Sciences*, *27*, 517–533. https://doi.org/10.1080/02640410802668668

Hardy, L., Jones, G., & Gould, D. (1996). *Understanding psychological preparation for sport: Theory and practice of elite performers*. John Wiley & Sons.

Hazan, K. P., Carlson, M. W., Hatton-Bowers, H., Fessinger, M. B., Cole-Mossman, J., Bahm, J., . . . Gilkerson, L. (2020). Evaluating the facilitating attuned interactions (FAN) approach: Vicarious trauma, professional burnout, and reflective practice. *Children & Youth Services Review*, *112*, 104925. https://doi.org/10.1016/j.childyouth.2020.104925

Health and Care Professions Council, HCPC. (2013). *Standards of proficiency: Dietitians*. www.hcpc-uk.org/assets/documents/1000050CStandards_of_Proficiency_Dietitians.pdf

Health and Care Professions Council, HCPC. (2015). *Standards of proficiency: Practitioner psychologists*. www.hcpc-uk.org/assets/documents/10002963SOP_Practitioner_psychologists.pdf

Health and Care Professions Council, HCPC. (2019). *Benefits of becoming a reflective practitioner.* www.hcpc-uk.org/globalassets/news-and-events/benefits-of-becoming-a-reflective-practitioner – joint-statement-2019.pdf

Hébert, C. (2015). Knowing and/or experiencing: A critical examination of the reflective models of John Dewey and Donald Schön. *Reflective Practice, 16,* 361–371. https://doi.org/10.1080/14623943.2015.1023281

Heeneman, S., & de Grave, W. (2017). Tensions in mentoring medical students toward self-directed and reflective learning in a longitudinal portfolio-based mentoring system: An activity theory analysis. *Medical Teacher, 39,* 368–376. https://doi.org/10.1080/0142159X.2017.1286308

Heidegger, M. (1977). *The question concerning technology and other essays.* Harper Row.

Henriksen, K., Diment, G., & Hansen, J. (2011). Professional philosophy: Inside the delivery of sport psychology service at team Denmark. *Sport Science Review, 10,* 5–21. https://doi:10.2478/v10237-011-0043-6

Hings, R. F., Wagstaff, C. R. D., Anderson, V., Gilmore, S., & Thelwell, R. C. (2018). Professional challenges in elite sports medicine and science: Composite vignettes of practitioner emotional labor. *Psychology of Sport and Exercise, 35,* 66–73. https://doi.org/10.1016/j.psychsport.2017.11.007

Hings, R. F., Wagstaff, C. R. D., Anderson, V., Gilmore, S., & Thelwell, R. C. (2020). Better preparing sports psychologists for the demands of applied practice: The emotional labor training gap. *Journal of Applied Sport Psychology, 32,* 335–356. https://doi.org/10.1080/10413200.2018.1560373

Hoffman, K. A., Aitken, L., & Duffield, C. (2009). A comparison of novice and expert nurses' cue collection during clinical decision-making: Verbal protocol analysis. *International Journal of Nursing Studies, 46,* 1335–1344. https://doi.org/10.1016/j.ijnurstu.2009.04.001

Holt, N. L., & Strean, W. B. (2001). Reflecting on initiating sport psychology consultation: A self-narrative of neophyte practice. *The Sport Psychologist, 15,* 188–204. https://doi.org/10.1123/tsp.15.2.188

Howell, W. C., & Fleishman, E. A. (Eds.). (1982). *Information processing and decision making.* Psychology Press.

Huntley, E. (2021). *Exploring reflective practice engagement and development within trainee sport and exercise scientists* (Unpublished Doctoral Thesis). Liverpool John Moores University.

Huntley, E., Cropley, B., Gilbourne, D., Knowles, Z., & Sparkes, A. (2014). Reflecting back and forwards: An evaluation of peer-reviewed reflective practice research in sport. *Reflective Practice, 15,* 863–876. https://doi.org/10.1080/14623943.2014.969695

Huntley, E., Cropley, B., Knowles, Z., & Miles, A. (2019). The BASES expert statement on reflective practice: The key to experiential learning. *The Sport & Exercise Scientist, 60,* 6–7.

Huntley, E., & Kentzer, N. (2013). Group-based reflective practice in sport psychology: Experiences of two trainee sport and exercise scientists. *Sport & Exercise Psychology Review, 9,* 57–68.

Hutchins, H. M., & Rainbolt, H. (2017). What triggers imposter phenomenon among academic faculty? A critical incident study exploring antecedents, coping, and development opportunities. *Human Resource Development International, 20,* 194–214. https://doi.org/10.1080/13678868.2016.1248205

Hutchison, A. J., & Johnston, L. H. (2013). Exploring the potential of case formulation within exercise psychology. *Journal of Clinical Sport Psychology, 7,* 60–76. https://doi.org/10.1123/jcsp.7.1.60

Ieva, K. P., Ohrt, J. H., Swank, J. M., & Young, T. (2009). The impact of experiential groups on master students' counselor and personal development: A qualitative investigation. *The Journal for Specialists in Group Work, 34*, 351–368. https://doi.org/10.1080/01933920903219078

Ingham, S. (2016). *How to support a champion: The art of applying science to the elite athlete.* Simply Said.

Ives, J. C., Neese, K., Downs, N., Root, H., & Finnerty, T. (2020). The effects of competitive orientation on performance in competition. *The Sport Journal, 41*. https://thesportjournal.org/article/the-effects-of-competitive-orientation-on-performance-in-competition/

Jackson, R. C. (2006). Reflections on the Athens Paralympics: Working with wheelchair rugby. *Sport and Exercise Psychology, 2*, 41–45.

Jain, A., & Aggarwal, P. (2020). What would be most helpful for us to talk about? Trainee perspectives on culturally effective supervision in the USA and India. *Journal of Psychotherapy Integration, 30*, 84–92. https://doi.org/10.1037/int0000184

Johns, C. (1994). Guided reflection. In A. Palmer, S. Burns, & C. Bulman (Eds.), *Reflective practice in nursing* (pp. 110–130). Blackwell.

Johns, C. (1995). The value of reflective practice for nursing. *Journal of Clinical Nursing, 4*, 23–30. https://doi.org/10.1111/j.1365-2702.1995.tb00006.x

Johns, C. (2006). *Engaging reflection in practice: A narrative approach.* Wiley Blackwell.

Johns, C. (2017). *Becoming a reflective practitioner.* Wiley Blackwell.

Johnstone, L., & Dallas, R. (2014). *Formulation in psychology and psychotherapy.* Routledge.

Johnstone, L., & Dallos, R. (2013). *Formulation in Psychology and psychotherapy, making sense of people's problems* (2nd ed.). Taylor and Francis.

Jones, H., George, K. P., Scott, A., Buckley, J. P., Watson, P. M., Oxborough, D., . . . Green, D. J. (2021). Charter to establish clinical exercise physiology as a recognised allied health profession in the UK: A call to action. *British Medical Journal: Open Sport & Exercise Medicine, 7.* http://dx.doi.org/10.1136/bmjsem-2021-001158

Jones, I. (2014). *Research methods for sports studies* (3rd ed.). Routledge.

Jones, R. L., Edwards, C., & Vitto Filho, I. A. T. (2016). Activity theory, complexity and sports coaching: An epistemology for a discipline. *Sport Education and Society, 21*, 200–216. https://doi.org/10.1080/13573322.2014.895713

Jonker, L., Elferink-Gemser, M. T., de Roos, I. M., & Visscher, C. (2012). The role of reflection in sport expertise. *The Sport Psychologist, 26*, 224–242. https://doi.org/10.1123/tsp.26.2.224

Kahneman, D. (2000). Experienced utility and objective happiness: A moment-based approach. In D. Kahneman & A. Tversky (Eds.), *Choices, vales, and frames* (pp. 673–692). Cambridge University Press.

Kahneman, D., & Riis, J. (2005). Living, and thinking about it: Two perspectives on life. In F. Huppert, N. Baylis, & B. Keverne (Eds.), *The science of well-being* (pp. 285–304). Oxford University Press.

Katz, J., & Keyes, J. (2020). Person-centred approaches. In D. Tod & M. Eubank (Eds.), *Applied sport, exercise and performance psychology: Current approaches to helping clients* (pp. 31–52). Routledge.

Keegan, R. (2016). *Being a sport psychologist.* Palgrave Macmillan.

Kember, D., Leung, D. Y., Jones, A., Loke, A. Y., McKay, J., Sinclair, K., . . . Yeung, E. (2000). Development of a questionnaire to measure the level of reflective thinking. *Assessment & Evaluation in Higher Education*, 25, 381–395. https://doi. org/10.1080/713611442

Kemp, S., Burt, C. D., & Furneaux, L. (2008). A test of the peak-end rule with extended autobiographical events. *Memory & Cognition*, 36, 132–138. https:// doi.org/10.3758/MC.36.1.132

Kiff, J., Holmes, G., & Cushway, D. (2010). Personal awareness/development groups and clinical training. *Clinical Psychology Forum*, 207, 30–34.

Kirk, A. (2019). Should reflection be used as a form of assessment? *Journal of Paramedic Practice*, 11, 255–257.

Knight, K., Sperlinger, D., & Maltby, M. (2010). Exploring the personal and professional impact of reflective practice groups: A survey of 18 cohorts from a UK clinical psychology training course. *Clinical Psychology & Psychotherapy*, 17, 427–437. https://doi.org/10.1002/cpp.660

Knowles, Z., Borrie, A., & Telfer, H. (2005). Towards the reflective sports coach: Issues of context, education and application. *Ergonomics*, 48, 1711–1720. https:// doi.org/10.1080/00140130500101288

Knowles, Z., & Gilbourne, D. (2010). Aspiration, inspiration and illustration: Initiating debate on reflective practice writing. *The Sport Psychologist*, 24, 504–520. https://doi.org/10.1123/tsp.24.4.504

Knowles, Z., Gilbourne, D., Borrie, A., & Nevill, A. (2001). Developing the reflective sports coach: A study exploring the processes of reflective practice within a higher education coaching programme. *Reflective Practice*, 2, 185–207. https:// doi.org/10.1080/14623940120071370

Knowles, Z., Gilbourne, D., Cropley, B., & Dugdill, L. (2014a). *Reflective practice in the sport and exercise sciences: Contemporary issues.* Routledge.

Knowles, Z., Gilbourne, D., Cropley, B., & Dugdill, L. (2014b). Reflecting on reflection and journeys. In Z. Knowles, D. Gilbourne, B. Cropley, & L. Dugdill (Eds.), *Reflective practice in the sport and exercise sciences: Contemporary issues* (pp. 3–14). Routledge.

Knowles, Z., Gilbourne, D., Cropley, B., & Dugdill, L. (2014c). Reflecting back and forwards. In Z. Knowles, D. Gilbourne, B. Cropley, & L. Dugdill (Eds.), *Reflective practice in the sport and exercise sciences: Contemporary issues* (pp. 185–191). Routledge.

Knowles, Z., Gilbourne, D., Tomlinson, V., & Anderson, A. G. (2007). Reflections on the application of reflective practice for supervision in applied sport psychology. *The Sport Psychologist*, 21, 109–122. https://doi.org/10.1123/tsp.21.1.109

Knowles, Z., Katz, J., & Gilbourne, D. (2012). Reflective practice within elite consultancy: Diary extracts and further discussion on a personal and elusive process. *The Sport Psychologist*, 26, 454–469. https://doi.org/10.1123/tsp.26.3.454

Knowles, Z., & Saxton, J. (2010). Needs analysis and reflective practice: Two important components of case studies. *The Sport and Exercise Scientist*, 25, 23.

Koh, K. T., Chew, M., Kokkonen, M., & Chew, W. (2017). The use of reflection-card by elite youth basketball players, head coach and team manager: Effects on players' performance and perceptions of users. *Reflective Practice*, 18, 291–311. https:// doi.org/10.1080/14623943.2016.1267001

Koh, K. T., & Tan, K. H. (2018). The use of group-based reflective practice to enhance badminton players' performance: An exploratory study. *Asian Journal of Coaching Science, 1,* 47–62. https://doi.org/10.29426/ajcs.201806_1(2).0001

Kolb, D. (1984). *Experiential learning: Experiences as the source of learning and development.* Prentice Hall.

Kuklick, C. R., & Gearity, B. T. (2015). A review of reflective practice and its application for the football strength and conditioning coach. *Strength and Conditioning Journal, 37,* 43–51. https://doi.org/10.1519/SSC.0000000000000159

Kuklick, C. R., Gearity, B. T., & Thompson, M. (2015a). The efficacy of reflective practice and coach education on intrapersonal knowledge in the higher education setting. *International Journal of Coaching Science, 9,* 23–42.

Kuklick, C. R., Gearity, B. T., & Thompson, M. (2015b). Reflective practice in a university-based coach education programme. *International Sport Coaching Journal, 2,* 248–260. https://doi.org/10.1123/iscj.2014-0122

Kuklick, C. R., Gearity, B. T., Thompson, M., & Neelis, L. (2015). A case study of one high performance baseball coach's experiences within a learning community. *Qualitative Research in Sport, Exercise and Health, 8,* 61–78. https://doi.org/10.1080/2159676X.2015.1030343

La Guardia, J. G. (2017). *Self-determination theory in practice: How to create an optimally supportive health care environment.* Independently Published.

Larner, R. J., Wagstaff, C. R. D., Thelwell, R. C., & Corbett, J. (2017). A multi-study examination of organisational stressors, emotional labor, burnout, and turnover in sport organisations. *Scandinavian Journal of Medicine & Science in Sports, 27,* 2103–2115. https://doi.org/10.1111/sms.12833

Lave, J., & Wenger, E. (1991). *Situated learning: Legitimate peripheral participation.* Cambridge University Press.

Le Meur, Y., & Torres-Ronda, L. (2019). 10 challenges facing today's applied sport scientist. *Sport Performance & Science Reports, 57,* 1–7.

Lee, J., Knowles, Z., & Whitehead, A. E. (2019). Exploring the use of TA within women's artistic gymnastics judging education. *Psychology of Sport and Exercise, 40,* 135–142. https://doi.org/10.1016/j.psychsport.2018.10.007

Lee, J., & Ryan-Wenger, N. (1997). The "think aloud" seminar for teaching clinical reasoning: A case study of a child with pharyngitis. *Journal of Paediatric Health Care, 11,* 105–110. https://doi.org/10.1016/s0891-5245(97)90061-4

Lee, S. M., Chesterfield, G., Shaw, D. J., & Ghaye, T. (2009). Exploring the potential of reflective learning in sport. *Reflective Practice, 10,* 285–293. http://dx.doi.org/10.1080/14623940903034556

Lee, S.-M., Fogaça, J., & Harrison, M. (2020). Can writing be wrong? Collaborative autoethnography as critical reflective practice in sport, exercise, and performance psychology. *The Qualitative Report, 25,* 3562–3582. https://doi.org/10.46743/2160-3715/2020.4357

Lees, A. (2019). The evolution of racket sport science. A personal reflection. *German Journal of Exercise and Sport Research, 49,* 213–220. https://doi.org/10.1007/s12662-019-00604-2

Lemyre, F., Trudel, P., & Durand-Bush, N. (2007). The learning experience of youth sport coaches. *The Sport Psychologist, 21,* 191–209. https://doi.org/10.1123/tsp.21.2.191

Lethbridge, K., Andrusyszyn, M., Iwasiw, C., Laschinger, H. K. S., & Rajulton, F. (2013). Assessing the psychometric properties of Kember and Leung's reflection questionnaire. *Assessment & Evaluation in Higher Education*, *38*, 303–325. https://doi.org/10.1080/02602938.2011.630977

Lieberman, M. D., Eisenberger, N., Crockett, M., Tom, S., Pfeifer, J., & Way, B. (2007). Putting feelings into words: Affect labeling disrupts amygdala activity in response to affective stimuli. *Psychological Science*, *18*, 421–428. https://doi.org/10.1111/j.1467-9280.2007.01916.x

Lindsay, P., Breckon, J. D., Thomas, O., & Maynard, I. W. (2007). In pursuit of congruence: A personal reflection on methods and philosophy in applied practice. *The Sport Psychologist*, *21*, 335–352. https://doi.org/10.1123/tsp.21.3.335

Lindsay, P., & Thomas, O. (2014). Reflections on being a neophyte sport psychologist in the media: Conversations with my younger self. *The Sport Psychologist*, *28*, 290–301. https://doi.org/10.1123/tsp.2012-0087

Lubit, R. (2001). Tacit knowledge and knowledge management: The keys to sustainable competitive advantage. *Organisation Dynamics*, *29*, 164–178. https://doi.org/10.1016/S0090-2616(01)00026-2

Lyle, J. (2002). *Sports coaching concepts: A framework for coaches' behaviour*. Routledge.

Lyle, J., & Cushion, C. (2010). Narrowing the field: Some key questions about sports coaching. In J. Lyle & C. Cushion (Eds.), *Sports coaching professionalisation and practice* (pp. 243–252). Churchill Livingstone Elsevier.

Mallett, C. J. (2010). Becoming a high-performance coach: Pathways and communities. In J. Lyle & C. Cushion (Eds.), *Sports coaching professionalisation and practice* (pp. 99–118). Churchill Livingstone Elsevier.

Malone, J. J., Harper, L. D., Jones, B., Perry, J., Barnes, C., & Towlson, C. (2019). Perspectives of applied collaborative sport science research within professional team sports. *European Journal of Sport Science*, *19*, 147–155. https://doi.org/10.1080/17461391.2018.1492632

Mamede, S., Figueiredo-Soares, T., Santos, S., Faria, R., Schmidt, H., & Gog, T. (2019). Fostering novice students' diagnostic ability: The value of guiding deliberate reflection. *Medical Education*, *53*, 628–637. https://doi.org/10.1111/medu.13829

Mamede, S., Schmidt, H. G., & Rikers, R. (2007). Diagnostic errors and reflective practice in medicine. *Journal of Evaluation in Clinical Practice*, *13*, 138–148. https://doi.org/10.1111/j.1365-2753.2006.00638.x

Mann, K., Gordon, J., & MacLeod, A. (2009). Reflection and reflective practice in health professions education: A systematic review. *Advances in Health Sciences Education*, *14*, 595–621. http://dx.doi.org/10.1007/s10459-007-9090-2

Mantzios, M., & Wilson, J. C. (2015). Mindfulness, eating behaviours, and obesity: A review and reflection on current findings. *Current Obesity Reports*, *4*, 141–146. https://doi.org/10.1007/s13679-014-0131-x

Mantzourani, E., Desselle, S., Le, J., Lonie, J. M., & Lucas, C. (2019). The role of reflective practice in healthcare professions: Next steps for pharmacy education and practice. *Research in Social and Administrative Pharmacy*, *15*, 1476–1479. https://doi.org/10.1016/j.sapharm.2019.03.011

Markula, P. (2003). The technologies of self: Sport, feminism, and Foucault. *Sociology of Sport Journal*, *20*, 87–107. https://doi.org/10.1123/ssj.20.2.87

Marshall, S. (1995). *Schemas in problem solving*. Cambridge University Press.

Marshall, T. (2019). The concept of reflection: A systematic review and thematic synthesis across professional contexts. *Reflective Practice, 20,* 396–415. https://doi.org/10.1080/14623943.2019.1622520

Marshall, T., Keville, S., Cain, A., & Adler, J. R. (2021). On being open-minded, wholehearted, and responsible: A review and synthesis exploring factors enabling practitioner development in reflective practice. *Reflective Practice, 22,* 860–876. https://doi.org/10.1080/14623943.2021.1976131

Martin, D. R. (1988). Truth, power, self: An interview with Michel Foucault. In L. H. Martin, H. Gutman, & P. H. Hutton (Eds.), *Technologies of the self: A seminar with Michel Foucault* (pp. 9–15). University of Massachusetts Press.

Martin, D. R. (2017). A nutritionist and an educator in professional horseracing: Using reflection to create 'my process'. *Reflective Practice, 18,* 589–599. https://doi.org/10.1080/14623943.2017.1304374

Martin, D. R., Quartiroli, A., & Wagstaff, C. R. D. (2022, ahead of print). A qualitative exploration of neophyte sport psychology practitioners' self-care experiences and perceptions. *Journal of Applied Sport Psychology.* https://doi.org/10.1080/10413200.2022.2046659

Martindale, A., & Collins, D. (2007). Enhancing the evaluation of effectiveness with professional judgment and decision making. *The Sport Psychologist, 21,* 458–474. https://doi.org/10.1123/tsp.21.4.458

Martschukat, J. (2021). *The age of fitness: How the body came to symbolize success and achievement.* Polity.

McCarthy, M. (2003). Detecting acute confusion in older adults: Comparing clinical reasoning of nurses working in acute, long-term, and community health care environments. *Research in Nursing and Health, 26,* 203–212. https://doi.org/10.1002/nur.10081

McDougall, M., Nesti, M., & Richardson, D. (2015). The challenges of sport psychology delivery in elite and professional sport: Reflections from experienced sport psychologists. *The Sport Psychologist, 29,* 265–277. https://doi.org/10.1123/tsp.2014-0081

McEwan, H., Tod, D., & Eubank, M. (2019). The rocky road to individuation: Sport psychologists' perspectives on professional development. *Psychology of Sport & Exercise, 45.* https://doi.org/10.1016/j.psychsport.2019.101542

McGreary, M., Eubank, M., Morris, R., & Whitehead, A. (2020). Thinking aloud: Stress and coping in junior cricket batsmen during challenge and threat states. *Perceptual and Motor Skills, 127,* 1095–1117. https://doi.org/10.1177/0031512520938911

McGregor, P., & Winter, S. (2017). A reflective case study of sport psychology support at the Lacrosse World Cup. *Case Studies in Sport and Exercise Psychology, 1,* 40–51. https://doi.org/10.1123/cssep.2016-0013

Mechbach, S., Wagstaff, C. R. D., Kenttä, G., & Thelwell, R. (2022, ahead of print). Building the "team behind the team": A 21-month instrumental case study of the Swedish 2018 FIFA World Cup team. *Journal of Applied Sport Psychology.* https://doi.org/10.1080/10413200.2022.2046658

Meyer, E., & Land, R. (2003). *Threshold concepts and troublesome knowledge: Linkages to ways of thinking and practising within the disciplines.* Occasional Report 4, May, ETL Project, Universities of Edinburgh, Coventry and Durham/ESRC.

Mezirow, J. (1981). A critical theory of adult learning and education. *Adult Education Quarterly, 32,* 3–24. https://doi.org/10.1177/074171368103200101

Mezirow, J. (1991). *Transformative dimensions of adult learning.* Jossey-Bass.

Michie, S., Ashford, S., Sniehotta, F. F., Dombrowski, S. U., Bishop, A., & French, D. P. (2011). A refined taxonomy of behaviour change techniques to help people change their physical activity and healthy eating behaviours: The CALO-RE taxonomy. *Psychology & Health, 26,* 1479–1498. https://doi.org/10.1080/088704 46.2010.540664

Miles, A. (2001, January). Supporting coach education – towards reflective practice. *Faster, Higher, Stronger, 10,* 15–16.

Mills, J. P., Gearity, B. T., Kuklick, C. R., & Bible, J. (2022, ahead of print). Making Foucault coach: Turning post-structural assumptions into coaching praxis. *Sports Coaching Review.* https://doi.org/10.1080/21640629.2022.2057696

MIND. (2022). *Tips on developing a healthy relationship with physical activity.* www.mind. org.uk/about-us/our-policy-work/sport-physical-activity-and-mental-health/ resources/tips-on-developing-a-healthy-relationship-with-physical-activity/

Miron-Shatz, T., Stone, A., & Kahneman, D. (2009). Memories of yesterday's emotions: Does the valence of experience affect the memory-experience gap? *Emotion, 9,* 885–891. https://doi.org/10.1037/a0017823

Moon, J. (2004). *A handbook of reflective and experiential learning: Theory and practice.* Routledge.

Morton, J. P. (2009). Critical reflections from a neophyte lecturer in higher education: A self-narrative from an exercise 'physiologist'! *Reflective Practice, 10,* 233–243. https://doi.org/10.1080/14623940902786230

Morton, J. P. (2014). Critical reflections from sport physiology and nutrition. Tales from pitch side to ringside. In Z. Knowles, D. Gilbourne, B. Cropley, & L. Dugdill (Eds.), *Reflective practice in the sport and exercise sciences: Contemporary issues* (pp. 124–136). Routledge.

Mulhall, S. (2000). *Heidegger and being and time.* Routledge.

Murrell, K. A. (1998). The experience of facilitation in reflective groups: A phenomenological study. *Nurse Education Today, 18,* 303–309. https://doi.org/10.1016/ s0260-6917(98)80047-6

Næss, A. (1986). The deep ecological movement: Some philosophical aspects. *Philosophical Inquiry, 8,* 10–31. https://doi.org/10.5840/philinquiry198681/22

Naess, A. (1987). Self-realization: An ecological approach to being in the world. *The Trumpeter, 4,* 35–42.

Nathan, V., & Poulsen, S. (2004). Group-analytic training groups for psychology students: A qualitative study. *Group Analysis, 37,* 163–177. https://doi. org/10.1177/0533316404042855

Neil, R., Cropley, B., Wilson, K., & Faull, A. (2013). Exploring the value of reflective practice interventions in applied sport psychology: Case studies with an individual athlete and a team. *Sport & Exercise Psychology Review, 9,* 42–57.

Nelson, R. (2013). Conceptual frameworks for PaR and related pedagogy: From 'hard facts' to 'liquid knowledge'. In R. Nelson (Ed.), *Practice as research in the arts: Principles, protocols, pedagogies, resistances* (pp. 48–70). Palgrave Macmillan.

Nelson-Jones, R. (1997). *The theory and practice of counselling and therapy.* Cassell.

Newman, S. (1999). Constructing and critiquing reflective practice. *Educational Action Research, 7,* 145–163. https://doi.org/10.1080/09650799900200081

Nguyen, Q. D., Fernandez, N., Karsenti, T., & Charlin, B. (2014). What is reflection? A conceptual analysis of major definitions and a proposal of a five-component model. *Medical Education, 48,* 1176–1189. https://doi.org/10.1111/medu.12583

Nugent, P., Moss, D., Barnes, R., & Wilks, J. (2011). Clear(ing) space: Mindfulness-based reflective practice. *Reflective Practice, 12*, 1–13. https://doi.org/10.1080/14623943.2011.541088

Nuss, K., Moore, K., Nelson, T., & Li, K. (2021). Effects of motivational interviewing and wearable fitness trackers on motivation and physical activity: A systematic review. *American Journal of Health Promotion, 35*, 226–235. https://doi.org/10.1177/0890117120939030

O'Sullivan, T. (2005). Some theoretical propositions on the nature of practice wisdom. *Journal of Social Work, 5*, 221–242. https://doi.org/10.1177%2F1468017305054977

Olson, K. L., & Emery, C. F. (2015). Mindfulness and weight loss: A systematic review. *Psychosomatic Medicine, 77*, 59–67. https://doi.org/10.1097/PSY.0000000000000127

Ong, C. W., Smith, B. M., Levin, M. E., & Twohig, M. P. (2020). Mindfulness and acceptance. In J. S. Abramowitz & S. M. Blakey (Eds.), *Clinical handbook of fear and anxiety: Maintenance processes and treatment mechanisms* (pp. 323–344). American Psychological Association.

Orbell, S., & Verplanken, B. (2020). Changing behavior using habit theory. In M. Hagger, L. Cameron, K. Hamilton, N. Hankonen, & T. Lintunen (Eds.), *Handbook of behavior change* (pp. 178–192). Cambridge University Press.

Owton, H., Bond, K., & Tod, D. (2014). "It's my dream to work with Olympic athletes": Neophyte sport psychologists' expectations and initial experiences regarding service delivery. *Journal of Applied Sport Psychology, 26*, 241–255. https://doi.org/10.1080/10413200.2013.847509

Pai, H. (2015). The effect of a self-reflection and insight program on the nursing competence of nursing students: A longitudinal study. *Journal of Professional Nursing, 31*, 424–431. https://doi.org/10.1016/j.profnurs.2015.03.003

Pai, H., Ko, H., Eng, C., & Yen, W. (2017). The mediating effect of self-reflection and learning effectiveness on clinical nursing performance in nursing students: A follow up study. *Journal of Professional Nursing, 33*, 287–292. https://doi.org/10.1016/j.profnurs.2017.01.003

Pais, L. G., & Felgueiras, S. (2016). Police decision-making at major events: A research programme. *European Police Science and Research Bulletin, 15*, 48–58.

Papastephanou, M., & Angeli, C. (2007). Critical thinking beyond skill. *Educational Philosophy and Theory, 39*, 604–621. https://doi.org/10.1111/j.1469-5812.2007.00311.x

Parikh, S. B., Janson, C., & Singleton, T. (2012). Video journaling as a method of reflective practice. *Counselor Education and Supervision, 51*, 33–49. https://doi.org/10.1002/j.1556-6978.2012.00003.x

Parker, P. (2018). *The art of gathering – How we meet and why it matters.* Riverhead Books.

Partington, M., Cushion, C., Cope, E., & Harvey, S. (2015). The impact of video feedback on professional youth football coaches' reflection and practice behaviour: A longitudinal investigation of behaviour change. *Reflective Practice, 16*, 700–716. https://doi.org/10.1080/14623943.2015.1071707

Pauline, J. S., Pauline, G. A., Johnson, S. R., & Gamble, K. M. (2006). Ethical issues in exercise psychology. *Ethics & Behavior, 16*, 61–76. https://doi.org/10.1207/s15327019eb1601_6

Peden-McAlpine, C., Tomlinson, P., Forneris, S., Genck, G., & Meiers, S. (2005). Evaluation of a reflective practice intervention to enhance family care. *Journal of Advanced Nursing, 49*, 494–501. https://doi.org/10.1111/j.1365-2648.2004.03322.x

Pentland, D., Kantartzis, S., Clausen, M., & Witemyre, K. (2018). *Occupational therapy and complexity: Defining and describing practice*. Royal College of Occupational Therapists.

Pettersson, S., & Ekström, M. (2014). Reaching balance and sustainability: Weight regulation in combat sports. A case study of a female boxer. *Reflective Practice, 15*, 66–77. https://doi.org/10.1080/14623943.2013.868796

Phillips, D. Z. (1992). *Interventions in ethics*. Macmillan Press Ltd.

Picknell, G., Cropley, B., Hanton, S., & Mellalieu, S. D. (2014). Where's the evidence? Empirical reflective practice interventions with different populations in sport. In Z. Knowles, D. Gilbourne, & L. Dugdill (Eds.), *Reflective practice in the sport and exercise sciences: Contemporary issues* (pp. 28–38). Routledge.

Picknell, G., Cropley, B., Mellalieu, S. D., & Hanton, S. (2022). Facilitating healthcare dieticians' communication skills: A reflective practice intervention [Manuscript submitted for publication]. *International Journal of Training and Development*.

Picknell, G., Mellalieu, S. D., Cropley, B., Hanton, S., & Al Shehhi, M. (2022). Who is it good for? Examining the relationship between reflective practice and mindfulness for promoting healthy lifestyles [Manuscript submitted for publication]. *Military Medicine*.

Platt, L. (2014). The 'wicked problem' of reflective practice: A critical literature review. *Innovations in Practice, 9*, 44–53. https://doi.org/10.24377/LJMU.iip.vol9iss1article108

Pleasants, N. (1999). *Wittgenstein and the idea of a critical social theory: A critique of Giddens, Habermas and Bhaskar*. Routledge.

Poncy, G. (2020). Skilful use of developmental supervision. *Journal of Psychotherapy Integration, 30*, 102–107. https://doi.org/10.1037/int0000162

Potrac, P., & Jones, R. L. (2009). Micropolitical workings in semi-professional football. *Sociology of Sport Journal, 26*, 557–577. https://doi.org/10.1123/ssj.26.4.557

Powell, J. H. (1989). The reflective practitioner in nursing. *Journal of Advanced Nursing, 14*, 824–832. https://doi.org/10.1111/j.1365-2648.1989.tb01467.x

Probyn, E. (1991). Ghosts in the (missing) text. In M. Lewandowska (Ed.), *Sight works* (pp. 111–124). Chance.

Raymond, J., Sealey, R., Naumann, F., Rooney, K., English, T., & Groeller, H. (2020). Development of core clinical learning competencies for Australian exercise physiology students. *Journal of Clinical Exercise Physiology, 9*, 1–9. https://doi.org/10.31189/2165-6193-9.1.1

Redelmeier, D., Katz, J., & Kahneman, D. (2003). Memories of colonoscopy: A randomized trial. *Pain, 104*, 187–194. https://doi.org/10.1016/S0304-3959(03)00003-4

Reid, B. (1993). "But we're doing it already!" Exploring a response to the concept of reflective practice in order to improve its facilitation. *Nurse Education Today, 13*, 305–309. https://doi.org/10.1016/0260-6917(93)90058-a

Reid, C., Stewart, E., & Thorne, G. (2004). Multidisciplinary sport science teams in elite sport: Comprehensive servicing or conflict and confusion? *The Sport Psychologist, 18*, 204–217. https://doi.org/10.1123/tsp.18.2.204

Renshaw, I., & Chappell, G. (2010). A constraints-led approach to talent development in cricket. In L. Kidman & B. J. Lombardo (Eds.), *Athlete-centred coaching: Developing decision makers* (pp. 151–172). IPC Print Resources.

Rhodius, A. (2012, February). *To graduation, certification and beyond: The importance of post-training peer support and reflective practice in sport psychology.* Paper presented at the National University Performance Psychology Conference.

Rhodius, A., & Huntley, E. (2014). Facilitating reflective practice in graduate trainees and early career practitioners. In Z. Knowles, D. Gilbourne, B. Cropley, & L. Dugdill (Eds.), *Reflective practice in the sport and exercise sciences: Contemporary Issues* (pp. 91–100). Routledge.

Rhodius, A., & Park, M. (2016). Who's supervising the supervisor? A case study of meta-supervision. In J. Cremades & L. Tashman (Eds.), *Global practices and training in applied sport, exercise, and performance psychology: A case study approach* (pp. 322–329). Routledge.

Rhodius, A., & Sugarman, K. (2014). Peer consultations with colleagues: The significance of gaining support and avoiding the 'Lone Ranger trap'. In J. Cremades & L. Tashman (Eds.), *Becoming a performance psychologist: International perspectives on service delivery and supervision* (pp. 331–338). Routledge.

Robson, M., & Robson, J. (2008). Explorations of participants' experiences of a personal development group held as part of a counselling psychology training group: Is it safe in here? *Counselling Psychology Quarterly, 21,* 371–382. https://doi.org/10.1080/09515070802602153

Rogers, C. R. (1961). *On becoming a person: A therapist's view of psychotherapy.* Houghton Mifflin.

Rogers, C. R. (1990). This is me. In H. Kirschenbaum & V. L. Henderson (Eds.), *The Carl Rogers reader* (pp. 6–29). Constable.

Rogers, E., Papathomas, A., & Kinnafick, F. E. (2021). Preparing for a physical activity intervention in a secure psychiatric hospital: Reflexive insights on entering the field. *Qualitative Research in Sport, Exercise and Health, 13,* 235–249. https://doi.org/10.1080/2159676X.2019.1685587

Ross, E., Gupta, L., & Sanders, L. (2018). When research leads to learning, but not action in high performance sport. *Progress in Brain Research, 240,* 201–217. https://doi.org/10.1016/bs.pbr.2018.08.001

Rowe, L., Moore, N., & McKie, P. (2020). The reflective practitioner: The challenges of supporting public sector senior leaders as they engage in reflective practice. *Higher Education, Skills, and Work-Based Learning, 10,* 783–798. https://doi.org/10.1108/HESWBL-03-2020-0038

Rowley, C., Earle, K., & Gilbourne, D. (2012). Practice and the process of critical learning: Reflections of an early-stage practitioner working in elite youth level rugby league. *Sport and Exercise Psychology Review, 8,* 35–50.

Roy, X., Gavrila, S., & Sercia, P. (2021, ahead of print). Reflective practice: Helping coaches improve their coaching. *International Journal of Strength and Conditioning.* https://doi.org/10.47206/ijsc.v1i1.55

Ryan, R. M., & Deci, E. L. (2000). Self-determination theory and the facilitation of intrinsic motivation, social development, and well-being. *American Psychologist, 55,* 68–78. https://doi.org/10.1037/0003-066X.55.1.68

Ryan, R. M., & Deci, E. L. (2017). *Self-determination theory: Basic psychological needs in motivation, development, and wellness.* The Guilford Press.

Schön, D. A. (1983). *The reflective practitioner: How professionals think in action.* Avebury.

Schön, D. A. (1987). *Educating the reflective practitioner.* Jossey-Bass.

Schön, D. A. (1995). The new scholarship requires a new epistemology. *Change, 27,* 26–35.

Scott, K., & McSherry, R. (2008). Evidence-based nursing: Clarifying the concepts for nurses in practice. *Journal of Clinical Nursing, 18,* 1085–1095. https://doi.org/10.1111/j.1365-2702.2008.02588.x

Shannon, V. R., & Zizzi, S. J. (2018). Professional and ethical issues in applied exercise psychology. In S. Razon & M. L. Sachs (Eds.), *Applied exercise psychology: The challenging journey from motivation to adherence* (pp. 445–452). Routledge.

Shetty, J. (2020). *Think like a monk: Train your mind for peace and purpose every day.* Thorsons.

Shogan, D. (1999). *The making of high-performing sport: Discipline, diversity and ethics.* University of Toronto Press.

Simmons, B., Lanuza, D., Fonteyn, M., Jicks, F., & Holm, K. (2003). Clinical reasoning in experienced nurses. *Western Journal of Nursing Research, 25,* 701–719. https://doi.org/10.1177/0193945903253092

Smallwood, J., & Andrews-Hanna, J. (2013). Not all minds that wander are lost: The importance of a balanced perspective on the mind-wandering state. *Frontiers in Psychology, 4, 441.* https://doi.org/10.3389/fpsyg.2013.00441

Smith, B., & Sparkes, A. (2009). Narrative analysis and sport and exercise psychology: Understanding lives in diverse ways. *Psychology of Sport and Exercise, 10,* 279–288. https://doi.org/10.1016/j.psychsport.2008.07.012

Sobral, D. (2000). An appraisal of medical students' reflection-in-learning. *Medical Education, 34,* 182–187. https://doi.org/10.1016/j.psychsport.2008.07.012

Sodhi, M. (2008). Embodied knowing: An experiential, contextual, and reflective process. *Adult Education Research Conference.* https://newprairiepress.org/aerc/2008/ papers/59.

Sparkes, A. C. (1998). Validity in qualitative inquiry and the problem of criteria: Implications for sport psychology. *The Sport Psychologist, 12,* 333–345. https://doi.org/10.1123/tsp.12.4.363

Stephenson, J., Cronin, C., & Whitehead, A. E. (2020). "Suspended above, and in action": TA as a reflective practice tool. *International Sport Coaching Journal, 7,* 11–21. https://doi.org/10.1123/iscj.2018-0022

Stevens, C., Lawrence, A., Pluss, M., & Nancarrow, S. (2018). The career destination, progression, and satisfaction of exercise and sports science graduates in Australia. *Journal of Clinical Exercise Physiology, 7,* 76–81. https://doi.org/10.31189/2165-6193-7.4.76

Stone, A. A., Broderick, J. E., Shiffman, S. S., & Schwartz, J. E. (2004). Understanding recall of weekly pain from a momentary assessment perspective: Absolute agreement, between- and within-person consistency, and judged change in weekly pain. *Pain, 107,* 61–69. https://doi.org/10.1016/j.pain.2003.09.020

Swann, C., Keegan, R., Cropley, B., & Mitchell, I. (2018). Professional philosophy. In G. Cremades & A. Mugford (Eds.), *Sport, exercise, and performance psychology: Theories and applications* (pp. 15–33). Routledge.

Sweet, J. (2010). Beyond reflective dogma. In H. Bradbury, N. Frost, S. Kilminster, & M. Zukas (Eds.), *Beyond reflective practice* (pp. 182–190). Routledge.

Swettenham, L., Eubank, M., Won, D., & Whitehead, A. E. (2020). Investigating stress and coping during practice and competition in tennis using TA. *International Journal of Sport and Exercise Psychology, 18,* 218–238. https://doi.org/10.1080/1612197X.2018.1511622

Swettenham, L., & Whitehead, A. E. (2021). Developing the triad of knowledge in coaching: Think aloud as a reflective tool within a category 1 football academy. *International Sport Coaching Journal, 9,* 122–132. https://doi.org/10.1123/iscj.2020-0122

Szedlak, C., Batey, J., Smith, M. J., & Church, M. (2021). Examining experienced S&C coaches' reflections on the effectiveness of psychosocial behaviors in coaching. *International Sport Coaching Journal, 9,* 1–9. https://doi.org/10.1123/iscj.2020-0092

Szedlak, C., Callary, B., & Smith, M. (2019). Exploring the influence and practical development of coaches' psychosocial behaviours in strength and conditioning. *Strength & Conditioning Journal, 41,* 8–17. https://doi.org/10.1519/SSC.0000000000000421

Szedlak, C., Smith, M. J., & Callary, B. (2021). Developing a 'letter to my younger self' to learn from the experiences of expert coaches. *Qualitative Research in Sport, Exercise and Health, 13,* 569–585. https://doi.org/10.1080/2159676X.2020.1725609

Szedlak, C., Smith, M. J., Callary, B., & Day, M. C. (2019). Using written, audio, and video vignettes to translate knowledge to elite strength and conditioning coaches. *International Sport Coaching Journal, 6,* 199–210. https://doi.org/10.1123/iscj.2018-0027

Szedlak, C., Smith, M. J., Callary, B., & Day, M. C. (2020). Examining how elite S&C coaches develop coaching practice using reflection stimulated by video vignettes. *International Sport Coaching Journal, 7,* 295–305. https://doi.org/10.1123/iscj.2019-0059

Tan, S. L., Koh, K. T., & Kokkonen, M. (2016). The perception of elite athletes' guided self-reflection and performance in archery. *Reflective Practice, 17,* 207–220. https://doi.org/10.1080/14623943.2016.1146582

Tang, Y. Y., & Leve, L. D. (2015). A translational neuroscience perspective on mindfulness meditation as a prevention strategy. *Translational Behavioral Medicine, 6,* 63–72. https://doi.org/10.1007/s13142-015-0360-x

Teixeira, P. J., Marques, M. M., Silva, M. N., Brunet, J., Duda, J. L., Haerens, L., . . . Hagger, M. (2020). A classification of motivation and behavior change techniques used in self-determination theory-based interventions in health contexts. *Motivation Science, 6,* 438–455. https://doi.org/10.1037/mot0000172

Tekavc, J., Wylleman, P., & Cecić Erpič, S. (2015). Perceptions of dual career development among elite level swimmers and basketball players. *Psychology of Sport and Exercise, 21,* 27–41. https://doi.org/10.1016/j.psychsport.2015.03.002

Tenenbaum, G., & Elran, E. (2003). Congruence between actual and retrospective reports of emotions for pre-and post-competition states. *Journal of Sport & Exercise Psychology, 25,* 323–340. https://doi.org/10.1123/jsep.25.3.323

Tenenbaum, G., & Filho, E. (2018). *Psychosocial measurement issues in sport and exercise settings.* Oxford Research Encyclopedia: Psychology.

Thomas International Ltd. (2020). *DISC personality test from Thomas international.* https://www.thomas. Co/resources/hr-blog/disc-personality-test-Thomas-International.

Thompson, K. (2010). Where does the sport physiologist fit in? *International Journal of Sports Physiology and Performance*, 5, 429–430. https://doi.org/10.1123/ijspp.5.4.429

Threlfall, S. J. (2014). How elite athletes reflect: An interview with Holly Bleasdale and Paul Bradshaw. *Reflective Practice*, 15, 495–503. https://doi.org/10.1080/1 4623943.2014.900025

Thue Bjørndal, C., & Tore Ronglan, L. (2021). Engaging with uncertainty in athlete development – orchestrating talent development through incremental leadership. *Sport, Education and Society*, 26, 104–116. https://doi.org/10.1080/13573322. 2019.1695198

Tod, D. (2007). The long and winding road: Professional development in sport psychology. *The Sport Psychologist*, 21, 94–108. https://doi.org/10.1123/tsp.21.1.94

Tod, D. (2014). 'Daddy and the meaning of service delivery.' Becoming an applied sport psychology practitioner. In P. McCarthy & M. Jones (Eds.), *Becoming a sport psychologist* (pp. 38–45). Routledge.

Tod, D., Hutter, R. I., & Eubank, M. (2017). Professional development for sport psychology practice. *Current Opinion in Psychology*, 16, 134–137. http://dx.doi. org/10.1016/j.copsyc.2017.05.007

Tonn, E., & Harmison, R. J. (2004). Thrown to the wolves: A student's account of her practicum experience. *The Sport Psychologist*, 18, 324–340. https://doi. org/10.1123/tsp.18.3.324

Toulmin, S. (2001). *Return to reason*. Harvard University Press.

Trede, F. V. (2010). Enhancing communicative spaces for fieldwork education in an inland regional Australian university. *Higher Education Research & Development*, 29, 373–387. https://doi.org/10.1080/07294360903470993

Trelfa, J. (2020). *Facilitating reflective practice in higher education professional programmes: Reclaiming and redefining the practices of reflective practice* (Unpublished thesis). University of Winchester, UK.

Trelfa, J., & Telfer, H. (2014). Keeping the cat alive: 'Getting' reflection as part of professional practice. In Z. Knowles, D. Gilbourne, B. Cropley, & L. Dugdill (Eds.), *Reflective practice in the sport and exercise sciences: Contemporary issues* (pp. 47–56). Routledge.

Tuffiash, M., Roring, R. W., & Ericsson, K. A. (2007). Expert performance in scrabble: Implications for the study of the structure and acquisition of complex skills. *Journal of Experimental Psychology: Applied*, 13, 124–134. https://doi. org/10.1037/1076-898X.13.3.124

Tummons, J. (2011). 'It sort of feels uncomfortable': Problematising the assessment of reflective practice. *Studies in Higher Education*, 36, 471–483. https://doi. org/10.1080/03075071003671794

Uphill, M. A., & Hemmings, B. (2017). Vulnerability: Ripples from reflections on mental toughness. *The Sport Psychologist*, 31, 299–307. https://doi.org/10.1123/ tsp.2016-0034

Urbiola, A., Willis, G. B., Ruiz-Romero, J., & Moya, M. (2018). Does a multicultural perspective shape unbiased minds? The moderating role of outgroup threat. *Journal of Applied Social Psychology*, 48, 608–617. https://doi.org/10.1111/jasp.12551

Vamplew, W. (2007). Playing with the rules: Influences on the development of regulation in sport. *International Journal of the History of Sport*, 24, 843–871. https:// doi.org/10.1080/09523360701311745

Vaughan, J., Mallett, C. J., Davids, K., Potrac, P., & López-Felip, M. A. (2019). Developing creativity to enhance human potential in sport: A wicked transdisciplinary challenge. *Frontiers in Psychology, 10, 2090.* https://doi.org/10.3389/fpsyg.2019.02090

Vaughan, J., Mallett, C. J., Potrac, P., López-Felip, M. A., & Davids, K. (2021). Football, culture, skill development and sport coaching: Extending ecological approaches in athlete development using the skilled intentionality framework. *Frontiers in Psychology, 12, 635420.* https://doi.org/10.3389/fpsyg.2021.635420

Wade, J. C., & Jones, J. E. (2014). *Strength-based clinical supervision.* Springer.

Wadsworth, N., McEwan, H., Lafferty, M., Eubank, M., & Tod, D. (2021, ahead of print). A systematic review exploring the reflective accounts of applied sport psychology practitioners. *International Review of Sport & Exercise Psychology.* https://doi.org/10.1080/1750984X.2021.1975304

Wagstaff, C. R. D. (2019). Taking stock of organisational psychology in sport. *Journal of Applied Sport Psychology, 31,* 1–6. https://doi.org/10.1080/10413200.2018.1539785

Wagstaff, C. R. D., Gilmore, S., & Thelwell, R. C. (2015). Sport medicine and sport science practitioners' experiences of organisational change. *Scandinavian Journal of Medicine and Science in Sports, 25,* 685–698. https://doi.org/10.1111/sms.12340

Wagstaff, C. R. D., Gilmore, S., & Thelwell, R. C. (2016). When the show must go on: Investigating repeated organisational change in elite sport. *Journal of Change Management, 16,* 38–54. https://doi.org/10.1080/14697017.2015.1062793

Walsh, B., Jamison, S., & Walsh, C. (2010). *The score takes care of itself: My philosophy of leadership.* Penguin Publishing Group.

Walsh, K., McAllister, M., & Morgan, A. (2002). Using reflective practice processes to identify practice change issues in an aged care service. *Nurse Education in Practice, 2,* 230–236. https://doi.org/10.1016/S1471-5953(02)00023-9

Walsh, N., & Driver, P. (2019). Developing reflective trainee teacher practice with 360-degree video. *Teaching & Teacher Education, 78,* 97–105. https://doi.org/10.1016/j.tate.2018.11.009

Wang, L. (2021). How self-reflection and resilience can affect pre-competition anxiety? Evidence from national competitive table tennis in adolescent players. *Current Psychology,* 1–11. https://doi.org/10.1007/s12144-021-02473-1

Watson, P. M., Dugdill, L., Pickering, K., Owen, S., Hargreaves, J., Staniford, L., . . . Cable, T. (2015). Service evaluation of the GOALS family-based childhood obesity treatment intervention during the first three years of implementation. *British Medical Journal Open, 5,* e006519. https://doi.org/10.1136/bmjopen-2014-006519

Watson, P. M., McKinnon, A., Santino, N., Bassett-Gunter, R. L., Calleja, M., & Josse, A. (2021). Integrating needs-supportive delivery into a laboratory-based randomised controlled trial for adolescent girls with overweight and obesity: Theoretical underpinning and 12-week psychological outcomes. *Journal of Sports Sciences, 39,* 2434–2443. https://doi.org/10.1080/02640414.2021.1939948

Weinberg, R. S., & Gould, D. (2019). *Foundations of sport and exercise psychology* (7th ed.). Human Kinetics.

Wenger, E. (1998). *Communities of practice: Learning, meaning, and identity.* Cambridge University Press.

Wenger, E. (2009). *A social theory of learning. Contemporary theories of learning: Learning theorists in their own words.* Routledge.

Wenger, E., McDermott, R., & Snyder, W. M. (2002). *Cultivating communities of practice: A guide to managing knowledge*. Harvard Business School.

Whitehead, A. E., Cropley, B., Miles, A., Huntley, T., Quayle, L., & Knowles, Z. (2016). 'Think Aloud': Towards a framework to facilitate reflective practice amongst rugby league coaches. *International Sport Coaching Journal, 3*, 269–286. https://doi.org/10.1123/iscj.2016-0021

Whitehead, A. E., & Jackman, P. C. (2021, ahead of print). Towards a framework of cognitive processes during competitive golf using the TA method. *Psychology of Sport and Exercise, 53*. https://doi.org/10.1016/j.psychsport.2020.101869

Whitehead, A. E., Taylor, J. A., & Polman, R. C. (2015). Examination of the suitability of collecting in event cognitive processes using TA protocol in golf. *Frontiers in Psychology, 6, 1974*. https://doi.org/10.3389/fpsyg.2015.01974

Whitehead, A. E., Taylor, J. A., & Polman, R. C. (2016). Evidence for skill level differences in the thought processes of golfers during high and low pressure situations. *Frontiers in Psychology, 6, 1083*. https://doi.org/10.3389/fpsyg.2015.01083

Whittaker, A., & Taylor, B. (2017). Understanding risk in social work. *Journal of Social Work Practice, 31*, 375–378. https://doi.org/10.1080/02650533.2017.1397612

Williams, D. E., & Andersen, M. B. (2012). Identity, wearing many hats, and boundary blurring: The mindful psychologist on the way to the Olympic and Paralympic Games. *Journal of Sport Psychology in Action, 3*, 139–152. https://doi.org/10.1080/21520704.2012.683090

Williams, R., & Grudnoff, L. (2011). Making sense of reflection: A comparison of beginning and experienced teachers' perceptions of reflection for practice. *Reflective Practice, 12*, 281–291. http://dx.doi.org/10.1080/14623943.2011.571861

Willis, S. (2010). Becoming a reflective practitioner: Frameworks for the pre-hospital professional. *Journal of Paramedic Practice, 2*, 212–216. https://doi.org/10.12968/jpar.2010.2.5.48162

Winter, S., & Collins, D. (2016). Applied sport psychology: A profession? *The Sport Psychologist, 30*, 89–96. http://dx.doi.org/10.1123/tsp.2014-0132

Wirtz, D., Kruger, J., Scollon, C. N., & Diener, E. (2003). What to do on spring break? The role of predicted, on-line, and remembered experience in future choice. *Psychological Science, 14*, 520–524. https://doi.org/10.1111/1467-9280.03455

Wittgenstein, L. (1968). *Philosophical investigations*. Basil Blackwell.

Wittgenstein, L. (1978). *Remarks on the foundations of mathematics*. Basil Blackwell.

Woodcock, C., Richards, H., & Mugford, A. (2008). Quality counts: Critical features for neophyte professional development. *The Sport Psychologist, 22*, 491–506. https://doi.org/10.1123/tsp.22.4.491

Xu, H., Ang, W. G. B., Soh, J. Y., & Ponnamperuma, G. G. (2021). Methods to improve the diagnostic reasoning in undergraduate medical education in the clinical setting: A systemtaic review. *Journal of General Internal Medicine, 36*, 2745–2754. https://doi.org/10.1007/s11606-021-06916-0

Yagata, K. (2018). Bildung as an essential disposition in becoming a reflective practitioner: Practical application of philosophical hermeneutics to second language teacher education. *Reflective Practice, 19*, 322–332. https://doi.org/10.1080/14623943.2018.1437409

Zeichner, K. M., & Liston, D. P. (1996). *Reflective teaching: An introduction*. Routledge.

Index

Page numbers in *italics* indicate figures and page numbers in **bold** indicate tables.

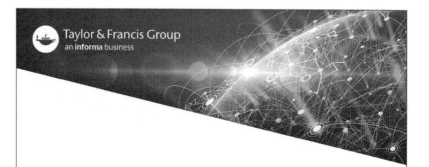